The Pronunciation of English in New York City

CONSONANTS AND VOWELS

Allan Forbes Hubbell

OCTAGON BOOKS

A DIVISION OF FARRAR, STRAUS AND GIROUX

New York   1972

Copyright 1950 by Allan Forbes Hubbell

Reprinted 1972
by special arrangement with Allan Forbes Hubbell

OCTAGON BOOKS
A DIVISION OF FARRAR, STRAUS & GIROUX, INC.
19 Union Square West
New York, N. Y. 10003

Library of Congress Cataloging in Publication Data

Hubbell, Allan Forbes.
    The pronunciation of English in New York City.
    Originally presented as the author's thesis, Columbia University, 1950.
    Bibliography: p.
    1. English language in the United States—Dialects—New York (City). 2. English language in the United States—Pronunciation. I. Title.

PE3101.N7H8 1972   427'.9'7471   72-6964
ISBN 0-374-94002-9

Printed in U.S.A. by
NOBLE OFFSET PRINTERS, INC.
NEW YORK, N.Y. 10003

ACKNOWLEDGMENT

During the preparation of this study I benefited greatly from the friendly criticism of a number of my seniors at the University. I should like to express my particular thanks to Professor W. Cabell Greet, under whom I first undertook the investigation and whose advice about the analysis of the phonetic facts and their presentation I found very helpful. Professors Elliott V. K. Dobbie and André Martinet were kind enough to read the early drafts and I have incorporated many of their suggestions in the final form. I want also to record my indebtedness to the late Professor Harry Morgan Ayres, and to Professors Jane D. Zimmerman and George W. Hibbitt, who also read the manuscript and made detailed comments which were very useful in revision. For similar criticism and for many discussions which I found both pleasant and profitable, I should furthermore like to thank Professor Victor A. Oswald, Jr., now of the University of California at Los Angeles.

I have made some supplementary use in the study of a series of phonographic recordings of nine *Linguistic Atlas* informants, which were made by me and by the late Mr. Walter Garwick in 1941. Although these recordings belong to Columbia University, I felt that it would hardly be proper for me to use them without the express permission of the editor of the *Atlas*, Professor Hans Kurath. I want to record my appreciation of his kindness in granting that permission very freely.

A. F. H.

New York City
August, 1949

CONTENTS

GENERAL OBSERVATIONS; LIMITATIONS OF THIS STUDY	1
INFORMANTS, METHODS AND SYMBOLS	12
THE CONSONANTS	20
The Stops	20
The Fricatives	33
The Affricates	43
Voiced Frictionless Consonants with Voiceless Fricative Variants	44
The Nasals	55
THE VOWELS AND DIPHTHONGS OF STRESSED SYLLABLES	58
Vowels That Do Not Occur as Word-Finals	58
Diphthongs of the [ɪ]-Series	64
Diphthongs of the [ŭ]-Series	70
Diphthongs of the [ə̆]-Series and Their Monophthongal Variants	73
THE VOWELS OF WEAK SYLLABLES	87
APPENDIX A: Primary Informants	91
APPENDIX B: Supplementary Informants	119
APPENDIX C: Test Sentences	125
NOTES	133
SELECTIVE BIBLIOGRAPHY	149
WORD INDEX	151

GENERAL OBSERVATIONS; LIMITATIONS OF THIS STUDY

1.1. Among the several regional types of American English, none perhaps is more distinctly set apart from others, both in fact and in the popular awareness of the fact, than that of New York City and its environs. Not all the phonological characteristics of the speech of this area are unique, of course, in the sense that they do not occur elsewhere in the United States. That is sometimes the case; but at least as frequently particular features of metropolitan pronunciation are shared by other dialects of American English. There are certain similarities between the pronunciation of New York and that of the coastal areas in the South. Other similarities link the city with the Middle Atlantic states, with eastern New England, or even with the Middle West. But despite all these partial resemblances, the metropolitan patterns resulting from the combination of many features are rather unlike those which appear in other varieties of spoken English.

This singularity of New York speech, though it is often apprehended well enough by those innocent of any linguistic training, has not always been adequately recognized by phoneticians. To be sure, many features of metropolitan pronunciation, and especially some of those which occur on the uncultivated level, have been described in detail. Students have even been conscious that the substandard speech of New York would not fit easily into any of the usual categories. But many of them have not been very familiar with the cultivated types of metropolitan pronunciation and have in any case been more interested in the dialects of other regions of the United States. As a result, they have often been content to accept what was in most respects an elocutionist's fiction: the concept of an eastern type of pronunciation that included the speech both of New York City and of eastern New England. The cultivated usage, at least, of these two areas was thought to exhibit a sufficient number of fundamental similarities to justify classing them together as a regional type distinct from other types of American English. And so the term "Eastern American" has been employed, not only in manuals of a prescriptive sort, but also in Kenyon's *American Pronunciation* and in the Kenyon and Knott *Pronouncing Dictionary*.

The accuracy of this term, however, has not gone unchallenged. Its most outspoken critic has been Charles Kenneth Thomas, who in several articles and in a recently published book,[1] has denied that the classification had any validity whatever.² In one of these articles, after listing what he takes to be the chief characteristics of eastern New England speech, he then sets against them the results of an extensive tabulation of metropolitan usage. The differences are so considerable that he concludes by stating: "Actually three major types, each with its standard, have their habitation east of the Hudson, and an amalgam, or higher synthesis, of the three has never been anything more than conversational."³

Some of Thomas' specific statements, I think, need to be qualified. His method is to tabulate the occurrences of particular pronunciations used by an undifferentiated group of speakers. Pronunciations heard from persons whose dialects are probably quite different are lumped together and, as a result, the patterns occurring in the speech of individuals are sometimes obscured. For example, his tables indicate that vowels approximating the so-called "intermediate quality" occur rather more frequently in metropolitan speech in *abandon, damp,* and *man* than in *ask* and *dance.* "It is impossible to avoid the conclusion," he therefore asserts, "that the 'broad a' category has no validity in downstate speech and that [a] is merely a lowered variety of the [æ] phoneme."⁴ An examination of the total pattern of successive individual speakers, however, will show something different. In the speech of a large number of New Yorkers, all these words contain the same vocalic phoneme (which is not /æ/),⁵ and one of the variants of this phoneme in the pronunciation of some speakers is a very low long vowel or a diphthong that begins at a very low position. But this is not the only type of pronunciation which occurs. Some speakers, most of them women, use the "intermediate vowel" rather consistently in the *ask*-group and do not use it elsewhere. Such speakers, it may be added, also often pronounce mid-central vowels without "*r*-coloring" in *third, turn,* etc., and may frequently round the vowel of *stop, possible,* and *volume.* These "eastern" patterns, to be sure, are not infrequently acquired ones, carefully drilled into the speaker in college or in finishing school. But that in a certain sense is beside the point. The fact remains that such a type of pronunciation does exist in New York and cannot be omitted from any description of the city's speech.

Individual patterns similarly disappear in Thomas' figures for the occurrence of /r/ in the preconsonantal and final positions. His tables show that the consonant is very frequently pronounced in *absorb, barn, course,* and the like. "New York City," he sums up, "agrees with eastern New England in the excrescent [r] of *idea*...but in little else in the treatment of *r*."⁶ These tabulations, however, conceal the fact that millions of New Yorkers rather regularly pronounce in the "*r*-less" fashion, according to which the consonant occurs only when immediately followed by a vowel. It might further be added that coastal New England is by no means so predomi-

nantly "r-less" as Thomas seems to assume. The maps of the
Linguistic Atlas make clear that in Massachusetts, for example, within fifty miles of Boston, there are communities in
which many speakers pronounce the consonant quite in the
General American manner. And the pronunciation of many other
persons who live east of the Connecticut River exhibits that
same haphazard irregularity that is so common in the city.
Undoubtedly, the occurrence of /r/ in the preconsonantal position is somewhat more frequent in New York than in eastern
New England; but that the two areas reveal no similarity in
regard to the occurrence of the consonant is simply not so.
 Nevertheless, though one may legitimately take issue with
Thomas about specific points, there can certainly be no quarrel with his general conclusion. The types of metropolitan
pronunciation that bear any marked resemblance to the speech
of eastern New England (in matters other than the occurrence
of /r/) are spoken only by a small minority of New Yorkers.
So far as the other dialects of the city are concerned, divergences from the New England pattern are far more numerous
than similarities. The [ɪ]- diphthongs in *third* and *turn*, the
same diphthongs in *boil* and *joint*, the retraction of the long
vowels or diphthongs in *cart* and in *law*, the absence of the
hoarse-horse distinction, the homonymy of *cod* and *card*, the
blade-alveolar affricate allophones of /t/ and /d/--these are
but a few of the characteristics of one or another of the
metropolitan dialects that have no counterparts in the speech
of eastern New England. The city and its suburbs must, as
Thomas insists, be considered a separate area in the linguistic geography of the country. The term "Eastern American"
should either not be used at all or should be restricted in
its application to the region east of the Connecticut.

1.2. Although one may properly speak of a distinct metropolitan dialect-area, one cannot similarly speak of a single
metropolitan dialect--for the speech-patterns heard in the
city and its environs are extraordinarily varied. The task of
the observer, as a result, is a somewhat different one from
that which would confront him in Ohio or in Montana. The phonetician studying the pronunciation of many parts of the
United States can practically leave out of account differences that may be correlated with varying degrees of cultivation and of social status. Nowhere, of course, do educated
and uneducated persons speak the same English. But in large
areas of America, so far as my limited knowledge goes, the
differences that occur are chiefly morphological, syntactic,
and lexical. A Middle Western farmhand whose formal schooling
had been rather limited and a member of a university faculty,
both of them natives of the same state, will certainly not
talk alike. The teacher will avoid certain verb-forms, for
example, which the other uses naturally. His sentences, even

in his most colloquial moments, are likely to exhibit a somewhat different syntactic arrangement, more influenced, for one thing, by the patterns of written English. And his vocabulary will be very different indeed. But in phonemic structure and in phonetic detail the speech of the two men will probably not be very far apart. In the Preface to the first edition, Kenyon describes his *American Pronunciation* as being based on the cultivated usage of the Western Reserve of Ohio. One wonders whether his work would have been very different had he chosen instead to describe the pronunciation of garage mechanics and soda clerks in the same region--or at least of those among them who were of the older American stock. Probably it would not be. The phonetic uniformity in cultivated and uncultivated speech in much of the United States is, in truth, one of the most striking aspects of American English.

In New York City this uniformity does not exist. Here too, as everywhere, cultivated and uncultivated English go their separate ways in many matters of morphology, syntax, and vocabulary. But in addition, a large number of marked differences in pronunciation serve to set apart from one another the speech-habits of individuals and of social groups. In some cases these variations involve the occurrence and distribution of phonemes, for example the distribution of /ɛɜ/ and /ɜɪ/. More commonly, they are of the kind which Jones calls diaphonic, that is, they are articulatory and acoustic differences in the pronunciation of what is phonemically the same vowel or consonant. As examples one might cite the varying articulation of intervocalic [r] before an unstressed vowel or the variations in quality of the first element of the diphthong /aɪ/. In either case, the result is that the pronunciation of two New Yorkers, both of them born and bred in the city, may exhibit far greater divergences than those that distinguish the speech of Wisconsin, let us say, from that of Oregon.

These variations in metropolitan usage are for the most part not chance, individual peculiarities, but as I have indicated, features of class-dialect. By this I mean that they can be brought into an approximate relation at least with the whole complex of such nonlinguistic factors as education, income, occupation, family background, and so forth. The pronunciation of a cab-driver whose father and grandfathers were also members of the working class will normally differ, both phonemically and phonetically, from that of a physician whose family has been well-to-do and college-educated for several generations. And the features that appear in the pronunciation of the two men are likely to recur in the speech of others of similar background and education. The correspondence between language and these nonlinguistic factors is never, of course, exact. In the pronunciation of this or that cultivated speaker, for example, one may observe some feature that is for the most part confined to uncultivated use. I have described the well-known homonymy of *curl* and *coil*, *learn* and *loin* as uncultivated, for although the diphthong /ɜɪ/ may appear in words like *curl* on all levels, in cultivated speech words like *coil* ordinarily exhibit the phonemically distinct /ɔɪ/. Nevertheless, I have a few times heard elderly persons of undoubted cultivation pronounce /ɜɪ/ in words of the *coil*-group also. But the correspondences, even if they are not one-to-one, do none the less exist; and any description of metropolitan speech in which pronunciations were not labeled as belonging to one or another class-dialect would be confusing and more or less meaningless. Throughout this study, therefore, I have tried to indicate as best I could on what levels particular pronunciations are likely to occur.

Now, when one employs terms like "cultivated" and "uncultivated," there is some danger that he will apply the former to pronunciations that he happens to like and the latter to those against which he has some merely personal prejudice. He is certain to falsify the record, of course, if he approaches his task with a preconceived idea of propriety, of a standard, as do the authors of so many prescriptive manuals. It may be that I have not entirely succeeded in avoiding such dangers myself. I have, however, tries to work without preconceptions and to ground my use of classificatory labels exclusively on nonlinguistic criteria. That is to say that I have begun with the facts of social life, as it were, and first roughly classified those whom I have observed on the basis of matters other than their use of spoken language. One informant, for instance, is an elevator operator, born in the Hell's Kitchen district of Manhattan. His father and paternal grandfather were both slaughterhouse workers. He has not completed the eighth grade of elementary education and the necessity of writing a claim-letter to the Veterans' Administration presents him with a difficult problem. Since leaving school he has held a succession of jobs, all of them relatively unskilled. The pronunciations that I have observed in the usage of this speaker and of others of comparable education and background I have classed as uncultivated. Another informant is a woman of education, the sister of a well-known novelist and poetess, and a descendant of two former presidents of Columbia College. The usage of this speaker and of others of comparable education and family background I have described as cultivated.[7]

1.3. There is another sort of variation that I think requires some comment, especially because it seems to be very rarely discussed in phonological writings. It has long been recognized that all dialects are in a sense mixed ones: particular linguistic changes, however regularly they may have been carried through in the forms of speech in which they first arose, do not spread uniformly across an area, and each word consequently has its own history and its own isogloss. But it is usually assumed that the resulting irregularities in the speech of a given area or of a given individual involve merely the lexical distribution of phonemes. Thus in one speaker's dialect Middle English "short o" may be represented by /ɔɝ/ in *dog* but by /aɝ/ in *log*. The historical correspondences are disturbed, presumably as a result of dialect mixture. The two phonemes /ɔɝ/ and /aɝ/ form, nevertheless, a set of exclusive categories, as do all the other phonemes of the dialect. Their actualizations in successive utterances may exhibit a good deal of phonetic variation, but normally within such limits that there is no overlapping in a particular position. As Bloomfield puts it: "In the ordinary case, there is a limit to the variability of the non-distinctive features: the phoneme is kept distinct from all other phonemes of its language. Thus we speak the vowel of a word like *pen* in a great many ways, but not in any way that belongs to the vowel of *pin*, and not in any way that belongs to the vowel of *pan*: the three types are kept rigidly apart."[8]

"In the ordinary case," this is of course true. If it were not, if there were no limits set to the variability of allophones, we could not talk at all and expect to be understood. But I have been impressed, in studying the usage of individual speakers, by the number of cases that are not ordinary. In some instances, in the speech of the same person, a particular opposition may appear and disappear in a rather bewildering fashion. In the speaker's dialect, that is to say, one may observe two phonemic patterns: he pronounces now according to one, now according to the other, and frequently in such a fashion that the phonemic situation is obscure. I became aware of these incomplete suspensions, as they might be called, when I noticed that it was often difficult in transcribing to decide to which of two contiguous phonemes the vowel in a particular utterance should be assigned. A few examples will serve to make this matter clear.

In the high-front vowel range, there is an opposition between /i/ and /iɝ/, which serves to distinguish (in the speech of "*r*-less" speakers) pairs like *bid-beard*, *Milly-merely*, and the like. But before /r/ it is often difficult in particular cases to decide whether this opposition is present or not. *Dearer*, for example, normally has a rather long monophthong; but *mirror* may be pronounced by the same person, now with a short vowel, so that it does not rime, and now with a longer one, so that it does. And often one hears vowels of intermediate length, so that one is quite at a loss to know whether in a phonemic transcription one should write /i/ or /iɝ/. The same difficulty may be present in the case of /a/ and /aɝ/ before /r/. In successive utterances a speaker may pronounce *sorry* so that it does not rime with *starry*, then so that it does, and then so that the listener cannot be sure.

These low-back vowels also furnish another example of the

same sort. In the pronunciation of "r-less" speakers, pairs like *shop-sharp, cot-cart, goggles-gargles* exhibit this same opposition between /ɑ/ and /ɑǝ̃/. Before certain consonants, however, the opposition tends to disappear, and *god* and *guard*, *gob* and *garb* may be homonymous. But the pronunciation of many persons is rather unpredictable. In their speech words like *guard* and *garb* normally have a long monophthong or a diphthong, and do not vary much. But the length of the syllabics in words like *god* and *gob* seems highly unstable: in successive utterances under similar conditions of stress one may hear long monophthongs, diphthongs with a pronounced glide, or vowels that are rather short. The speech of such persons appears to be forever oscillating between one pattern according to which a difference in length (and often in quality also) serves to constitute an opposition before these consonants, and another pattern according to which the opposition is suspended.

It may be that irregularities like these--and many more examples may be found in the body of this study--are to be observed everywhere. Perhaps they may occur even in the speech of small, homogeneous, and isolated communities. But I am inclined to suspect that they are peculiarly characteristic of the dialects of large cities like New York. In such cities, where so many different patterns exist cheek-by-jowl, the pronunciation of a particular speaker may never reach a state of phonemic equilibrium, as one might call it. From childhood, his speech is affected by all sorts of diverse influences. As a consequence, his usage may exhibit a degree of variability that it would not have if he had grown up in a community of another sort--a community in which all the persons whom he imitated when he learned to talk spoke what was in general the same dialect.

1.4. As the subtitle indicates, this account of New York pronunciation is a partial one, dealing only with the vowel and consonant phonemes of the various metropolitan dialects. Certain matters have not been discussed at all, chiefly because including them would have resulted in a study of such length that it would be impossible for me to publish it. I have, therefore, excluded any consideration of intonation patterns or of juncture phenomena, although in the latter case a good deal of incidental information is contained in the discussion of the separate phonemes. I have in addition made two other major limitations, which should be clearly understood.

In the first place, I have arbitrarily confined my attention to the city proper. Such a restriction, of course, is a wholly artificial one: the speech-patterns of the metropolis do not suddenly disappear at the North River or the Nassau County line. Beyond Yonkers, many features of metropolitan pronunciation die out rather quickly, but the suburban communities of Nassau County and the near-by towns of Hudson

County, New Jersey, are linguistically part of the city. If one does not set an arbitrary limit to the area being considered, however, he is faced with the task of establishing a separate isogloss for each major feature of the New York dialects. The determination of these boundaries, I have felt, might properly be made the subject of a separate investigation and I have not undertaken it here. I do have a good deal of material in the speech records of Columbia College undergraduates from these suburban areas, on the basis of which certain isoglosses might be determined--at least for the speech of those under thirty years of age. An analysis of this material I hope to publish later.

The second limitation I have set is implied in the statement that this study deals with the pronunciation of New Yorkers who have no immediate foreign language background.[9] No information is given, except incidentally, regarding the many subdialects that arise from the blending of English and other languages in the speech of the foreign born or of their children. Since the number of persons living in the five boroughs of New York City who fall into these categories is greater than the population of some sovereign states, this is a very considerable restriction indeed. Nor would the detailed investigation of the usage of such speakers be unprofitable. An extended account of the varied substitutions and "contamination-forms" in the English of bilingual New Yorkers would not only be of interest to linguists, but of great practical value to teachers of pronunciation. But this too is a subject for half-a-dozen other monographs--and before any of them can be written, a more detailed description than has hitherto appeared of those types of New York speech that are not the result of bilingualism is required. It has been my aim to perform this more restricted task.

Perhaps it may be objected that such a limitation is based on a rather dubious assumption. New York is a multilingual city, in whose streets one may hear all the languages of the Western World. Some of them, particularly Yiddish and Italian, are spoken by large groups among the city's population. Is it at all possible, one might ask, to ignore these other languages in studying any aspect of the city's speech? Let us put the case of a working-class family of the older stock, one which has lived in the city for a number of generations. In such a family, normally, nothing but English is spoken or understood. But the children go through the public schools with the boys and girls who hear Italian, Yiddish, Greek, or Polish at home. Later on they work in factories or offices with people of similarly diverse backgrounds. Is it not absurd to think that their speech will be unaffected by all these intimate contacts? Indeed, is it not probable that many of those features that distinguish their pronunciation from that of Kentuckians or Yorkshiremen have resulted from the influence of these foreign tongues?

GENERAL OBSERVATIONS 9

In attempting to answer such questions as these, one might have recourse to certain generally accepted conclusions of historical linguistics. It has been pointed out time and again that when foreigners enter a country, not as conquerors but as immigrants, their influence on the language of the older native groups is very slight. And this is true even if they come in considerable numbers. Usually borrowing does not go beyond the taking over of a few words and phrases. A small number of Yiddish words, for example, have passed over into American slang, and Americans call certain foods by their German or Italian names. But details of morphology, of syntax, or of phonemic structure are normally not adopted at all. The newcomer imitates as best he can the speech of the native speaker, but his own usage is not similarly imitated.

Granting, however, that this principle is perfectly valid when applied to American English as a whole, it may be that conditions in New York City are so very special that one cannot apply it here. Certainly nowhere else in the United States are there such vast concentrations of the foreign born. The not unnatural tendency, furthermore, of the foreign-language groups to congregate in particular neighborhoods undoubtedly results in a slowing down of the process of cultural assimilation. So certain very definite foreignisms may often be observed in the pronunciation of Columbia College freshmen who are monoglot speakers of English, but whose grandparents spoke Yiddish or Italian. Hence, because of the sheer weight of numbers and because of the persistence of foreign traits within certain groups at least, an influence might possibly be exerted on the speech of the older native stock that would not be exerted elsewhere in America. It would not be wise, therefore, to lay much stress on this general principle.

More to the point is the fact, already alluded to, that so many features of metropolitan pronunciation recur in other areas where foreign influence can be discounted. (As I have said, it is often merely the particular combination of these features which is unique in the city's speech.) The New York [ï]-diphthongs, for example, in words like *third* and *turn* are also heard very commonly in coastal Southern speech, even though the exact quality may not be quite the same. With similar slight qualitative differences, the retraction of the first element of the diphthong in *ride* and *fly* also appears in other dialects. The dental affricate or stop in *the* and *this* may occur in the substandard speech of many regions. Again, the pronunciation of many New Yorkers differs, as I have said, from most types of spoken English in that words like *guard* and *god*, *large* and *lodge*, *garb* and *gob* are homonyms. But only the pattern here is unusual; for the absence of /r/ in the preconsonantal position is to be observed in other areas, and so is the unrounding and lengthening of Middle English "short o" before certain consonants. And these are but a few of the resemblances, partial or complete, which might be pointed out.

A certain residue of unique features, to be sure, would remain even after one had made an exhaustive catalog of such similarities. One might mention the occurrence before a pause of monophthongal variants of /iə̆/ and /ɛə̆/ (in words like *clear* and *hair*). Or the occurrence between a stressed and an unstressed vowel of a strongly lip-modified allophone of /r/ (*very, fear it*). Or the peculiar dentalized blade-articulation of the alveolar consonants. The difficulty in such cases is that analogous features do not appear in the languages from which borrowing might conceivably have taken place.[10] One cannot, after all, label metropolitan pronunciations "foreignisms" merely because speakers in Chattanooga and Evanston do not use them. A foreignism in pronunciation involves the substitution of a particular feature of the foreign language, the hypercorrection of such a feature, or a contamination (as when a German produces the English [r] with the tongue-point raised to the back of the alveolar ridge, but with velar friction as well). In any event one must find something in the foreign pattern which might reasonably be considered the source of the English pronunciation. And this, so far as I have been able to determine, cannot be done in the case of the several peculiarities of metropolitan English.

This matter may be further clarified if we approach it from the opposite direction. Let us consider certain pronunciations which very definitely are foreignisms. The difficulty, for example, that many persons whose first language is Yiddish have in distinguishing between *reed* and *rid, feel* and *fill* is well known. The source of this difficulty is also very apparent. Many dialects of Yiddish have obliterated the distinction between the Middle High German short and long vowels. In the high-front range they have as a consequence only one phoneme. Many Yiddish speakers, therefore, hear no marked difference between the English /i/ and /iː/ and so confuse them. But despite the large number of such speakers in the metropolitan area, this confusion never appears in the speech of New Yorkers of the older stock. (In fact, it is only in extraordinary cases that the American-born children of Yiddish-speaking parents show any trace of it.) A more striking instance is afforded by the foreigner's failure to distinguish between /ŋ/ and the sequence /ŋg/. The English pattern exemplified in the series *sinker-linger-singer* does not appear in any European language that I know of. In Yiddish, Italian, Spanish, Greek, and the Slavic group the *singer*-type is lacking, with the result that speakers of these languages commonly pronounce the velar stop in such words. This mispronunciation, possibly because the /ŋ/-/ŋg/ distinction is semantically unimportant in English, persists very frequently in the speech of the first American-born generation. Indeed, among those of Yiddish or Italian back-

ground, it is common in the pronunciation of the immigrant's
grandchildren. It does not appear, however, in the speech of
those who do not have one of these languages in their own
family backgrounds. Among Columbia freshmen, for example,
this foreignism is extremely common. It occurs in the speech
of a large majority of those who hear Yiddish or Italian at
home, and it is also frequent among those in whose families
these languages went out of use a generation ago. But in the
pronunciation of students of the older English and Dutch
stocks, or those whose families took part in the mid-nine-
teenth-century German immigration, or those of Irish descent,
I have not once encountered it.[11]

1.5. The reader, making his laborious way through the later
sections of this study, might perhaps think that I had made
another major omission, of which I have so far not spoken.
Where, he might ask, is the Brooklyn accent? There is a great
deal of comment about the levels on which particular pronunciations may appear, but where is the corresponding information about the geographical distribution of variants within
the city? And it is true that I have not at any place marked
a certain pronunciation as being predominantly the usage of
Brooklyn, or of Staten Island, or of the Borough of Queens.
But the reason for this silence is a very simple one: there
is no evidence, so far as I have been able to discover, that
any purely geographical variation in speech-patterns really
occurs within the city. Certain pronunciations, of course,
may have a much higher frequency in one neighborhood than in
another. For example, a careful sampling of the usage of a
large number of speakers would undoubtedly show that the
homonymy of *learn* and *loin* was far more frequent in Elmhurst
in the Borough of Queens than in the east Sixties between
Fifth and Lexington Avenues. But such facts as this can be
better explained in social, than in geographic terms. During
the past fifteen years phonographic recordings of the pronunciation of several thousand students from the city have been
made at Columbia College, both as part of the freshman speech
test and during the work of an undergraduate course. An observer, listening to these records with a sufficient knowledge of the metropolitan dialects, could make very shrewd
guesses about the family background of the various speakers,
the *kind* of neighborhoods they grew up in, and so forth. But
I am quite convinced that no observer, however keen his ear
or considerable his knowledge, could sort the speakers out by
boroughs. The "Brooklyn accent" is merely uncultivated New
Yorkese: it may be heard in all the boroughs, and in Jersey
City and Hoboken as well. The use of the term I take as a
tribute to the peculiar vitality of the life in my native
borough, which has come in a sense to stand for the whole
city in the popular consciousness. It certainly is not the
accurate expression of any linguistic reality.

INFORMANTS, METHODS AND SYMBOLS

2.1. The thirty persons who have served as primary informants during the preparation of this study are listed in section 13.1. In each case certain pertinent facts about the informant are noted, such as his age, education, and occupation, the education of his parents, and, when known, of his grandparents, the occupation of his father and, when known, of his grandfathers. All the informants were born in New York City and with minor exceptions, the details of which are given in 13.1, have always lived here. With similar unimportant exceptions, the parents of all informants were also native New Yorkers, and in some cases the families have been established in the city since before 1700. I have also made some use of phonographic recordings of certain other New Yorkers whom I have not listed because the material I got from them was rather scanty--I made these records at a time when I did not sufficiently appreciate the necessity of getting really adequate samples of each individual's speech.

2.2. In addition, I have studied a number of recordings of the speech of nine other New Yorkers, who are listed in section 13.2. These records were made in 1941 at Columbia University of *Linguistic Atlas* informants whom Dr. Guy S. Lowman, Jr., interviewed while he was working in this area. The brief biographical comments are from Dr. Lowman's notes.

2.3. The data offered by these informants constitute the core of this study; but in addition I have frequently gone on to discuss the pronunciation of particular words that do not occur in my recorded material. To cite only a few examples, I have spoken in one place or another of the pronunciation of *Connecticut, dirigible, hundred, lasso, Lenox, lilacs, liverwurst, Loeser* (the name of a Brooklyn department store), *moire, monger, radish, sarsaparilla, Schermerhorn* (a family name, and street name in Brooklyn), *temperature,* and *vanilla.* For the methodological looseness involved here, I make no particular apology. In working with my informants, I was primarily interested in discovering what patterns emerged when one scrutinized rather closely the usage of individual speakers--for instance, in the phonetic distribution of particular vowels. I could not possibly include in my test material (which ran to fifteen typewritten pages as it was) all the words whose pronunciation was in any way of interest. Yet when I came to writing, it seemed to me that whatever value my account might have would be considerably decreased if I restricted it to those words alone which occurred on my records. I thought it desirable to note that a common local pronunciation of *Schermerhorn* is /'skemə‚hoʊn/; that the pronunciation which I have most frequently heard in the city for *dirigible* is not recorded in most dictionaries and is listed in Kenyon and Knott's *Dictionary* only as a British variant; that, as in some other parts of the country, an old pronunciation /'redəʃ/ *radish* survives in the usage of some speakers; and that the dictionary pronunciation of *sarsaparilla* is one that I have never heard in New York. Such information as this I have added on almost every page.

2.4. The material examined in this study includes test sentences, the *Rat* selection, and extemporaneous conversation. As for the first, I prepared at the beginning of my investigation a set of 365 fairly simple sentences, composed to include large numbers of those vowels and consonants that are particularly variable in New York speech. For example, more than one hundred and forty words of the Middle English "short o" group occur, because I was particularly interested in studying individual patterns in the pronunciation of the low-back vowels. There is an even larger selection of words containing vowels in the low-front range. These sentences will be found in section 13.3.

2.5. When I first began interviewing informants, my method was to have them work slowly through the test sentences, often repeating a particular sentence after an interval, while I made notes on their pronunciation in as close a transcription as seemed feasible. Then when the sentences had been completed, I made brief recordings of their unrehearsed conversation, of the *Rat* story, and sometimes of a short selection of sentences. The whole procedure usually took at least two full afternoons to complete. Because of this, I found that it was rather difficult to persuade people to serve as informants. A number who at first seemed willing to assist me balked when they learned that seven or eight hours of their time would be required. As a consequence, I began recording everything--sentences, the *Rat*, and conversation--and so proceeded with the majority of my informants. In the listing of informants I have indicated in each case what material was recorded.

2.6. I adopted the method of using written test material because I do not know of any other way in which certain aspects of pronunciation can be conveniently studied. It might seem that the best procedure would be to record nothing but unrehearsed conversation, preferably in such a way that the speaker did not know that a recording was being made. But this method has the serious disadvantage that the speaker may not happen to use the words which the investigator is especially interested in; one might record a person's conversation for several hours, for example, without getting a sufficient number of words in the *oil*-group to make any judgment concerning them. In a study of vocabulary or of selected features of morphology and syntax, the best procedure is undoubtedly that employed by the *Linguistic Atlas* workers. But in an exclusively phonological investigation, one may be interested in the pronunciation of many words that cannot be easily elicited in directed conversation. For this purpose, the use of specially composed test material seems best.

As everyone knows, certain distortions of the natural speech-patterns occur when a person reads. Because of this fact, objections have sometimes been raised to the use of written material. These objections, I feel, are not particularly convincing, for the distortions that appear in reading are pretty obvious and can be taken into account. The most important variation from ordinary conversational speech is in the frequently altered pattern of intonation and stress. (A study of intonations based on an analysis of read material would admittedly be of doubtful value.) As a result of changes in stress, strong forms will often appear in positions where the weak ones would be usual. Furthermore, open juncture between consecutive stops will sometimes replace the normal close juncture, and the glottal stop will occur more frequently before initial vowels. Assimilatory changes will not appear as frequently. But the reader's practice in regard to these matters will never be consistently unnatural and one can usually discover without much difficulty what his natural habits are.

In most respects, the pronunciations that occur in reading do not differ from those that may be observed in ordinary conversation. In the first place, although the reader may be aware in a general way that his pronunciations are not the same as those of other speakers, he is usually not conscious of the specific differences. Most of those New Yorkers, for example, who strongly affricate the stop of *time* and *return* do not hear the affricated stop and the merely aspirated one as being at all unlike. And even when a speaker is conscious of a particular difference, say between the glottal and the alveolar stop in *bottle,* and even when he wishes to avoid his natural pronunciation because it has excited ridicule, he is often quite unable to do so, either in conversation or in reading. He is not a phonetician, after all, who has trained himself to produce all sorts of sounds at will. He may have come to dislike his pronunciation [ˈbɑʔɫ], but he uses it willy-nilly because he cannot pronounce the word in any other way.

But it sometimes happens that a speaker is able to pronounce according to two different patterns: one, the pattern he acquired as a child and, the other, the one he has come to

INFORMANTS, METHODS AND SYMBOLS 15

prefer. In this case, his reading and his ordinary conversation will probably not be the same. The substitution of the preferred type will be more frequent in reading, because he is more conscious of the speech-process then, and because he actually has the written symbols before his eyes. But such substitutions are usually easy to detect, again for the reason that the speaker is likely to make them in an inconsistent fashion. The extemporaneous material also serves as a check on these changes. Indeed, I have found that the comparison of a speaker's reading and his unrehearsed conversation often brings out interesting facts about his usage. That there is an element of spelling-pronunciation, for instance, in many New Yorkers' tendency to pronounce /r/ in the preconsonantal position is shown by the fact that the consonant often occurs much more frequently in records of read material than in those of conversation. So also, one learns something about metropolitan speech when he hears an informant read *which* as /hwitʃ/ and then pronounce it repeatedly in conversation as /witʃ/.

2.7. The phonemic symbols used in this study are the following:

a) *For Consonant Phonemes*

1. *Stops*
/p/	pit
/b/	bid
/t/	tell
/d/	den
/k/	keen
/g/	give

2. *Fricatives*
/f/	fill
/v/	vane
/θ/	thin
/ð/	this
/s/	soap
/z/	zone
/ʃ/	ship
/ʒ/	vision
/h/	hold

3. *Affricates*
/tʃ/	chip
/dʒ/	jar

4. *Voiced Frictionless Consonants*
/r/	ride
/l/	lift
/w/	west
/j/	year

5. *Nasals*
- /m/ mill
- /n/ nest
- /ŋ/ sing

b) For Vowel and Diphthong Phonemes

1. *Vowels That Do Not Occur as Word-finals*
   - /i/ pit
   - /e/ best
   - /æ/ bat
   - /ɑ/ pot
   - /u/ push
   - /ʌ/ cut

2. *Diphthongs of the [ĭ]-series*
   - /iĭ/ peace
   - /eĭ/ wage
   - /aĭ/ fine
   - /ɔĭ/ noise
   - /ɜĭ/ third

3. *Diphthongs of the [ŭ]-series*
   - /aŭ/ house
   - /oŭ/ road
   - /uŭ/ food
   - /ɨŭ/ new

4. *Diphthongs of the [ə̆]-series*
   - /iə̆/ fear
   - /ɛə̆/ fair
   - /æə̆/ stand
   - /aə̆/ ask
   - /ɑə̆/ far
   - /ɔə̆/ war
   - /uə̆/ poor
   - /ɜə̆/ third
   - /ʌə̆/ occur

5. *Vowels of Completely Unstressed Syllables*
   - /ə/ soda

This table is given chiefly for purposes of recognition, and the headings consequently are not exhaustive descriptions. Thus /θ/ and /ð/ are listed merely as fricatives, although in the pronunciation of many New Yorkers they have allophones that are dental or interdental stops or affricates. Certain allophones of /r, l, w, j/ are voiceless fricatives. Among the phonemes listed as diphthongs many, for example /iĭ/, /uŭ/, and those in group *b* 4 have monophthongal allophones. A detailed description of such variants will be found in the discussion of the separate phonemes.

INFORMANTS, METHODS AND SYMBOLS   17

In the table above, twenty-five vocalic phonemes are listed.
The reader should understand that not all of them would appear in any given speaker's dialect. For example, a category
/ʌə̆/ is included in order to describe the pronunciation of
those who make a threefold distinction between *a curd* [ə kɜɪd],
occurred [ə'kʌə̆d, ə'kʌ·d], and *a cud* [ə kʌd]. In the speech
of others, however, either *a curd* and *occurred*, or *occurred*
and *a cud* are identical and the third category is unnecessary.
The category /ɨŭ/ is not needed to describe the pronunciation
of most speakers, since they pronounce all the words in which
it might appear either with /uŭ/ or with the sequence /juŭ/.
Similarly, /aə̆/ is a category which is not required in describing the speech of most New Yorkers.
     Even when such a qualification has been made, some phonologists will consider that twenty or so categories are about
three times as many as are needed to set forth the vowel-
system of any form of English.[1] Put the conception of the
long vowels and diphthongs as unitary phonemes still seems to
me the soundest one. Analyzing them as sequences of "checked"
vowels plus consonants has little to recommend it except mere
orthographic simplicity. Such an analysis involves the forced
collocation of such disparate sound-types that "phonetic
similarity" becomes quite meaningless as a criterion of phonemic identity. I must confess that I have myself applied
this criterion a bit loosely in several instances. In one
case, I have followed Trager in assigning [ʔ] in certain positions to /t/, a classification that some may object to,
because the articulatory positions are so far apart. I have
justified this, to myself at least, on the grounds that the
similarity exists for those who speak in this fashion; that
speakers who pronounce *bottle* as ['bɑʔl̩] and have never become conscious of this as a "different" pronunciation apprehend the glottal stop here as /t/ and would do so (I believe)
even if they knew no spelling. Secondly, I have treated the
unstressed vowels of *running* and of *soda* as allophones of the
same phoneme--which is admittedly going rather far. But such
an analysis does serve to bring out clearly what I regard as
one rather important characteristic of New York English: that
unstressed [i] and [ə], so far as I can see, are not significantly opposed to each other, as they are in Southern British,
but occur in a variation that is either free or determined by
position. No such purpose is served, however, by the identification of the off-glide of the [ə̆]-diphthongs with /h/. As
Einar Haugen and W. F. Twaddell have remarked,[2] this analysis
tells us nothing about English pronunciation which we did not
know before.
     To underline my conviction that the diphthongs (and their
monophthongal variants) are best conceived as unitary phonemes, I have written their second elements with symbols
which are not used to represent any other phonemes, namely by
[ɪ̆], [ŭ], and [ə̆]. In other words, the /iə̆/ of *hear* is not to

be interpreted as a sequence composed of the vocalic phoneme of *hit* followed by the first vocalic phoneme of *attempt*. It is an indivisible unit.

2.8. For reasons of economy, I have not used an elaborate set of finely graded phonetic symbols, one for each allophone and for each of the diaphones of different dialects, although I have described such variants in a fairly detailed fashion. Of necessity, however, I have employed a small number of specifically phonetic symbols. These symbols, which do not occur in phonemic transcription, are the following:
 a) [ʔ] is used for the glottal stop.
 b) Syllabic consonants are indicated by the usual modifier: [n̩, l̩, r̩], etc.
 c) The hyphen is used to mark position in syllables. Initial position is indicated by a following hyphen, final position by a preceding one. Ambisyllabic position is shown by two hyphens, thus: [-p-].
 d) The monophthongal variants of the [ɞ]-series of diphthongs are indicated by the symbol for the first element followed by a raised period: [i·, ɛ·, a·], etc.
 e) The symbol [ɒ] is used to indicate a lower low-back, rounded vowel. (In a few references to British English, it is used as a phonemic symbol.)
 f) The modifiers [˔, ˕, ˒, ˓] are used in the senses "raised," "lowered," "advanced," "retracted," respectively. The modifier [˜] indicates nasality.

2.9. Only a few other comments on the use of symbols are necessary:
 a) In direct quotation from other writers, I have of course allowed their symbols to stand unaltered.
 b) In phonemic transcription, I have followed the practice of the Kenyon and Knott *Dictionary* in indicating what might be called "movable /r/" by /(r/: /hiɞ(r/ *here*, /faɞ(r/ *far*. For the reason advanced on page 138, note 38, I do not consider that anything is gained by analyzing the two forms of a word like *far* as phonemically equivalent, even though their occurrence is positionally determined. I employ this device merely to avoid writing every word of this sort twice.
 c) I have already referred to the mixed pattern of many New York speakers in the matter of the occurrence of /r/ in the preconsonantal position. In generalized transcriptions I have normally cited words in their "r-less" form, thus: /biɞd/ *beard*, /fɔɞk/ *fork*. But all such transcriptions should be read in the light of the section devoted to /r/.
 d) As the reader will already have observed, I have adopted the device, employed by Bloch and Trager, of enclosing symbols within square brackets when they were phonetic and within diagonals when they were to be interpreted as phonemic class-markers. In many specific cases, of course, either device

might be used with equal justification. Thus, in speaking of the distribution of the low-front vowels, one might say: "Within the word, /εə̆/ does not occur before /p, t, k/," or "Within the word, /εə̆/ does not occur before [-p, -p-, -t, -t-, -k, -k-]." In such cases, I have ordinarily employed diagonals, although I am not sure that the reader will not find occasional inconsistencies.

THE CONSONANTS

THE STOPS

3.1. /p/. In cultivated speech, the following allophones may be distinguished:

a) A voiceless aspirated stop occurs initially[1] in stressed syllables: *pound, appoint*. The position assumed by the lips may be influenced to some extent by the nature of the preceding or following phones: they may be protruded slightly, for example, in articulating the [p] of *paw* and *poor*.[2] After the stop, the allophones of /l/ (*plaid*), /r/ (*profit*), and /j/ (*pure*) are regularly voiceless fricatives or begin as such.

b) When preceded by /s/ and followed by a vowel, unless an onset of stress falls between the consonants, a lax unaspirated bilabial stop occurs, whose phonemic classification has frequently been discussed. A similar problem arises in the classification of the alveolar and velar stops and, as will be seen, of certain other consonants as well. Since the difficulty in all these cases is the same, I have chosen to deal with the entire matter here.

(Excursus: It has often been pointed out that in words like *spill, still,* and *skill* phones are employed in American English which are phonetically different from the initial stops of *pill, till,* and *kill*. From the examples usually cited, one might infer that phones of this type occur only before stressed vowels in the same word. This is not the case, however, for similar stops may be observed in words like *whisper, boasting,* and *whiskers,* and also before initial vowels when /s/ plus a stop constitutes a word-final cluster in a word which is part of a closely knit phrase: *wisp of straw, cost of living, risk of death*.[3] Furthermore, parallel examples may be observed in the case of the labio-dental fricatives (*sphere* and similar words) and the palato-alveolar affricates (*question* and the like). Under these conditions the oppositions /p/-/b/, /t/-/d/, /k/-/g/, /f/-/v/, and /tʃ/-/dʒ/ do not occur. In the case of pairs like *disperse-disburse, discussed-disgust,* which might seem to provide minimal contrasts, either the onset of stress in *disburse, disgust* separates the consonants, so that the examples are not valid for establishing an opposition; or the stress-onset precedes or falls within the fricative, and the pairs are homonymous. The former type of pronunciation, in my observation, is artificial and uncommon, and the words are usually pronounced alike.

Whenever an opposition is suspended in a particular position, the question how one is to classify the phones arises.[4]

To label them archiphonemes or to establish a separate phonemic category in each instance of the sort is undoubtedly the procedure least open to attack. But most phoneticians, desiring for one reason or another to work with the smallest possible number of categories, assign the phones in the position of suspension to one member of the suspended pair. This procedure seems to me defensible enough so long as one recognizes it as arbitrary and makes no exaggerated claims for its rigidly scientific character. In the case of the stops, almost all writers agree in assigning the phones in *spill, still,* and *skill* to /p/, /t/, and /k/, respectively. I have followed the usual practice here, in part at least because I do not want to give the impression that metropolitan pronunciation differs from other types of American English in respect to this matter.[5] At the same time it may be questioned whether the assumption that these phones are always voiceless is entirely true. In transcribing from records, one may at times be inclined to think that the voice sets in *before* the following vowel, particularly if the vowel is unstressed.[6] Putting the matter another way, it may be asked whether in American English there is regularly an observable phonetic difference between the stops in *whisper* and *slumber*, or between those in *poster* and *launder*. Examining such phones by instrumental methods to discover how often the ones classified as /p/, /t/, and /k/ were voiced might have some interesting results.)

In the sequences /spl, spr, spj/, unless the stop begins a stressed syllable, fully voiced allophones of /l, r, j/ are usual: *split, spring, whispering* (disyllabic), *spew.*

c) A voiceless bilabial stop, somewhat less strongly aspirated than the [p] of *pound*, occurs as a word-initial before unstressed vowels: *Patricia, perhaps.* In the ambisyllabic position (*slipper, shopping*), the aspiration is weaker still and may be absent. But the substitution of voiced stops in this latter case, which is reported as occurring in certain other types of American English,[7] I have not observed.

d) In final position before a pause there is free variation between
 1. a voiceless unreleased bilabial stop;
 2. the same, accompanied by a simultaneous glottal closure;
 3. an aspirated stop;
 4. a stop which is lightly released without any real explosive effect.

e) Before following initial consonants, both released and unreleased varieties of /p/ occur. Before /l/, for example, a weak release is usually heard, while before stops there is normally no explosion, although as the lips open a weak release may sometimes be observed if the following stop is not homorganic. When the following consonant is a fricative, whatever release might otherwise be heard is absorbed. The unexploded stop or one whose release is absorbed in a following fricative is also used in final clusters: *apt, lapse*. Labio-dental articulation may occur before /f/ and /v/, for example in *cupful*.

f) Nasal release occurs before the syllabic variant of /m/ which is sometimes heard in rather negligent pronunciation as a result of assimilation in words like *happen* and *open*. The stops in words like *Chapman, ripeness*, whose articulation Daniel Jones also classifies under this head,[8] in New York English are better considered as examples of the unreleased type referred to above. There is normally so little pressure behind the closure that when the velum drops, no particular effect of nasal plosion is heard.

The practice of uncultivated metropolitan speakers does not differ, except in minor phonetic respects, from that already described:

a) In the speech of some, the aspiration of the initial stop before a high-stressed vowel is sometimes heavier than is ordinarily the case in cultivated English. Occasionally an affricated stop may be heard; but it is neither so striking nor so common as the affricated allophone of /t/ (see page 26).[9]

b) There is sometimes an incomplete labial closure in the position between a stressed and an unstressed vowel (*slipper, stop it*) and in the final clusters /ps/ and /pθ/ (*ships, depth*). The lips come together at the sides but do not quite meet in the center. Such pronunciations may also be heard occasionally in the negligent speech of the cultivated.

3.2. /b/. A voiced bilabial stop occurs initially and finally in syllables, in the ambisyllabic position, and in certain initial and final clusters: *buy, crab, robber, bray, blast, ribs, robbed, de Kalb*. The allophones that are used in these various positions require only a few brief comments. In general, cultivated and uncultivated speakers articulate the stop in the same fashion.

As in the case of the other stops, both released and unreleased varieties of the final stop may be heard before a pause. When a release is heard, it is ordinarily very weak and voiceless. Before following initial consonants, both types also occur, the unreleased stop being usual before other stops (though a barely audible release may sometimes be heard in words like *subcommittee, subgroup*). Before other consonants, the release, if it is heard at all, is also very weak. When the following consonant is /f/ or /v/, the stop is sometimes labio-dental (*cab fare, mob violence*).

Nasal plosion occurs before the syllabic variant of /m/ in the negligent pronunciation of words like *cabin-boy*.

In the speech of those whose articulation is in general very slipshod, there may be an incomplete labial closure in

the position between a stressed and an unstressed vowel (*cabbage, rub it*), and in the final cluster /bz/ (*ribs*).
The complete loss of the stop is uncommon. I have occasionally heard a substandard pronunciation of *submarine*, in which the stop had been lost as a result of assimilation. For *probably*, /ˈprɑbliĭ/, with the loss of a syllable, is rather frequent on all levels; in uncultivated pronunciation both stops may disappear: /ˈprɑliĭ/.

3.3. /t/. In cultivated pronunciation the following allophones may be distinguished:

a) A voiceless aspirated alveolar stop occurs initially in stressed syllables: *time, attain*. The stop is usually somewhat retracted in the cluster /tr/ (*try*). The allophone of /r/ which occurs in this position, like that of /w/ (*tweed*), is a voiceless fricative or begins as such.

b) When preceded by /s/ and followed by a vowel, unless an onset of stress falls between the consonants, a lax unaspirated alveolar stop occurs, which is here arbitrarily assigned to /t/: *still, misty, It cost a dollar*. In the sequence /str/ under similar conditions (*string, mystery*), a fully voiced allophone of /r/ occurs.

c) A weakly aspirated voiceless alveolar stop may occur, in interchange with phones (a voiced tap or a rapid voiced stop) that I would arbitrarily assign to /d/:

1) Between a stressed and an unstressed vowel: *city, courtesy, Let him go*. Under these conditions, /d/ may occur in the preposition *to* (*Go to the door*) and as a word-initial in *today, together, tonight, tomorrow*. Usually, however, in words of this pattern, for example in *telegrapher, terrific, toboggan*, the aspirated voiceless stop is regular and /d/ does not occur.

2) Between two unstressed vowels: *liberty, riveter, I know that he does*.

3) Between two stressed vowels if an onset of stress immediately follows the consonant: *light opera, right answer* (compare *high tide*).

4) Between an unstressed and a stressed vowel if an onset of stress immediately follows the consonant: *secret agent, at Albany* (compare *a tall man*).

The relative frequency of /t/ and /d/ in these cases varies from speaker to speaker and also according to style. In deliberate and consciously careful enunciation, such as might be employed in formal reading, the occurrence of /t/ is likely to increase noticeably. This increase, I believe, is only in part due to a feeling for "correctness" derived from the spelling.

The assignment of what is ordinarily called "voiced *t*" to the phoneme /d/ may require some justification. When a voiced tap is used in *atom, latter,* or *kitty*, the words become homonyms of *Adam, ladder,* and *kiddie,* which are also most commonly pronounced with a voiced tap. The /t/-/d/ opposition is thus suspended in this position.[10] One might of course establish a separate phonemic category to include these phones, but assigning them arbitrarily to /d/ seems the simplest and most reasonable procedure.[11]

d) A weakly aspirated voiceless stop, in variation with a rapid voiced stop, occurs after /l/ between vowels unless an onset of stress falls between the consonants: *cultivate, It fell to the ground, I felt it*. But even when the stop is voiced, contrasts like *melted-melded, bolted-folded* remain (although the contrast seems at least partly dependent on a difference in length of the sequence /el/ or /oŭl/). So also the opposition /nt/-/nd/ under the same conditions is stable, so that *center* and *sender* are not homonyms and *counter* and *flounder* do not rime. But between unstressed vowels (for example, in *seventy* and *lavender*) the stops sometimes seem identical to my ears.

e) A voiceless unreleased alveolar stop, often accompanied by a simultaneous glottal closure, occurs finally in stressed and unstressed syllables before a pause or an initial consonant. Before a pause it is in free variation with the aspirated stop, which may be used in distinct, emphatic utterance, and a stop which is lightly released without any noticeable explosion. Before initial consonants, both released and unreleased varieties occur, the latter being usual before stops. But when /t/ is final in many consonant clusters, it may be released even before stops in careful utterance (*textbook, chipped beef, district court*), although in many of these clusters it is often lost. The loss of the stop is also rather common when it stands, preceded by another consonant, before /s/: *lifts, corrupts, compacts*. Sometimes the glottal stop is substituted for [-t] before a following initial consonant: *it means, that boy*.

f) A laterally released voiceless alveolar stop occurs before the syllabic form of /l/, interchanging with /d/: *battle, shuttle, myrtle*. In the latter case, words like *metal* and *meddle, petal* and *pedal* fall together. The occurrence of /d/ is perhaps not as common in this position as it is between vowels in words like *British* and *city*.

g) A nasally released voiceless alveolar stop, sometimes accompanied by a simultaneous glottal closure, occurs before the syllabic form of /n/: *cotton, matinee*. When the stop is preceded by another consonant, both nasal and oral release may be observed: *Fulton, mountain, Boston, Upton*. Precise and careful utterance favors the orally released stops, but the relative frequency of the two types is also in part dependent on the nature of the preceding consonant. Thus [ˈmaŭntņ] is almost regular, [ˈfultņ] very common, and [ˈʌptņ] rare. It may be noted that in the "r-less" type of metropolitan pronunciation nasal plosion often occurs in *eastern, western,* and *lantern*.[12]

h) A voiceless dental or interdental stop occurs before /θ/ in the same syllable (*eighth* and, in the pronunciation of many speakers, *breadth, width, hundredth*) and finally before a following /θ/ or /ð/ (*that thing, sit there*). It is sometimes accompanied by a simultaneous glottal closure.

In the less cultivated speech of the city the phonemic patterning of /t/ is in general the same (for an exception, see page 36), but several rather striking phonetic differences occur. The most important of these is the articulation of [t] (and of the other alveolar consonants) with the tongue-point in contact with the inner surfaces of the upper or, more commonly, the lower front teeth. The stop is not a true dental, however, for the primary closure is made between the blade of the tongue and the alveolar ridge. Often the interdental aperture is very small; many New Yorkers, indeed, find it extremely difficult to articulate any alveolar consonant if the jaws are wedged apart with the finger-tip.

The blade-articulation of the alveolar consonants, with the related affrication of certain allophones of /t/ and /d/, is certainly one of the more important differentiae of less cultivated metropolitan speech today. Although this type of articulation is not particularly recent in the New York dialects,[13] there is some reason to believe that it has become much more common in the past two generations. Among the oldest generation of uncultivated speakers, I have noticed that many do not employ it, while in the speech of those, say, under thirty-five it is extremely common. In fact, among younger persons, it may be observed on a level considerably removed from the completely uncultivated one. The affrication of [t-] and sometimes of [d-] appears, for example, in the speech of many university students from middle class families. (I have indicated in section 13.1 which of my informants pronounce these affricated stops.)

It is sometimes said that this peculiar manner of articulating the alveolar consonants is a foreignism in New York speech. Though the "substratum" language is usually not specified, the writers often seem to have Yiddish in mind.[14] This seems to me quite unlikely. It is true that blade-articulation is common in the pronunciation of Jews in the city; but it is also common in the speech of those who are not likely to be imitating Jewish practice, either consciously or unconsciously. For example, it appears very frequently in the pronunciation of Columbia College freshmen whose parents were born in Ireland and whose primary and secondary education has been exclusively parochial. In Yiddish itself, blade-articulation, and the affrication of [t] *in word-initial position* (*tog, teler, tochter*) occur, so far as my limited knowledge goes, only in the speech of Jews of the American-born generations. I have been informed[15] that this type of articulation is not known in European Yiddish and that in the pronunciation of Jews whose Yiddish is not spoken with an English accent the initial allophone of their /t/ is a tongue-point stop that is often less strongly aspirated than the corresponding North German one.[16]

The allophones of /t/ found in uncultivated metropolitan speech, arranged in the same order as above, are the following:

a) In place of the moderately aspirated alveolar stop, a heavily affricated blade-alveolar stop may be employed initially in stressed syllables: *time, attain*. The release is relatively slow; and as the tongue-blade moves away from the gum-ridge, it passes momentarily through a position not unlike that of the fricative, [s]. Frequently as the release takes place the jaw drops down, the tongue and jaw moving as one. Even in the cluster /tr/ (*try*) the tip of the tongue may remain in contact with the lower teeth during the articulation of both consonants.

b) In the sequence /st/ before a vowel, unless an onset of stress falls between the consonants, a lax unaspirated blade-alveolar stop may occur.

c) Intervocalically under the conditions described above, the voiced tap, in occasional variation with a fully articulated voiced stop, is rather general and /t/ much less common than it is in cultivated speech. The articulation is sometimes blade-alveolar.[17] In indistinct articulation, the intervocalic consonant may occasionally disappear: [ˈpri-iɪ̆ ˈgud] *pretty good*.[18]

d) After /l/ and /n/ before unstressed vowels, the stop may lost entirely. This loss is more common after /n/ than after /l/ and more common in certain words than in others: pronunciations of *twenty* riming with *penny* and of *want a, want to* riming with *Donna* are extremely frequent. (Nor are they unknown in cultivated speech.) The voiced tap may also occur and, particularly in emphatic articulation, the affricated blade-alveolar stop. (Those among my students who normally rime *twenty* with *penny,* if they are asked to "pronounce the *t,*" will frequently use an affricated stop. The regular occurrence of the affricated stop in this position, however, I have observed chiefly in the pronunciation of persons with a Yiddish-language background.) An anomalous word is *ninety*, which is often pronounced with a fully articulated voiced stop.

e) In the articulation of the final stop, the following deviations from the pattern described above may be mentioned:

1) Blade-articulation is common.
2) The substitution of the glottal stop is more frequent.
3) A final stop, if exploded before a pause, may sometimes be heavily affricated.[19]
4) The loss of the stop from many final clusters is extremely common. Many speakers are completely unable to articulate clusters like /sts/, /pts/, and /fts/ and regularly simplify them. In the sequence vowel plus /ts/, the stop

frequently disappears in contracted forms: /'lɛs 'goŭ/ *Let's go*, /ˌðæs 'rɔ̃əŋ/ *That's wrong*, /'wʌs ˌgoŭən 'a˞n/ *What's going on?*, /ˌɪs 'dʒʌs ˌwʌd iĭ 'wɑnts/ *It's just what he wants*.

5) Sporadic losses of the final stop occur before initial consonants, even when it is not part of a cluster: for example, in *that* and *what (That doesn't matter; What does he want?)*, in *let me, sit down*, and in *pocketbook*. Except for /'pɑkəˌbuk/, these pronunciations may also be heard in cultivated use.

6) The voiceless stop may occur in a frequent pronunciation of *hundred* as /'hʌnət/. (Another pronunciation of this word might also be mentioned here, namely /hʌn/, which is not used in most contexts, but may occur in phrases like *121st Street* /ˌhʌn ˌtwɛniĭ 'fɜĭs ˌstriĭt/.)

f) Pefore the syllabic form of /l/, the laterally ploded stop may be accompanied by a glottal closure, but more commonly the glottal stop occurs in place of it: ['bɑʔl̩] *bottle*. The voiced stop (/d/) is also frequent. These varying pronunciations may all be used by the same speaker.

g) Pefore the syllabic form of /n/ in words like *kitten, cotton*, the stop may be accompanied by a glottal closure, or the glottal stop may occur in place of it. Orally released [t], not uncommon in cultivated speech when certain consonants precede *(Fulton, Boston)*, is less frequently employed; when it is, the stop may be affricated.

h) The final cluster /tθ/ does not occur in the speech of many less cultivated speakers, the stop being lost. As a result, *eighth* rimes with *faith*. Finally before a following /θ/ or /ð/, [-t] may be glottalized, or the glottal stop may occur in place of it. For the appearance of /d/ in words like *the* and *this* when preceded by /t/, see page 37.

3.4. /d/. In cultivated pronunciation the following allophones may be distinguished:

a) A voiced alveolar stop occurs initially in stressed and unstressed syllables: *dime, adopt, decay, Ogden*. In the cluster /dr/ (*dry*), the stop is often retracted to the back of the alveolar ridge and the allophone of /r/ that occurs in this position normally has some fricative quality.

b) A voiced alveolar tap, in free variation with a voiced stop, appears between vowels unless the stress-onset precedes (as in *adopt* above): *budding, radio, said it, salad oil*. The occurrence of the same phones, interchanging with allophones of /t/, in words which in certain other types of English are pronounced with /t/ alone, has already been discussed in the preceding section.

c) Finally in stressed and unstressed syllables, before a pause or a following initial consonant, both released and unreleased varieties of the voiced stop occur. When it is exploded before a pau'se, the release is usually voiceless. The unreleased stop is regular before other stops except in certain cases where it is in turn preceded by a consonant, as in *creamed potatoes*. But from many of these final clusters, particularly /ld/ and /nd/, the stop is frequently lost before initial consonants (*cold cream, bandstand*). It may similarly disappear from the final clusters /ldz/ and /ndz/.

d) A voiced laterally released alveolar stop occurs before the syllabic variant of /l/ in words like *paddle, medal* and may occur beside /t/ in *rattle, metal* and the like.

e) A voiced nasally released alveolar stop occurs before the syllabic variant of /n/ in *sudden, didn't, rod and gun*, etc. When the stop is preceded by another consonant, both nasal and oral release may be heard. The former is most common if the preceding consonant is /l/ (*Belden, golden*); after /n/ in *London* nasal release, though it occurs, would strike some speakers as slipshod. After other consonants (*Ogden, loved and lost, gazed and gazed*), oral release is usual in careful utterance, though the other type may also be heard.

f) A voiced dental or interdental stop occurs in the cluster /dθ/ (*breadth, width*) and finally before a following /θ/ or /ð/ (*sad thing, read this*). For /t/ in *breadth, width, hundredth*, see page 25 above.

In uncultivated metropolitan speech the deviations from the pattern just described parallel those that appear in the case of /t/:

a) In place of the alveolar stop, a dentalized blade-articulated alveolar affricated stop may occur initially in stressed syllables (*dime, adopt*); in unstressed initial syllables (*decay, dessert*) it is less frequent. The primary closure is made between the blade of the tongue and the gum-ridge, while the tip of the tongue is usually in contact with the inner surfaces of the lower front teeth. As the stop is released, the tongue passes momentarily through a position somewhat like that of the fricative, [z]. It should be noted that the affricated allophone of /d/ is less common than that of /t/: many persons whose [t-] in *time* is strongly affricated pronounce a blade-articulated but unaffricated stop in *dime*.

b) Intervocalically under the conditions described above, the voiced tap occurs, in occasional variation with a fully articulated voiced stop. These allophones are sometimes dentalized and blade-articulated (but see page 136, note 17). For /d/ in words like *city, butter*, see pages 23-24; for /d/ in those like *the, other*, see pages 37-38.

c) Finally before a pause or a following initial consonant, a dentalized, blade-articulated stop may occur. If the stop is exploded before a pause, it may have a voiceless affrication. The loss of the stop from final clusters is more extensive than it is in cultivated speech: it may occur before a pause (*He's my friend*) or before a following initial vowel (*a friend of mine*). So also after /n/ intervocalically within the word (*wonderful, fundamental, finding*), the stop may be weakened and is often lost.

THE CONSONANTS   29

d) Before the syllabic allophone of /l/, the laterally released stop is often dentalized and blade-articulated. The occurrence of /d/ in words like *little, metal, cattle* is common, /d/ interchanging here with the glottal stop and a glottalized, blade-articulated voiceless stop (see page 27).

e) Before the syllabic allophone of /n/, a nasally ploded blade-articulated stop occurs. Nasal plosion may occur in the word *modern*, a pronunciation also used, at least occasionally, by some educated speakers. Conversely, oral plosion may sometimes occur in words like *wooden* and *hidden*, and in the contracted forms *didn't, couldn't,* etc.[20]

f) The final cluster /dθ/ does not occur in the speech of many uncultivated speakers, the stop being lost. As a result, *breadth* and *breath, width* and *with* are often homonyms (in the speech of some, *width* is /wiθ/ and *with* is /wit, wid/--see page 36).

As has already been pointed out on page 25, dentalized, blade-articulated stops are not universal in the uncultivated speech of the city. Some--particularly among the oldest generation--pronounce ordinary alveolar stops that do not differ in any noticeable way from those employed in cultivated speech.

3.5. /k/. In cultivated pronunciation the following allophones may be distinguished:

a) A voiceless aspirated velar stop occurs initially in stressed syllables: *kind, account*. After the stop, the allophones of /r/, /l/, /w/, and /j/ (*crew, claim, queen, cube*) are regularly voiceless fricatives or begin as such.

b) When preceded by /s/ and followed by a vowel, unless an onset of stress falls between the consonants, a lax unaspirated velar stop occurs, which is here arbitrarily assigned to /k/: *school, disgust, risky* (see pages 20-21). In the sequence /skr/ under similar conditions, the voiceless fricative allophone of /r/ does not appear (*scrawl, discretion*).

c) A voiceless velar stop, somewhat less strongly aspirated than the [k] of *kind*, occurs as a word-initial before unstressed vowels (*canoe, compare*). Elsewhere before unstressed vowels (*maker, cookery, make it*), the aspiration is weaker still and may be absent. For the sporadic occurrence of /g/ in the intervocalic position in words usually pronounced with /k/, see the next section.

The varieties of the stop so briefly listed in these three paragraphs in actual fact comprise a rather extended series of allophones, although it would be impracticable to note them separately. The differences between these stops depend on the fact that the point on the soft palate (or the posterior hard palate) at which the occlusion is made varies with the following vowel. As in other types of English, the stop is articulated farther forward before a front vowel than before a back vowel. To a lesser extent the point of occlusion is also affected by preceding vowels: the [k] in *maker* may be somewhat more advanced than that of *cookery*.

d) In final position before a pause there is free variation between
  1) an unreleased voiceless velar stop;
  2) the same, accompanied by a simultaneous glottal closure;
  3) an aspirated stop;
  4) a stop that is lightly released without any real explosive effect.

e) When the stop is final before initial consonants, a release is normally not heard. If the following consonant is a fricative, the explosion occurs after the articulating organs have taken the fricative position and it is not apprehended separately. Before other stops, the unreleased type is regular.

f) Nasal plosion may sometimes be heard in a rather negligent pronunciation of participial forms like *taking* and of phrases like *chicken coop*. For the question of nasal plosion in words like *Beekman* and *sickness*, see the brief discussion of the parallel cases of /p/ and /t/ on pages 21 and 135, note 12.

The usage of uncultivated speakers does not differ much from that which has just been described, and the differences are not phonemic:

a) The aspiration of the initial stop is sometimes heavier in uncultivated speech than is usually the case in cultivated pronunciation. When the syllable is heavily stressed, a somewhat affricated stop may occasionally be heard. But such pronunciations are far less frequent than the affrication of the alveolar stop: many speakers whose [t-] before a stressed vowel is strongly affricated pronounce in words like *kind* and *car* the same moderately aspirated stop that is found in the speech of the cultivated.

b) Those whose articulation is in general very slipshod occasionally pronounce in certain positions a variety of /k/ with an incomplete closure. (I have noticed this chiefly in words like *action* and *lecture*.)[21] The fricative quality of this phone is very weak.

The stop is frequently lost in a less cultivated pronunciation of *accessory* as /ə'sesərɪ̈/, used by some of my informants. I have sometimes heard a similar pronunciation of *eccentric*.

3.6. /g/. A voiced velar stop occurs initially and finally, in ambisyllabic position, and in certain initial and final clusters: *give, leg, ragged, green, glare, rugs, dragged*.
The following differences in the articulation of the various allophones may be mentioned:

As in the case of /k/, the point on the soft palate (or the posterior hard palate) at which the occlusion is made varies

with the following vowel: the stop is articulated farther
forward before front vowels than before back. To a lesser extent, the position is affected by preceding vowels, the [g]
of *dig* often being made slightly farther forward than that of
dog.
  Like the other stops, /g/ occurs in both released and unreleased varieties when it is final before a pause. When the
stop is exploded in this position, the release is normally
very weak and voiceless. Similarly weak releases may sometimes be heard before initial consonants, but the unreleased
stop is common, and is regular before other stops.
  Nasal plosion may sometimes be heard in the negligent pronunciation of participial forms like *lagging, rigging*, and of
phrases in which /ŋ/ replaces /n/ as a result of assimilation
(*dog in the manger*). For the question of nasal plosion in
words like *dogma, signature*, see the parallel cases on page
22 and page 135, note 12.
  The occurrence of /d/ in place of /t/ in words spelled *t* or
tt, which has been discussed already, is occasionally paralleled in the pronunciation of the velar stops. I have sometimes heard the voiced stop in *package, ticket, Take it away*,
and a few other cases. But such pronunciations are sporadic
and infrequent. For *Look out!*, however, the pronunciation
/ˌluˈgaut, lə-/ is very common on all levels (note the syllable-division).
  In negligent articulation there is sometimes an incomplete
closure between the back of the tongue and the roof of the
mouth, so that a weakly fricative variety of /g/ is produced
in words like *bigger* and *hugging*.
  As in other regional types of pronunciation, /g/ is not infrequently omitted from *England* and *English*. Other losses of
the stop after /ŋ/ occur in less cultivated speech in *language, distinguish, extinguisher*, and it is sometimes very
weakly articulated after /ŋ/ in other cases, for example in
angry and *single*. But the complete and regular loss of /g/
after /ŋ/ in *finger, single, younger*, etc. is a foreignism
resulting from the influence of German or the Scandinavian
languages, or occurring as a hypercorrect pronunciation in
the speech of those who are attempting without sufficient information to avoid the foreign insertion of /g/ in words like
singer and *singing*.
  The common uncultivated pronunciation /ˈrekəˌnaiz/ for *recognize* is, of course, not an instance of the loss of the stop,
but a survival of older usage.

3.7. [ʔ]. The glottal stop may appear in the following situations:
  a) It often occurs initially before vowels in emphatically
stressed syllables (*That's ALL you'll get; I didn't say
"thirty"--I said EIGHTY"*) and serves here as one of the components of what Bloomfield calls the secondary phoneme of
loudest stress.

b) It may also occur as a nondistinctive sound before vowels at the beginning of syllables which do not bear an emphatic stress. Many speakers, for instance, pronounce the stop before every vowel that would otherwise be initial after a pause. Within the breath-group it may sometimes be used in place of the more usual smooth transition, after final vowels (*the other man*) and final consonants (*most authors*). If /r/ is not pronounced in the word-final position in cases like *Mr. Andrews, greater interest, four others*, or in those like *Utica Avenue, law office* (see page 47), the second vowel may be preceded by the glottal stop.

c) The voiceless stops [p, t, k] when they are final in syllables are often produced with a double closure, one oral and one glottal. These glottalized stops are in free variation with the simple oral stops, and are merely allophones of /p, t, k/

d) Without any oral articulation [ʔ] alone may occur at the end of syllables, chiefly as a substitute for the voiceless alveolar stop. The chief cases are:

1) Before a following initial nonsyllabic consonant: *department, that one, what boy, But look here*, etc. This use may be observed in cultivated pronunciation in some cases, but is commoner on the uncultivated and intermediate levels.

2) Before the syllabic form of /l/: *metal, bottle, hospital*. Here the use of [ʔ] is extremely widespread on the uncultivated and intermediate levels of New York speech. Indeed, pronunciations like [ˈmeʔl̩] and [ˈbɑʔl̩] for *metal* and *bottle* have become one of the chief shibboleths of New Yorkese. Cultivated speakers do not use the glottal in this position.

3) Before the syllabic form of /n/: *button, kitten, mountain*, and often *lantern* also. Here some cultivated speakers pronounce stops with a double closure, alveolar and glottal. The complete substitution of the glottal stop in words like *button* and *kitten* is uncultivated.

4) Occasionally after a vowel before /s/ in cases like *Let's go, That's right*. The glottal here is a sort of intermediate stage in the complete loss of the alveolar stop; pronunciations like /ˈlɛs ˈgoŭ/ and /ˌðæs ˈraɪt/ may also be heard in negligent and uncultivated speech.

5) Sometimes at the end of syllables before a pause: *Are you leaving tonight?, He's gone out.*

6) Sometimes, although not commonly, at the end of a syllable before an initial vowel: *right answer, not only*. I have observed this chiefly in reading, and the alveolar consonants, voiced or voiceless, are usually employed in this position.

One may not be altogether certain how the glottal stop in these cases should be classified. Some writers, in discussing its occurrence under similar conditions in other forms of English, do not concern themselves with this question, others treat [ʔ] as an allophone of /t/. This latter analysis will probably serve, although one may consider it a bit strained to describe two stops, one made at the alveolar ridge and one at the glottis, as phonetically similar. The occurrence of [?] in place of other voiceless consonants (with the complete loss of the oral articulation) might make such an analysis difficult if it were more common, but it is actually unusual and need hardly be thought of as a part of normal pronunciation.

E. H. Babbitt half a century ago reported that the glottal stop was common in uncultivated speech intervocalically in words like *letter* and *butter*.[22] In present-day pronunciation [?] does not normally occur in this position.

THE FRICATIVES

4.1. /f/. In all positions /f/ is a voiceless labio-dental fricative, the lower lip articulating against the upper incisors. The fricative occurs initially and finally, in the ambisyllabic position, and in certain initial and final clusters: *fill, official, cliff, rafter, tougher, flame, free, cliffs, raft*. As in the other forms of English pronunciation with which I am familiar, positional variants sufficiently distinct from one another to require discrimination do not occur. Nor are there many significant differences in the articulation of the fricative between the various class-dialects of the city.

In the sequence /ft/ plus vowel some uncultivated speakers rather frequently accompany the labio-dental articulation with a simultaneous glottal stop. In *fifty* the lip-movement sometimes disappears entirely: one of my informants pronounced [ˌfiʔtiĭ 'fɜĭs striĭt] for *Fifty-first Street*. (I have not observed this in other words.)

The occurrence of /f/ in place of /v/ as a result of assimilation to a following voiceless consonant is almost regular in *have* before the infinitive in the sense of "must." Otherwise this assimilatory change is unusual. The pronunciation of *thereof* with /f/ instead of the now usual /v/, which is recorded as a variant both by Jones and by Kenyon and Knott, is used by one of my older informants in a recorded reading of the Twenty-fourth Psalm.

In *nephew* /f/ is usual, although a few cultivated speakers pronounce /v/, perhaps in conscious imitation of British usage. I have noted a spelling-pronunciation of *Stephen* with /f/ in the speech of some undergraduates, but /v/ is generally pronounced.

As elsewhere, /f/ is lost from *half* in the colloquial pronunciation of *half-past two, -six*, etc. The omission occurs only in this phrase.

In words spelled with *-phth-* pronunciations with /fθ/ and /pθ/ both occur, as they do in other forms of English. The comparative frequency of the two pronunciations depends in general on the familiarity of the words. Thus in *naphtha*, a

household word, /f/ is uncommon and it is probably the less
frequent pronunciation in *diphtheria;* in *diphthong,* /f/ occurs more often and in *monophthong* I have never heard /p/.
But in *ophthalmology, ophthalmologist, ophthalmia,* and
exophthalmic, which are hardly among the commonest words, /p/
is very frequently pronounced.

4.2. /v/. A voiced labio-dental fricative occurs initially
and finally, in ambisyllabic position, and in a few final
clusters: *village, obvious, live, savior, liver, lives, lived.*
Like the other voiced fricatives, /v/ has a partially voiceless allophone that occurs finally before a pause; but except
for this the phones appearing in the various positions differ
so slightly that they do not need to be distinguished. Nor
have I observed any differences in the way the fricative is
articulated by cultivated and uncultivated speakers.

As in the other regional types of English pronunciation,
the fricative is often lost in colloquial speech from the unstressed form of the preposition *of* when it is followed by a
consonant (*the top of the hill, ten pounds of potatoes*). The
same loss in *have* (*I could have come*) is much less frequent
in the usage of the cultivated, but appears very commonly on
other levels. The omission of the fricative when final after
a stressed vowel occurs in uncultivated speech in a few cases:
in *give me* (here the loss may also occur in the negligent
speech of the cultivated) and sometimes in certain other
verbs before the pronoun *me,* for example in *leave me alone;*
I have also noticed the omission rather frequently in the
numeral *five* (and *twenty-five, thirty-five,* etc.), but only
when it preceded the word *dollar(s)* or the word *cent(s).*

4.3. /θ/. In cultivated pronunciation, a voiceless dental or
interdental fricative occurs in initial and final position,
ambisyllabically, and in certain initial and final clusters:
thought, sympathetic, booth, mythical, thrill, thwart, depth,
etc. The allophones that are employed in these various positions do not differ appreciably from one another. Before /θ/,
the consonants /t, d, n/, normally alveolar, usually have
dental allophones and the allophones of /s/ and /z/ often
have a somewhat advanced position. After /θ/, /r/ is often
represented by a tap or a reduced trill.

The fricative may be lost in all but the most careful articulation of some of the final clusters: *sixths* is [sikss]
very frequently and *months* is often [mʌn(t)s][23] Even when the
fricative is not lost, its articulation may be much reduced
in these difficult clusters.

As in other types of American English, both /θ/ and /ð/
occur in *with.* Some speakers use both pronunciations in an
apparently random fashion, others pronounce only /θ/ or only
/ð/. While the statement in the Kenyon and Knott *Dictionary*
under *with* that the voiceless fricative in this word "is

clearly not substandard" is more or less valid as applied to
metropolitan speech, there is, nevertheless, a strong tendency in cultivated pronunciation to prefer /ð/, and a corresponding tendency in other types of metropolitan speech to
use only the voiceless consonant. And it should be noted that
the uncultivated pronunciation with /t/ and /d/ (see below)
presumably is a development of [wiθ].

Among cultivated speakers practice in regard to the pronunciation of the plurals *baths, booths, laths, moths, mouths, oaths, paths, sheaths, troths, truths, wreaths, youths* does not differ from that found elsewhere in the United States. Some plurals, for example *baths* and *paths*, have /ðz/ almost exclusively, others vary between /ðz/ and /θs/.[24] But in the pronunciation of many of the less cultivated, the cluster /ðz/ occurs only in verbal forms and in the plurals of those nouns like *lathe* which have /ð/ in the singular: in all plurals like *baths, paths, moths* such speakers use /θs/ only. Nor is this practice confined to that type of metropolitan speech which is at the farthest remove from cultivated English--it may often be observed on the intermediate levels, for example in the speech of many Columbia College freshmen.

In a few words that occur infrequently in spoken English, /θ/ is sometimes used in place of /ð/, presumably as a sort of spelling-pronunciation. Many speakers say /'θiðə(r/ for *thither*. Several years ago, when *Blithe Spirit* was playing on Broadway, I noticed that the adjective was rather often pronounced /blaɪθ/. Conversely, I have often heard /ð/ in the verb *froth*, particularly in the participial form.

Two other words require mention. In *trough*, /θ/ was pronounced by several of my older informants, one of whom told me that this pronunciation was very common when she was a girl. In cultivated pronunciation /haɪt/ is rather generally used for *height*, but the variants /haɪtθ/, /haɪθ/ are common in the speech of the less educated. For the absence of /t/ in /haɪθ/, as in *eighth*, see page 27 above.

The equivalents of the Standard English fricative that occur in the speech of many New Yorkers have been frequently remarked and are among the more striking characteristics of the uncultivated speech of the city. In the literary representation of New York dialect, these equivalents are indicated by *t* or *t'*: *t'roo, toity-sixt', eighteent'*, and so forth. As will be seen below, such spellings are phonemically justifiable in a few cases, but not in most. There are a few situations, that is to say, in which /t/ appears in place of /θ/ or in which the /t/-/θ/ opposition found in cultivated English is absent; but in most positions the dental affricate or dental stop that the uncultivated speaker employs in place of the fricative is still distinct from the allophones of his /t/-phoneme.

Initially before a stressed vowel (*thirty, authority*), the following variants occur:

a) A dental or interdental voiceless affricate. In articulating it, the tongue-tip makes contact against the back surfaces or the lower edge of the upper teeth, in the same position as that taken for the fricative of cultivated speech. But instead of resting lightly against the teeth, the tongue makes a complete closure, which is then released into a weakly articulated dental fricative. This affricate differs from the affricated allophone of /t/ that occurs in *time* not only in regard to the place of articulation and the shaping of the tongue, but also because it is, relatively, a lenis. Words like *thanks* and *tanks* are never homonyms.

b) A weakly articulated dental or interdental unaspirated voiceless stop, identical with the preceding variant except for its lack of any appreciable fricative component.

c) The voiceless fricative that occurs in the various cultivated types of English pronunciation. Very few uncultivated speakers pronounce the dental affricate or stop with anything like consistency; more commonly, such speakers pronounce all three types more or less at random.

In the initial cluster /θr/ the same variants may occur, but the distinction between /θr/ and /tr/ seems occasionally to disappear. One may sometimes hear pronunciations of words like *three* and *thread* that sound exactly like the same speaker's pronunciation of *tree* and *tread* (see my comments on the usage of Informants #29 and #30). But it is difficult to be certain about the matter.

Intervocalically before an unstressed vowel within the word, the same variants--affricate, stop, fricative--occur. In this position (as in *Arthur, ether, method*), there is no question but that the phones must be assigned to /θ/. *Nothing*, however, which in cultivated pronunciation has /θ/ intervocalically, in uncultivated speech often rimes with *button*, being pronounced with a glottalized blade-articulated stop or with the glottal stop.

The variants mentioned above also occur when /θ/ is final in the syllable, as in *path, booth, birth, wealth*, etc. But there are one or two exceptions. The word *with* frequently has /t/, replaced by /d/ before a following vowel: *with a* often rimes with *bitter* and *bidder*; in *with you*, /tʃ/ is pronounced, just as it is in *meet you*. I have also observed /t/ a number of times in *Catholic*, pronounced as a disyllable (dentalized, blade-articulated stop with a simultaneous glottal closure, the same articulation that occurs in *Butler, Scotland, at last*, and the like. Or there may be a complete substitution of the glottal stop.)

4.4. /ð/. In cultivated pronunciation, a voiced dental or interdental fricative occurs initially and finally, in the ambisyllabic position, and in a few final clusters: *this, smooth, mother, bathed*. Finally before a pause or a following voiceless consonant, the fricative may end voicelessly. Ini-

THE CONSONANTS 37

tially in weak syllables the articulation is often very much
reduced and very weak variants of /ð/ may also be heard in
the final clusters /ðz/ and /ðd/. But except for these minor
variations, the positional allophones of /ð/ do not differ
noticeably from one another. Before /ð/ the consonants whose
articulation is normally alveolar are usually dentals, just
as they are before /θ/: *fight them, hide them*, etc.

In negligent pronunciation, the initial fricative is sometimes assimilated to certain preceding consonants. In phrases
like *all the men, on that corner, Who's there, miss the train*,
/l l, n n, z z, s z (s s)/ may replace /l ð, n ð, z ð, s ð/,
respectively. The double consonants that result are sometimes
simplified. These assimilations appear rather regularly in
the pronunciation of many less cultivated speakers.

Perhaps as a result of such assimilations, certain words
have variant forms without the fricative which may occur even
when not preceded by /l, n, s, z/. Thus for the demonstrative
that, /æt, æd/ occur beside /ðæt, ðæd/. This variant is rarely used in cultivated speech except jocularly (*'Attaboy*, etc.).
The pronunciation /ən, n/ for *than*, not infrequently heard
from uncultivated speakers, is uncommon in cultivated use, at
least among adults. A similar loss of /ð/ in initial position
may sometimes be observed in certain other words (I have
noticed it in *this, these, those*, but not in *the*).

The occurrence in uncultivated pronunciation of a dental
affricate or dental stop instead of the voiceless fricative
of *thank, method* is paralleled rather exactly in the case of
/ð/. Usually in free variation with the fricative, the following may appear:

a) A voiced dental or interdental affricate, distinct acoustically and in its manner of formation from the affricated
allophone of /d/ which may occur in the less cultivated pronunciation of words like *dime* and *adopt*.

b) A voiced dental stop, differing from the preceding variant only in the absence of any noticeable fricative component.
This stop, like the dental affricate, may appear in any position, but is most common initially.

These allophones are indicated in dialect writing by the
spelling *d*: *de, dis, dose*, etc. The person who does not pronounce them himself hears them as phones resembling or identical with his own /d/. But in the dialect speaker's pronunciation they are distinct from and opposed to /d/. There are
certain cases, however, in which such spellings are phonemically justifiable. In other words, alongside the dental stop
and affricate, phones may occur which must be assigned to the
/d/-phoneme (tip- or blade-articulated stop or tap). In initial position /d/ may appear at least occasionally in all the
common words, but most frequently in the word *the* preceded by
an unstressed vowel (*to the, of the*) or by /t/ or /d/ (*at the
movies, He heard the whistle*). Medially, I have observed /d/

in *other* (making it a homonym of *utter* and *udder* when these words are part of the vocabulary) and occasionally in *brother* and *mother*, but not in most other cases: it does not occur, for example, in participles like *bathing*, in *northern, southern* (never a homonym of *sudden*), *either, further,* and so forth. Nor have I observed /d/ in place of /ð/ in word-final position: *breathe* and *breed* are never identical, nor are *smooth-rude, bathe-blade* rimes in uncultivated speech. But for /d/ in *with* before a vowel, see the preceding section.

As has been pointed out, the affricate and dental stop allophones of /ð/ (and /θ/) occur in free variation with the fricative, and the substitution of /d/ (and /t/) is also never regularly carried through. Such pronunciations occur very frequently in the speech of many New Yorkers, but I have not observed any speaker who did not use the fricatives also, at least occasionally. On the intermediate levels of New York speech, it frequently happens that a speaker will in most positions pronounce fricatives identical with those of cultivated English, but will sometimes pronounce the variants discussed in these paragraphs in *with* and in words in which /ð/ is initial (*the, this, that*, etc.).[25]

One further fact about the occurrence of the affricate and dental stop allophones or of /t/ and /d/ in place of the fricatives is that such pronunciations appear far more commonly in the speech of men and boys than in that of women and girls. This comes out rather clearly in the speech of my less cultivated informants and may in fact be observed on every side.

4.5. /s/. A voiceless blade-alveolar fricative occurs initially and finally, in ambisyllabic position, and in a large number of initial and final clusters: *seal, miss, message, spin, slight, blast, risk, else, once*, etc. When the fricative precedes /θ/ or /ð/ (*esthetic, miss the train*), the tongue-position is often somewhat advanced.

The dentalization of the alveolar consonants that is characteristic of so much of the speech of the city occurs frequently in the articulation of the alveolar fricatives. The tip of the tongue, instead of being raised close to the upper gum-ridge, is held against the lower front teeth. In his account of Southern British pronunciation, Jones describes a variety of [s] made with the tongue-tip held in a similar position, but adds that it is hardly to be distinguished acoustically from the more common type.[26] Kenyon also refers to the articulation of the fricative by some speakers with the tongue against the back of the lower teeth, but says nothing of any resulting differences in acoustic quality.[27] In like fashion, the articulation of the fricative may be observed to vary somewhat in the speech of the cultivated in New York City. But the uncultivated metropolitan variety is to be distinguished from the types mentioned by Jones and

Kenyon, because the hiss is decidedly more prominent and also usually seems lower in pitch. The difference perhaps depends in part on a greater degree of expiratory force, but is chiefly the result, I believe, of a wider aperture between the blade of the tongue and the gum-ridge. In Jones' palatograms of the fricative,[28] first as it is made with the tip raised, then with it lowered, the rill in the latter case is only slightly wider than in the former.

In English pronunciation generally, it quite commonly happens that /z/ in final position ends voicelessly when it occurs before a pause or a following voiceless consonant. If another consonant precedes, the fricative may be voiceless throughout its entire length. The /s/-/z/ opposition in these cases is normally preserved as a distinction between fortis and lenis. There are some New Yorkers, however, who often unvoice the final fricative and at the same time make it rather fortis. As a result, /s/ may sporadically replace /z/ before a pause. Similar fortis unvoicings may be heard before following voiceless consonants (*Doctors' Hospital, he was careful*, etc.). Some cultivated speakers occasionally pronounce in this fashion, but I have observed the unvoicing more commonly on the less cultivated levels. The substitution is always sporadic--I have not heard anyone who regularly and consistently pronounced /s/ in these cases.

Such pronunciations are, of course, to be distinguished from the few cases like *used to* (= "was accustomed to"), where the occurrence of /s/ is universal, and like *has to* (= "must") and *newspaper*, where it is extremely common.

4.6. /z/. A voiced blade-alveolar fricative occurs initially and finally, in the ambisyllabic position, and in a number of final clusters: *zeal, raise, visit, raised, builds, runs*, etc. Partially or wholly voiceless allophones occur in final position before a pause or a following voiceless consonant. Before /θ/ and /ð/, the tongue-position of the fricative may be somewhat advanced. Otherwise, there are no appreciably different varieties that must be distinguished. Like /s/, the voiced fricative is often articulated by less cultivated speakers with the tip of the tongue held against the lower front teeth and perhaps with a somewhat wider aperture between the blade of the tongue and the gum-ridge.

In all types of English, there are a number of words that vary in their pronunciation between /s/ and /z/. In some cases, both variants are found very widely in America and in England; in others, a pronunciation frequently used in one country is rare in the other or is not heard at all. With respect to most of the words in question, metropolitan usage does not differ from that of America generally. For the sake of brevity, therefore, I shall enumerate only those few words whose pronunciation I have observed to differ in some way from that recorded in the Kenyon and Knott *Dictionary:*

Adhesive, exclusive, explosive, persuasive, and the like
have variants with /z/; so also does the word *illusory*. These
pronunciations are perhaps survivals, perhaps analogical re-
formations influenced by the voiced consonant of *adhesion,
exclusion,* etc. They are not confined to uncultivated speech.
The voiced fricative seems to be commoner in some words than
in others: I have heard it, for example, more often in *adhesive* than in *exclusive.*

Because is very frequently pronounced with /s/ on the less
cultivated levels. Many persons use both /s/ and /z/, apparently at random.

Business in the pronunciation of some usually less cultivated speakers is /'biznəz/, which may be a survival of an
older pronunciation now rather generally given up.

In *casserole* I have sometimes heard /z/.

Desolate and *desolation* occasionally have /z/ in less cultivated pronunciation.

Dis-: *Disaster* has both /s/ and /z/. Kenyon and Knott record /z/ as a variant in *disable, disarm, disdain, disgust,
dishonest, dishonor, dismay, disorder,* and *disown.* I have not
observed /z/ in these words in metropolitan speech.

Fricassee has a variant with /z/.

Jesus is sometimes /'dʒiĭzəz/ on the less cultivated levels.

Joseph has a rather common variant with /s/, which I have
heard chiefly on the less cultivated levels.

Resource and *resourceful* frequently have /z/ (at the beginning of the stressed syllable). This variant is not confined
to uncultivated speech.

4.7. /ʃ/. A voiceless lip-modified palato-alveolar fricative
occurs initially and finally, in the ambisyllabic position,
in the initial cluster /ʃr/ and the final cluster /ʃt/:
shine, insure, dish, mission, shrill, mashed. In the speech
of those who pronounce /r/ in the preconsonantal position,
the cluster /rʃ/ also appears. The degree of lip-modification
may vary in the pronunciation of different speakers from none
at all to moderate rounding and protrusion.[29] There is also
some tendency to round the consonant more strongly before a
stressed vowel than in other positions. Except for this minor
matter, however, noticeably different allophones of the fricative do not occur.

In uncultivated pronunciation, the fricative is sometimes
articulated with that type of dentalization which has already
been described in preceding sections: the tip of the tongue,
that is to say, may be held against the back of the lower
front teeth. This type of articulation, which is not nearly
so common as the dentalization of [s], results in a somewhat
"thinner" and more [s]-like sound.

Rather regularly, as in other types of English, /ʃ/ replaces
/s/ when final before /ʃ/ initial in the following syllable:
a close shave, tortoise-shell, this shocking story. The

double consonants which result are sometimes simplified. In
less cultivated speech the same assimilation frequently occurs as a consequence of the loss of [t] medially in words
like *question, suggestion:* /'kweʃʃən, 'kweʃən/, *etc.*
Sporadically /ʃ/ (or /ʃ j/) also occurs by assimilation
from /s j/ (*this year, Is this yours?,* etc.). This assimilation and the parallel occurrence of /ʒ/ (or /ʒ j/) for /z j/
(*as you know, close your eyes*) are somewhat less common than
the appearance of /tʃ/ and /dʒ/ in *I've caught you* and *Let me
read you the letter* (see pages 43-44).[30]

In the phonetic and lexical distribution of /ʃ/, metropolitan speech does not differ from American English generally;
differences from Southern British involve only a small number
of words, for example, *issue* and *tissue,* which regularly have
/ʃ/, and *Persia,* which regularly has /ʒ/. *Asia* usually has
/ʒ/, although some of my older informants pronounce /ʃ/. The
word *wurst* and its compounds require particular mention: beside /wɜ̆st, wrst/, used by many, especially among the more
educated, there is also a very common pronunciation /wuʃt/,
in which the vowel and the /ʃ/ are presumably taken from the
German dialects and Yiddish. A pronunciation /wust/ is also
used by some. I have not heard */wɜ̆ɪst/.

4.8. /ʒ/. A voiced lip-modified palato-alveolar fricative occurs initially in syllables which do not begin words: *luxurious, regime* (as a word-initial /ʒ/ may appear only in a few
learned words like *genre* which are pronounced in a more or
less Frenchified fashion); in the ambisyllabic position:
pleasure, vision; finally: *corsage, rouge* (but see below);
and in the final cluster /ʒd/: *rouged.* As in the case of /ʃ/,
the extent to which the lips are rounded and protruded varies
somewhat but is usually not great. The articulation of the
consonant by uncultivated speakers with the tip of the tongue
held against the lower front teeth may sometimes be observed.

On the uncultivated and intermediate levels, /ʒ/ often does
not occur as a word-final in most of the words of fairly recent French origin like *camouflage, corsage, garage, massage,
rouge,* /dʒ/ being pronounced instead. Usually this replacement is not regularly carried through: a speaker will pronounce /dʒ/ in some words (for example, *camouflage, garage*)
and /ʒ/ in some (for example, *beige* and *rouge*). As in other
parts of America, /dʒ/ is occasionally heard in educated
speech in some of these words, but there is a widespread prejudice against such pronunciations.

As a word-final, /ʒ/ quite commonly replaces /z/ before /ʃ/
initial in the next word in phrases like *as she said, he's
sure.* The occurrence of /ʒ/ in cases like *as you know, close
your eyes* has been referred to in the preceding section.

The lexical distribution of /ʒ/ does not differ from that
found generally in American English. But an odd occurrence of
the consonant is found in the name *Loeser* (a well-known Brook-

lyn department store), which is pronounced /'loŭʒə(r/. I have, furthermore, heard /ʒ/ pronounced by a few speakers in *misery* and *miserable*.

4.9. /h/. A glottal fricative occurs initially in syllables. As in other types of English pronunciation which contain this phoneme, there are strictly speaking as many allophones of the consonant as there are vowels, since the tongue- and lip-position of each vowel is approximated during the articulation of the preceding fricative. But no purpose is served by distinguishing these varieties.

Differences in the articulation of /h/ by cultivated and uncultivated speakers do not occur. So far as its phonetic distribution is concerned, metropolitan speech differs from that of much of America in that the initial cluster /hw/ (in words like *when* and *white*) does not occur in the pronunciation of most New Yorkers, who say /wen, waĭt/ (see page 52). Furthermore, the initial cluster /hj/ (in words like *huge* and *humorous*) is very frequently lacking on the uncultivated and intermediate levels: /juŭdʒ, 'juŭmərəs/ (see page 54). If words in which these clusters may occur are left out of consideration, the lexical distribution of the fricative is in general the same on all levels and does not differ from that found in the other varieties of American English.

Place- and family-names in *-ham*, when they do not have spelling-pronunciations with /θ/ or /ʃ/ (*Waltham, Wickersham*), have no /h/ if they are of two syllables (*Chatham, Fordham, Bingham, Burnham*), but they are pronounced with /h/ if they are longer (*Birmingham, Nottingham, Sydenham*).[31] When the longer names, however, are applied to British places and persons, the British pronunciations may be used by those among the more educated who know them. Similarly, *Amherst* and *Haverhill* are pronounced /'æməst/ and /'heĭvərəl/ by those to whom they are familiar, but spelling-pronunciations may also be heard.

Of those words in which '/h/ is normally not pronounced between a stressed and an unstressed vowel, I have not heard it inserted in *annihilate, Graham, nihilism, vehement;* in *vehicle* it is not infrequently pronounced by less cultivated speakers; for *rehabilitate* and *prehistoric* both pronunciations occur. Of words in which orthographic *h* is preceded by *ex-, exhale* is /ˌeks'heĭl/ and I have never heard /əɡ'zeĭl/, but /h/ does not occur in the other words (*exhaust, exhort, exhibit,* etc.).

Usage in regard to the omission of /h/ in the unstressed forms of *he, his, him, her, have, has, had* does not differ from that found elsewhere. In a stressed syllable /h/ is frequently lost in *Come here* /ˌkʌ'miə̆(r, kə-/.

In a few words in which /h/ is often not pronounced in Southern British English, I have not heard it omitted in New York speech: *historical, horizon, hotel*, the second syllable of *hedgehog* and *household*, and the phrase *at home*.

Orthographic *h* is "silent" in *heir, hour, honor, honest*, and their derivatives, as in other dialects. For *humble*, I have heard only /'hʌmbəl/. *Herb* has both pronunciations. In *homage*[32] and *hostler*, which are book-words to many, it is perhaps only the dictionary entries that keep the older pronunciations without /h/ in use at all.

THE AFFRICATES

5.1. /tʃ/. A voiceless palato-alveolar affricate occurs initially and finally, in the ambisyllabic position, and in certain final clusters: *chin, fracture, ditch, butcher, reached, branch, filch*. The lips may be held in a neutral position or may be slightly rounded and protruded. In uncultivated pronunciation, the affricate is sometimes articulated with the tongue-tip in contact with the lower front teeth.

In less cultivated speech, the stop-component of the affricate is sporadically weakened or lost in certain cases where cultivated pronunciation preserves it. Thus after /s/ (*question, suggestion*), /p/ (*rupture*), /k/ *actual, fracture, lecture*), the fricative alone may occur, so that, for example, *action* and *actual* contain the same consonant sequence. Finally after a vowel, the stop may sometimes also be weakened and is sporadically lost, with the result that *much* may occasionally be pronounced like *mush* and *search* so as to rime with the name *Kirsch*. After /n, l/, as in other forms of English, there is really no /tʃ/-/ʃ/ opposition (*branch, filch*): the stop-component is sometimes present, sometimes absent, although, as elsewhere in America, the loss is not as frequent as in British English. But the stop is never heard in the uncultivated pronunciation of words like *conscious* and *ancient* in which /n/ is represented merely by a strong nasalization of the preceding vowel (see page 55).

The affricate frequently results from the reciprocal assimilation of /t/ and a following /j/ in cases like *meet you* and *caught you*. The assimilation is avoided by some speakers (especially by those who aspire to speak well and are at the same time very unconfident of their own natural usage) but is very common on all levels. There is also the same variation between /tʃ/ and the sequence /tj/, in some words like *literature* and *congratulate*, which is to be found in other types of English. Like American English generally, metropolitan usage differs from British in the case of a few words, /tʃ/ being ordinarily pronounced in *aperture, overture, bestial, celestial, Christian*. Furthermore, certain words which frequently have /dʒ/ in Southern British (*ostrich, sandwich, spinach*, and place-names like *Greenwich* and *Norwich*) are regularly pronounced with /tʃ/ in New York.

5.2. /dʒ/. A voiced palato-alveolar affricate occurs initially and finally, in the ambisyllabic position, and in several final clusters: *job, majestic, cage, Dodgers, edged, lunge, bulge,* Like /tʃ/, the voiced affricate may be articulated by some speakers with a certain rounding and protrusion of the lips. A dentalized variety may sometimes be observed in uncultivated speech. When final before a pause or a following voiceless consonant, the fricative component may be partly or entirely voiceless. Ordinarily, this voiceless fricative phone is a lenis, but some speakers pronounce words like *college* with what might be written [dʃ]. This type of articulation, which appears in the speech of several of my informants (see section 13.1), I have observed most frequently in less cultivated speech, but it may occur as an individual peculiarity on all levels. The substitution of the entirely voiceless affricate is always, I think, a foreignism.

Paralleling /tʃ/, /dʒ/ very frequently results from the assimilation of /d/ and a following /j/ in cases like *Would you mind?, I heard you,* etc. Within the word there is the usual variation between /dʒ/ and the sequence /dj/ in words like *educate* and *procedure*.

As in America rather generally, /dʒ/ is very commonly pronounced by less cultivated speakers in a number of words of French origin that in educated English have /ʒ/ exclusively or predominantly: *barrage, garage, massage,* and the like (see page 41).

For the absence of a /dʒ/-/ʒ/ opposition after /n, l/ (*fringe, bulge*), see the parallel case in the preceding section.

VOICED FRICTIONLESS CONSONANTS WITH VOICELESS FRICATIVE VARIANTS[33]

6.1. /r/. The following allophones of the consonant may be distinguished:

a) Initially before stressed vowels and as a word-initial before unstressed vowels (*red, arrange, resign*), a voiced post-alveolar or alveolar lip-modified frictionless consonant occurs. The sides of the tongue are in contact with the lateral gum-ridges and with the inner surfaces of the upper molars. The tongue-point is raised, usually opposite the back of the alveolar ridge, although more advanced varieties occur; it is not turned back into the palatal arch, as often seems to happen in the pronunciation of General American speakers. As a result of the raising of the sides and point, the blade is held in a somewhat concave position. Accompanying this action of the tongue, there is usually a secondary lip-articulation: the lips approach each other, closing at either side, without being markedly protruded.

In the speech of some less cultivated speakers, /r/ in this position is articulated in a manner analogous to that which has already been described in the account of /t/ and /d/. The point of the tongue rises very little, if at all, and may

be held against the lower front teeth; the blade is higher
than the point. When articulated in this fashion, the consonant would give no palatogram, for the sides of the tongue
touch the molars but do not make contact with the lateral
gum-ridges. Perhaps as a compensation for this weakened
tongue-action, the action of the lips is often rather pronounced. (This secondary articulation is frequently labio-
dental.) This kind of articulation is by no means universal
in less cultivated speech--many persons articulate the consonant in a manner no different from that found in the pronunciation of the cultivated.[34]

b) When preceded in the same syllable by other consonants,
allophones of /r/ occur that exhibit modifications of the
same basic tongue and lip articulation. After the voiceless
stops, /r/ may be represented either by a voiceless fricative
or by an allophone that begins voicelessly. But when these
stops are in turn preceded by /s/, as in *spring, street,
scrawl*, the voiceless fricative does not appear. After /d/
also, as in *draw* and *drill*, the consonant tends to be a fricative, but in this case is always voiced. Flapped articulation may occur in the initial cluster /θr/ (*three, thrifty*),
as the tongue-point moves smartly back from the teeth and
strikes the posterior alveolar ridge. In /fr/ and /ʃr/ (*free,
shrill*) there may be some slight initial unvoicing, but in
general the other clusters show no noticeable modifications.

Some uncultivated speakers employ in these initial clusters
the same type of articulation with reduced point-action which
has already been described. In the word *tray*, for example,
the tongue-point may be held against the lower front teeth
throughout the entire word.

The loss of the consonant from initial clusters in unstressed syllables may be observed in a few cases, chiefly in
uncultivated speech. The pronunciation /'hʌnət/, referred to
on page 27, is hardly an example of such loss, for it is undoubtedly the local representative of the older metathesized
form. But *from* when unstressed is often /fəm/, and the loss
may occasionally occur in the initial syllables of words like
prepared, prescription (pronounced without the consonant by
Informant #39). In these latter cases, however, the omission
is very possibly due to a confusion of prefixes; the opposite
tendency appears in /prə'hæps/, one pronunciation of *perhaps*.

c) Within the word between a stressed and an unstressed
vowel or between two unstressed vowels (*Sarah, very; watering*), a voiced frictionless consonant occurs, the tongue
gliding up and away from the position described in *a* above.
Some speakers, however, articulate the consonant in this position in the fashion described by Thomas,[35] in which the
point of the tongue remains low, while the body arches up
close to the posterior hard palate.

The lip-modification of this allophone is reduced or entirely absent in the usage of the cultivated; but in some

uncultivated metropolitan speech it occurs here also in a
pronounced form. Such speakers, in uttering the word *very*,
for example, may raise the lower lip for the [r] as vigorously as they do for the [v]. (Here again, Informants #20
and #30 may serve as illustrations.) In the articulation of
this phone, the tongue-point may remain in contact with the
lower front teeth.

Flapped articulation of the consonant in intervocalic position is rarely heard in metropolitan speech. I have observed it chiefly in the professional dialect of elocutionists and it is without doubt an acquired pronunciation.

Within the word, the consonant is stable in the ambisyllabic position and the tendency, observable in certain types of
Coastal Southern speech, to omit it in words like *very*, *carry*,
and *Carolina*, is not found in metropolitan usage.[36] There are
several cases, to be sure, in which /r/ may not be present
between vowels: *temperature* is often /ˈtempəˌtʃuə̆(r, -tʃə(r/
in negligent and less cultivated speech and a similar pronunciation of *literature* may sometimes be heard. *Veterinary*
often suffers the same loss, even in educated pronunciation.
The omission of the consonant in these words, however, is
hardly a phonetic phenomenon, but is probably the result of
analogical re-formation on the pattern of *armature*, *furniture*,
dictionary, *seminary*, and the like.

Among the forms in which the consonant occurs between vowels are *aren't* /ˈɑə̆rənt/ and *weren't* /ˈwʌrənt/. In addition,
daren't is usually read by students as /ˈdɛə̆rənt/, although
this form is hardly part of their everyday usage. Such pronunciations are regular on the less cultivated levels; they
may also frequently be heard from cultivated speakers, although some use the monosyllabic pronunciations that are
usual in other types of English.

d) In the more common types of New York City pronunciation,
there is a regular alternation, like that of Southern British English, between word-final sequences containing /r/ and
those that lack it. When a word like *here* or *car* is followed
by another beginning with a vowel, the consonant appears; it
does not occur, however, when such a word stands before a
pause or before a word beginning with a consonant. The alternations are as follows: /iə-iə̆r/ (*hear*), /ɛə̆-ɛə̆r/ (*share*),
/ɑə̆-ɑə̆r/ (*far*), /ɔə̆-ɔə̆r/ (*war*), /uə̆-uə̆r/ (*poor*), /ɜ̆-ɜ̆r,
ʌ-ʌr, ʌə̆-ʌə̆r/ (*fur*),[37] /ə-ər/ (*whisper*).[38] So also /r/ appears
before suffixes beginning with a vowel: *hearing*, *fairest*,
starry.

In this type of pronunciation, as in Southern British English, /r/ in the word-final position is very commonly omitted even before an initial vowel in words like *emperor*, *horror*, and *terror*, in which the final vowel is in turn preceded
by /r/. Unlike the British practice,[39] however, the omission
is not usual unless the final vowel is unstressed: it would
not ordinarily be made in closely knit phrases like *rare example* and *rear admiral*.

Elsewhere the tendency to omit the word-final variety of /r/ before a following vowel is common enough, although not so frequent as in Coastal Southern speech. When the omission is made, the transition is sometimes smooth (as is usually the case in those varieties of Coastal Southern which I have observed); but often the second vowel is preceded by a glottal stop.

As in the south of England and the eastern part of the New England states, so in New York City many speakers pronounce /r/ before a following vowel, not only in words like *loafer, dear, car,* and *lore,* but also in those of the type of *sofa, idea, Utah,* and *law,* in which /r/ never appears in General American pronunciation. Put another way, in the speech of such persons the sequences /ə/ plus vowel, /iə̆/ plus vowel, /ɑə̆/ plus vowel, and /ɔə̆/ plus vowel ordinarily do not occur. This phenomenon, which is usually called "intrusive r," a term hardly warranted in descriptive phonetics, is not confined, of course, to uncultivated speech. The pronunciation of such words with /r/ is almost universal on the lower levels; but there are also many among the cultivated who pronounce in this fashion.[40] In his description of Southern British, Jones refers to the frequent occurrence of /r/ in phrases like *china and glass, a vanilla ice, the sonata in F,* but then adds that "the use of intrusive *r*" in words like *Shah* and *law* "is not very common among educated speakers."[41] One might make a not entirely dissimilar statement about metropolitan pronunciation: some cultivated speakers who would often pronounce /r/ in words like *china, vanilla,* and *sonata* would rarely do so in those like *Shah* and *law*.[42] But in the speech of the city as a whole, the occurrence of /r/ in phrases like *Utah is the home of the Mormons* and *the law of the land* is very common.

The usual omission of /r/ at the end of words after an unstressed vowel that is in turn preceded by /r/ (*emperor, horror*) has been referred to above. Similarly, I have not heard /r/ pronounced as a word-final in *camera, Clara, Dora, orchestra, Sinatra,* and the like.

The allophones that occur in word-final position before a following vowel are the same as those that appear intervocalically within the word: the tongue-point may glide up towards and away from the back of the alveolar ridge, or the body of the tongue may move up towards and away from the posterior hard palate. Flapped articulation occurs as an occasional affectation.[43] The uncultivated variants discussed in c above also appear in this position.

When /r/ occurs in words like *planner* and *steeper,* two slightly differing types of pronunciation may be observed, one resembling the Southern British, the other the General American. That is to say, one sometimes hears a sequence composed of an unstressed vowel plus [r]; but in other utterances, the tongue moves so rapidly to the [r]-position that no vowel is separately perceived.

e) In the speech of those whose usage we have been considering so far, /r/ does not occur in the preconsonantal position within the word, just as it does not appear in the word-final position before a following initial consonant or before a pause. Thus, /r/ does not occur in *beard, speared; scarce, cares; sharp, cars; port, shores; cures, poorly; third, furs; custard, glittered*. This type of pronunciation is still in my observation the most common one in the speech of the city.⁴⁴ It is not the only type, however, heard from native residents of New York. Some speakers--not very many--pronounce /r/ in the preconsonantal position as regularly and consistently as do speakers of General American. In their speech the [r]-articulation before consonants and pauses is often somewhat weaker than in General American pronunciation and strong retroflexion or other "r-coloring" of the preceding vowel is uncommon. The vowels before /r/, furthermore, are likely to keep that length which is characteristic of the city's speech: *sharp*, that is to say, is [ʃɑ·rp], not [ʃɑrp].

The pronunciation of a very large number of New Yorkers exhibits a pattern in these words that might most accurately be described as the complete absence of any pattern. Such speakers sometimes pronounce /r/ before a consonant or a pause and sometimes omit it, in a thoroughly haphazard fashion. In many cases this irregularity is a result of the conscious attempt, only partly successful, of originally "r-less" speakers to pronounce the consonant because they feel that it is more "correct" to do so. But often no conscious effort is involved. The speaker hears both types of pronunciation about him all the time, both seem almost equally natural to him, and it is a matter of pure chance which one comes first to his lips.

When /r/ is pronounced in the preconsonantal position, the articulation may resemble either of the two types described in *c* above. The tongue-point may be raised towards the back of the alveolar ridge, or the body of the tongue may rise towards the posterior hard palate.

The pronunciation of /r/ as a word-final in *law, sofa*, and the like occurs sometimes before a pause (*Obey the law; They sat on the sofa*) or before a following initial consonant (*law school, sofa cushion*).⁴⁵ Such occurrences are undoubtedly a reflection of the frequently irregular pronunciation of words like *sore* and *loafer*. A person whose usage is predominantly of the "r-less" type, but who nevertheless sometimes pronounces /r/ in *loafer* and *sore* before a pause or an initial consonant may treat *sofa* and *saw* in exactly the same fashion.⁴⁶

Another rather interesting result of the mixture of dialect-types referred to above is the pronunciation of /r/ in words like *sofa* and *saw* by speakers who have come to pronounce words with orthographic *r* more or less consistently in the General American fashion. I have come across a number of undergraduates from the city who, while reading the *Rat*-selection as part of the freshman speech test, have managed to pronounce /r/ three times in *saw Arthur*.

Those New Yorkers who regularly or frequently pronounce /r/ in *arm, court,* and the like also commonly pronounce words such as *first* and *turn* in a fashion like that of General American, with the tongue-point turned towards the back of the alveolar ridge or the body of the tongue lifted towards the posterior hard palate and in contact with the lateral gum-ridges. When treating such pronunciations, phoneticians differ only slightly or not at all in their account of the phonetic facts. They are not in the same agreement, however, regarding the analysis of these facts or the way in which to represent such syllabics in transcriptions that are intended as phonemic. Kenyon speaks of a "retroflex vowel" and has devised a widely used special symbol for it. Bloch and Trager analyse the same pronunciation as a sequence composed of the vowel in *cup* plus /r/. Bloomfield conceives of the syllabic in such words as an allophone of /r/ (the only regular case in English of a stressed syllabic consonant) and transcribes [tr̩n], [fr̩st], etc. Kenyon's method of transcription seems to me unfortunate because it obscures the connection between the syllabic of *turn* as pronounced in the General American manner and the initial phone of *red*, a connection that even an illiterate speaker would, I believe, be aware of. The analysis of Bloch and Trager is a necessary part of their attempt to demonstrate that all English syllables contain one or another of a very limited number of vowels. If one considers this attempt in general unconvincing, as I do, he will feel under no compulsion to adopt their practice in this case I myself prefer Bloomfield's conception of these phones, and his transcriptions; they have the advantage of neatness and simplicity, and they furthermore bring out plainly the close relationship, based on phonetic similarity, between the phones occurring as syllabics in these words and those phones that occur in *red, very,* and the like.

/r/ may also occur as a stressed syllabic in the speech of many who do not otherwise pronounce it in the preconsonantal position. My own usage is of this sort: I pronounce /biə̆d/ *beard*, /kɛə̆d/ *cared*, /hɑə̆d/ *hard*, /kɔə̆t/ *court*, /kjuə̆d/ *cured*, but /trn/ *turn*. So also do several of my informants, as I have noted in sections 13.1 and 13.2. This practice is the same as that mentioned by Kenyon as occurring in certain sections of the South;[47] it also resembles in part the usage of some British speakers referred to by Jones.[48]

6.2. /l/. In metropolitan pronunciation, as in the other regional varieties of English, the phoneme /l/ comprises a whole series of phones that differ from each other chiefly as a result of the different shape assumed by the body of the tongue. A fairly simple classification of these phones may be arrived at by grouping together all those that are similar acoustically and in their manner of formation.

In cultivated speech the following allophones may be distinguished:

a) The so-called clear varieties of /l/:

1) A voiced alveolar lateral consonant with front-vowel resonance occurs initially in syllables and in the initial clusters /bl/ and /gl/: *life, load, relation, deeply, blame, glass*. The point and blade of the tongue articulate against the alveolar ridge, while the forward part of the sides makes contact with the lateral gum-ridge and with the molar teeth. The front of the tongue is raised somewhat toward the hard palate. The "clearness" of this allophone is of course a relative matter. Compared, say, to the [l] of Stockholm Swedish, the consonant even in this position is comparatively "dark," and it often seems "darker" too than the initial [l] of Southern British. Furthermore, as in other types of English, the tongue-position tends to accommodate itself somewhat to that of a following vowel, so that the consonant may have a "clearer" resonance before high-front than before low-back vowels.

2) A voiceless alveolar lateral fricative with the tongue position of the preceding allophone occurs in the initial clusters /pl/ and /kl/: *play, apply, clear, acclaim*. Often, unless the syllable is heavily stressed, only the first part of the consonant is unvoiced. After other voiceless consonants in the same syllable (*flame, sleep*), some slight initial unvoicing may also occur.

3) A voiced alveolopalatal lateral consonant occurs finally before initial [j] in words like *William* and *bullion*. It also replaces the word-final "dark" [l] before initial [j] in the following word: *Will you go?, Bill Young*.[49] Its articulation resembles that of the initial allophone, but the contact along the mid-line of the tongue extends somewhat farther back on the roof of the mouth. The employment of this type of [l] is not universal. Some persons pronounce in *William, will you,* and the like the "dark" [l] of *will* and *bold;* others a partially vocalized [l] by failing to raise the tip and blade high enough to make contact with the roof of the mouth. Sometimes the consonant disappears entirely: [ˈwijəm] *William* [ˈte juÜ] *tell you*. Such pronunciations are not exclusively or even predominantly confined to uncultivated speech. They may occur on any level and in fact occur so frequently that a descriptive phonetician is somewhat loath to label them misarticulations in the usual sense.

b) The so-called dark varieties of /l/:

1) A voiced alveolar lateral continuant with back-vowel resonance occurs finally in syllables, as the first member of many final clusters, and in medial intervocalic position before an unstressed vowel: *bell, pole, feeble, culture, valve, field, bulb, telephone, collar*. The point and blade articulate against the alveolar ridge. The forward part of the sides touches the lateral gum-ridge and the molar teeth, but this contact does not extend as far back as in the case of the "clear" [l]. The central body of the tongue is low. The

back is raised and in the speech of some seems to make a second contact along its mid-line against the velum.[50]

In the type of Southern British described by Jones, the "dark" [l] does not occur intervocalically in words like *telephone* and *collar*, a "clear" variety of the consonant being used in this position. Furthermore, in Southern British the "clear" [l] replaces the "dark" in words like *tell* and *fill* before a closely linked following vowel (as in *tell it* and *fill up*).[51] In New York speech, on the other hand, although the intervocalic [l] is often not quite so "dark" as final [l], the definitely "clear" varieties that are used by many British speakers and that frequently occur in Southern American speech are not heard, except as an occasional affectation.

2) In the final cluster /lθ/ (*health, filth*) and finally before /θ/ and /ð/ (*all things, healthy, sell them*), the area of contact usually extends farther forward: the tongue-point may articulate against the back of the upper incisors.

These allophones often occur in free variation with other, vowel-like varieties of /l/, in the articulation of which the tip and blade of the tongue rise somewhat, but do not make contact with the alveolar ridge. Sometimes the back of the tongue seems to articulate against the velum, sometimes there is not contact of any sort. Such partially vocalized phones are common in the pronunciation of many persons and are not confined to uncultivated speech.

The dentalized blade-articulation of the alveolar stops that occurs in uncultivated metropolitan pronunciation has already been described. A similar articulation of the lateral may often be observed. The tip of the tongue rests against the lower front teeth, while the blade rises to make contact with the alveolar ridge. Initially and in initial clusters, the [l] that is so produced is often quite "dark"; finally and in final clusters, there is often no alveolar contact.

6.3. /w/. In metropolitan pronunciation on all levels, the following allophones of this consonant may be distinguished:

  a) Initially in stressed and unstressed syllables a voiced labio-velar frictionless consonant occurs, the lips ordinarily moving from a rounded, and the tongue from a high-back position to that of a following vowel. As in other forms of English, the degree of lip-rounding and the height to which the back of the tongue is raised are in general dependent on the nature of the vowel that is preceded by /w/. That is to say, the lips are normally more closely rounded and the initial tongue-position higher in words like *woo* and *wool*, which contain a high-back rounded vowel, than in those like *wash* and *wax*, whose syllabics are unrounded and lower.

  In negligent speech, the lip-articulation is often very much reduced and may be entirely absent, resulting in variants whose movement begins at the position of a high-back unrounded vowel.

In place of the usual frictionless consonant, one of my informants (#7) regularly uses a weakly articulated voiced velarized bilabial fricative. The generally old-fashioned quality of this person's speech leads one to believe that in her usage a type of pronunciation survives which once may have been rather common.[52] I have not, however, observed this fricative in the speech of other New Yorkers.

Spelling-pronunciation has rather generally restored /w/ to those place- and family-names in which it once was lost before an unstressed vowel. British place-names like *Norwich, Harwich,* and *Berwick* are pronounced in the British fashion by those among the educated to whom they are familiar. Others pronounce them according to the spelling. In similar American place-names the spelling-pronunciations are general. *Greenwich (Village, Avenue)* is an exceptional case, being very commonly pronounced /ˈgrenətʃ/, although /ˈgriĭnˌwitʃ/ may also be heard, even from educated speakers.

b) When preceded in the same syllable by /t/ (*twin, between*), a voiceless labio-velar fricative occurs. In emphatic utterance, a similar fricative may be used after /k/ in words like *queen* and *quick,* and some initial unvoicing may be observed in the clusters /sw/ and /θw/ (*sweet, thwart*). After /d/ (*dwarf, dwindle*), the consonant may also have some fricative quality under high-stress, but in this case is always voiced.

In words of the type of *whale, wheel, when,* the cluster /hw/[53] may occur, but the most common pronunciations on all levels of metropolitan speech are /weĭl, wiĭl, wen/, etc. Speakers who employ /hw/ consistently in all the words of this historical class are rather rare.[54] In uncultivated speech, /w/ is universal; on the intermediate and cultivated levels, /hw/ may not infrequently be heard, but its use more often than not is sporadic--the speaker will employ it only in a restricted number of words or will pronounce the same word now in one way and now in the other. C. K. Thomas' tabulations[55] show a majority of /w/-pronunciations in all but one minor instance, and one suspects even so that the surprisingly large figures for the other type would be smaller if the downstate counties outside the city were excluded. There can be little doubt that the /hw/-pronunciations are for the most part consciously adopted ones, adopted because of the widespread notion that pronouncing *whale* and *wail, whet* and *wet* as homonyms is "incorrect."[56]

New Yorkers of Irish birth usually employ /hw/ or some variant of it in these words, but the pronunciation rarely survives in the speech of the second generation. Here it may be added parenthetically that, despite the often alleged clannishness of Irish-Americans and the existence of a number of predominantly Irish neighborhoods, Irish speech-ways disappear very quickly in New York.[57] In such neighborhoods, one may hear Irish accents very frequently if he listens to

THE CONSONANTS 53

adults, but the children in the streets speak New Yorkese of
purest ray.

6.4. /j/. In all class-dialects the following allophones of
this consonant may be distinguished:
a) Initially in stressed and unstressed syllables a voiced
palatal frictionless consonant occurs: *yes, unit, population,
accurate, communist, onion, valuable.* The front of the tongue
is raised towards the hard palate and the sides touch the
lateral gum-ridges and the molar teeth. The space between the
tongue and the roof of the mouth is narrowest when /j/ precedes a high-front vowel as in *yeast, yield;* before lower
vowels the tongue-front ordinarily does not rise so high.
 An unhistorical /j/ appears in a few cases. As in other
types of English, *February* is frequently pronounced /'febjuŭ-
ˌeriY/ on the analogy of *January.* (I have also sometimes
heard /'febuŭˌeriY/.) Chiefly in less educated speech,
/'kaljəm/ may occur for *column.* The loss of /j/, on the other
hand, appears in the occasional variant /iYst/ for *yeast.*[58]
At the beginning of unstressed medial syllables, its omission
is rare--it may sometimes be lost in *regular* and *particular,*
but is generally preserved in other words. A few words like
garrulous and *virulent,* however, in which the consonant would
be preceded by /r/, are a special case: here /j/ is very commonly omitted.
 The same frictionless consonant is employed in initial
clusters the first member of which is one of the voiced consonants /b, v, m/ *beauty, view, mute*) and also in the clusters /dj, gj, zj, nj, lj/ (*due, gubernatorial, resume, new,
lunacy*) when these occur (see below). But some friction may
be audible after /d/ in *due, dubious,* etc. The group represented by *beauty* includes *carburetor* and related words in the
pronunciation of some educated speakers; more commonly, however, /j/ is omitted.
 b) When preceded in the same syllable by /p/ or /k/ (*pure,
cube*), a voiceless palatal fricative occurs. If the syllable
is not heavily stressed, only the first part of the consonant is voiceless. When the initial cluster /tj/ occurs in
words like *tube* and *Tuesday* (see below), the aspiration also
tends to unvoice the palatal to some extent. But there is
usually not as much fricative quality observable in this case
as in words like *tree* and *twin,* probably because speakers unconsciously avoid a pronunciation that would resemble [tʃ].
When the stops are in turn preceded by /s/ (*spew, student,
obscure*), the voiceless fricative does not occur.
 After other voiceless consonants in the same syllable, an
allophone with some slight initial unvoicing may also appear,
for example in *few,* and similarly in *enthusiasm* and *suitable*
if /j/ is pronounced in such words. The same type of consonant occurs after /h/ in *huge, humidor, Huron,* and the like.
In these words there is much less tendency than in Southern

British to replace the cluster by a single fricative phone. On the uncultivated and intermediate levels of New York speech the cluster /hj/ very often does not occur, all words like *huge* being pronounced with /j/ alone. (Such pronunciations are very common in the speech of Columbia undergraduates who come from the city.) The distinction recorded in our dictionaries between /j/ as a variant in *humor* and its derivatives, and /hj/ alone in the other words of this group appears in the speech of Informants #2, #6, #11, #15, and #25. But more commonly New Yorkers are consistent in pronouncing all these words with /hj/ or all with /j/.

Variations in the occurrence of /j/ in initial clusters in words of that class which in Early Modern English contained the diphthong /iu/ may be summed up in the following general statements:

1. After /p, b, m, f, v, k/ (*pew, beauty, mute, feud, view, cubic*), /j/ is regular on all levels. But *pubic, puberty* and related words are exceptional in that they have variant pronunciations that lack the consonant: /'puŭbək/, etc., may be heard rather frequently, even from educated speakers. Similarly, /j/ is often not pronounced in *recuperate*. Words in which /gj/ might occur as a cluster initial in syllables are uncommon; perhaps as a result /j/ is very frequently omitted from *gubernatorial* and *lugubrious*. Conversely, the group represented by *cubic* often includes *coupon*: the pronunciation /'kjuŭˌpɑn/ is widespread in less educated use and is also employed by some cultivated speakers. In *percolate* and *percolator* the fairly frequent introduction of /j/ is perhaps due to the analogy of *circulate*.

2. After /t, d, n/ (*tube, duty, new*), /j/ does not appear on the uncultivated level: /tuŭb, 'duŭdiĭ ('duŭtiĭ), nuŭ/. The usage of more cultivated speakers is divided and often very irregular. Some persons pronounce /j/ consistently in words of this class, others never do. Very frequently a speaker's pronunciation will vary between the two types; he will pronounce /j/ in some words but not in others, or will pronounce the same word differently in successive utterances. This irregularity, which is very common in the speech of my informants, is presumably evidence that the pronunciations with /j/ are often acquired ones.[59]

3. After /θ, s, z/ (*enthusiasm, suit, resume*), /j/ does not occur on the less cultivated levels, nor is its use very frequent in cultivated speech. Many who pronounce /j/ regularly or rather often after /t, d, n/ rarely or never do so after these consonants. Its occurrence is more frequent in some words than in others: I have observed it more often, for example, in *suit* than in *superintendent*, and have never heard it in *Susan*.

4. The initial cluster /lj/ in words like *lewd, lunatic*, and *absolutely* is uncommon: /luŭd, 'luŭnəˌtik/, etc. are regular in uncultivated speech and are overwhelmingly the more common pronunciations in the speech of the more cultivated.

THE CONSONANTS 55

5. After /r, ʃ, tʃ, dʒ/ (*rule, chute, chew, June*), and after /l/ preceded by another consonant (*fluid, glue*), /j/ does not appear on any level.
The occurrence of the diphthong /ɨu/ in some of the above words is discussed on pages 72-73.

THE NASALS

7.1. /m/. A voiced bilabial nasal occurs initially and finally, in ambisyllabic position, in the initial cluster /sm/, and in a few final clusters: *mill, clam, hammer, smooth, glimpse, warmth, brooms, climbed*. When the consonant is followed by /f/, as in *comfort, emphasis, triumph*,[60] it is sometimes labio-dental, but except for this, differences in the articulation of the nasal in various positions may be ignored.

In negligent pronunciation, /m/ may sometimes occur in place of /n/ by assimilation to a preceding or following /p/ or /b/, or to a following /m/ (*open, cabin, by-and-by, standpoint, on Monday*), and the labio-dental allophone may sometimes be heard in words like *oven* and *seven*. In less cultivated speech, this assimilation may also appear in the participial forms of verbs ending in /p/, /b/, or /v/ (*slipping, rubbing, leaving*) and in one pronunciation of the word *something*, /'sʌmpm/. One of my uncultivated informants pronounced the word *seventy* as ['semnit̬].

The abrupt cutting off of nasal resonance before the labial closure is released when /m/ preceded a voiceless consonant, as a result of which /p/ has been added to *empty, glimpse, Sampson, something, warmth*, and the like, may sometimes be heard in less cultivated speech when /m/ is final in the word. I have heard it most frequently before a following /t/, for example in *home town, I came to Columbia*.

7.2. /n/. A voiced alveolar nasal occurs initially and finally, in the ambisyllabic position, in the initial cluster /sn/, and in certain final clusters: *new, win, runner, snail, since, tent, bind*. Before /θ/ and /ð/ (*month, on Thursday, clean them*), the articulation is usually dental or interdental, and a similar allophone may appear after these fricatives, as in *Nathan* and *heathen*. The tongue-tip is normally withdrawn to the back of the alveolar ridge when the consonant is followed by /r/, as in *enrage, row on row*. But except for these minor variations, differences between the phones occurring in the various positions are slight and may be ignored.

Like the other consonants that are alveolar in cultivated English, this nasal is often dentalized and blade-articulated in uncultivated metropolitan speech. The tip of the tongue is in contact with the teeth (most often the lower teeth), while the blade rises to the gum-ridge.

When the nasal occurs in certain final clusters or is final before certain initial consonants, particularly voiceless fricatives, many less cultivated speakers often fail to make the alveolar contact and strongly nasalize the preceding vowel. A number of such pronunciations occur on my records and I have observed them frequently in the speech of undergraduates in words like *conference, confidence, in fact; conversation; length, strength* (see below); *ancient, conscious; friendly, kindly, only, Stanley; sandwich.*

As in other regional types of English, /n/ is often pronounced in place of /ŋ/ in verbal and nominal forms like *feeling, reading, going,* and in *anything, everything, nothing, something.*[61] Among the cultivated, pronunciations of these words with /n/ are not very common, although many use them occasionally. In uncultivated speech, they occur frequently. Less cultivated speakers also often pronounce /n/ instead of /ŋ/ in *length*, which may be [lenθ], [leĭnθ], or [lẽĭθ] (for this last pronunciation, see the preceding paragraph and for the allophones of /θ/ in final position, see page 36 above). Similar pronunciations occur for *strength, lengthen,* and *strengthen.*

7.3. /ŋ/. A voiced velar nasal occurs in ambisyllabic position, finally, and in certain final clusters: *hanger, ring, length, sings, hanged.* As in English generally, the point at which the contact is made between the tongue and the roof of the mouth may vary somewhat, depending on the tongue-position of the preceding vowel. But the differences are slight, and it is not necessary to distinguish between these various allophones. Nor are there noticeable differences in the articulation of the nasal in cultivated and uncultivated speech, although there is a considerable difference in the frequency of its occurrence on the various levels, as a result of the much greater tendency of uncultivated speakers to use /n/ in the participial forms. In the pronunciation of those who customarily articulate with a very narrow jaw-angle (see page 25), the tongue-front may sometimes make contact behind the alveolar ridge at the same time that the back of the tongue rises to the velum; but this variant does not make the impression on the ear of a palatal nasal.[62]

The phonetic distribution of the nasal does not differ from that found in other regional varieties of American English. So far as the lexical distribution is concerned, there is also little that requires mention. In regard to the alternation between /n/ and /ŋ/ before the velar stops, metropolitan pronunciation, like American English generally, shows a somewhat greater preference for /n/ than does Southern British, although the differences are not very important. *Concourse, Congreve, conquest, idiosyncrasy,* for example, which Jones records as being predominantly pronounced with /ŋ/, more often have /n/ in New York City. In like manner, /n/ often occurs in words like *synchronize* and *syncopate*, in which Jones records only /ŋ/. There is also less tendency to assimilate the nasal to the position of the stop in unstressed initial syllables (*conclusion, engagement, inclosure,* and the like).

The assimilation of /n/ to a preceding velar stop may occasionally be heard in negligent pronunciation in cases like *bacon fat, taken sick.*[63]

THE VOWELS AND DIPHTHONGS OF STRESSED SYLLABLES

VOWELS THAT DO NOT OCCUR AS WORD-FINALS

8.1. /i/. In *hit, hid, big,* and the like the syllabic is a somewhat retracted lower high-front vowel. Even in the speech of most cultivated speakers, the position is usually slightly farther back than that of the corresponding vowel in Southern British English;[1] and in uncultivated speech, the retraction often reaches the lower high-central position.[2] Many speakers use noticeably more centralized vowels before /l/, as in *bill, until,* than elsewhere. As a result of the retraction, the interval between /i/ and /u/ is somewhat diminished: I have sometimes observed less cultivated speakers who pronounced *Willie* and *wooly* almost as homonyms.

Before /r/, the phonemic pattern is not very regular, the older opposition between /i/ (*mirror, delirious*) and /iə̆/ (*Vera, mysterious*) having partially disappeared. For the details, the reader is referred to the discussion under /iə̆/ on pages 73-75.

Except before /r/, where metropolitan pronunciation differs from General American on the one hand and from Southern British on the other, the phonetic distribution of the phoneme in stressed syllables is the same as in these other types. The lexical distribution also requires little comment. In the stressed form of *can*, /i/ often occurs on the uncultivated level. For *Schermerhorn* (family-name, street-name in Brooklyn), /ˈskimə͵hoə̆n/ may be heard beside the more usual /ˈskemə͵hoə̆n/. (Spelling-pronunciations of this name are also frequent, even in the speech of some native New Yorkers.) Another street-name, *Coentes (Slip, Alley)*, was once pronounced /ˈkwinsiĭ/ according to two of my older informants, but the spelling-pronunciation /͵koŭˈentiĭz/ is now general. In the first syllable of *engine, engineer,* /i/ may be pronounced by uncultivated speakers; in *get* it occurs very frequently. The pronunciation /dəˈridʒəbəl/ for *dirigible*, which Kenyon and Knott list merely as a British variant, is extremely common in the city. For a few words in which /i/ and /iĭ/ may both be heard, see page 65.

The vowels of the final syllables in words like *city* and *valley*, those of the medial syllables in words like *carrier* and *period*, and those of the unstressed prefixes spelled *de-, pre-, re-,* etc. are dealt with on page 37. For the occurrence of lower high-front vowels and of vowels approaching that position in other unstressed syllables and for their phonemic classification, see pages 88-90.

8.2. /e/. The height of the vowel in words like *bet, bed*, and *beg* varies somewhat in the lower mid-front range. As in the case of /i/, the direction of variation is chiefly backward toward a more central placement. Again as in the case of /i/, the retraction is greatest and most frequent in uncultivated speech.³

The phonetic distribution of /e/ is like that found in Southern British; metropolitan practice differs from General American (or from some types of General American) in its preservation of the /e/-/ɛɚ̆/ and the /e/-/æ/ oppositions before /r/. So far as the lexical distribution is concerned, a few words must be mentioned. In less cultivated speech, *orchestra* often has /e/ under secondary stress: /'ɔã͜ˌkestrə/, and in the stressed syllable of *vanilla*, /e/ instead of /i/ is common. In *marshmallow*, /e/ instead of /æ/ is the more common vowel, even in cultivated speech (it is used by all but a few of my informants). For *err* and *erring*, which are book-words to many, /er/ and /'erəŋ/ are frequent, presumably because of the analogy of *error*. (It may be noted that /er/ is a complete anomaly in New York speech, no other examples of this word-final sequence occurring.) In *measure, treasure, eggs, keg, leg*, the use of /e/ is general.⁴ In *again* and *against*, a few among the educated pronounce /eĭ/, but /e/ is the usual vowel. The pronunciation /'redəʃ/ for *radish* may sometimes be heard, but /e/ is much less common than /æ/.⁵ *Catch* is generally /ketʃ/ in less cultivated usage, nor is this pronunciation unknown in the familiar speech of the cultivated.

In certain words metropolitan pronunciation, like the other types of American English, has /e/ under secondary accent where Southern British has an unstressed vowel: *accent, convent, nonsense, Somerset*. In *object, subject* (nouns), /e/ often occurs, although /ə/ may also be heard and is probably the more frequent pronunciation in cultivated speech. In *actuary, cemetery, customary, dictionary*, and the like, where Southern British has lost the secondary stress, metropolitan pronunciation, like American English generally, retains it. The British pronunciations are occasionally imitated, but usually only in one or two words of the group. In related words, in which secondary shifts to primary stress, /ɛɚ̆/ may occur, e.g., in *arbitrarily, honorarium, secretariat*.

For the occurrence of /e/ in weakly stressed initial syllables (*except, exhibit, endanger*, etc.), see page 146, note 6.

8.3. /æ/. The vowel in *cap, back, match* is intermediate low-front. It normally has a somewhat lower and more retracted position than the corresponding Southern British vowel and, when it varies, does so toward a still lower and more retracted placement, rather than toward [e] as in Southern British. This tendency is carried to a rather grotesque extreme in the speech of some individuals: thus in the pronunciation of some of my students the vowels in such words as *cap* and *match* vary at times to [a] and even [ɑ⁴]. (And see, for another example, the comments on the usage of Informants #39, page 124.)[6] The vowel is frequently nasalized, especially in less cultivated speech.

The phonetic distribution of /æ/ in the usage of many metropolitan speakers, particularly but not exclusively on the lower levels, differs markedly from that found in certain other regional types of English. Only under certain phonetic conditions does /æ/ occur in everyone's speech; in other positions it is replaced in the pronunciation of many, regularly or sporadically, by the phonemically distinct /ɛə̆/ (or /æə̆/). This replacement, which was first described in detail by Trager,[7] and the variations in New York pronunciation are dealt with below on pages 75-79. I shall not anticipate that discussion here, but merely indicate that /æ/ is found regularly before /p/, /t/ (including the /t/ that interchanges with /d/ in words like *batter*), /k/, /tʃ/, /l/, /ŋ/, /r/ when intervocalic in words not derived from others in which it is final, /ð/ except in plurals like *paths*, and /ʒ/ (*cap, sat, sack, match, shallow, anger, carry, gather, azure*). Before other consonants, /æ/ is regular under certain conditions and /ɛə̆/ may be used elsewhere.

Aside from this major variation from the pattern of some other dialects, there are a few words that might be specially mentioned. For *radio*, /'rædiɪ̯ˌoŭ/ may be heard on the uncultivated level although it is not, I think, so common as it was a few years ago. *Radiator*, however, is still often pronounced with /æ/ by uncultivated speakers. *Faucet* usually has /ɔə̆/, but /æ/ (and /ɛə̆/) sometimes occurs in old-fashioned, and in uncultivated speech. For *combatant*, the most usual pronunciation on all levels is /kəm'bætnt/; I have rarely heard the pronunciations recorded in the dictionaries.

Certain words with long Latin *a* vary between /æ/ and /eɪ̆/ as they do generally in America, for example, *apparatus, data, status, stratum*. In *ration* also, both /æ/ and /eɪ̆/ are heard, the latter being probably more frequent than it is in certain other parts of the United States.

8.4. /ɑ/. The vowel in *stop, not, rock*, as such words are most commonly pronounced, is advanced lower low-back, unrounded. In the speech of many, its quality is identical with that of the monophthongal variant of /ɑə̆/, length alone often serving to distinguish *cot* from *cart*, *shop* from *sharp*, *goggles* from *gargles*, and *toddy* from *tardy*. This is not the case, however, in the pronunciation of those whose /ɑə̆/ is of the retracted variety discussed on page 79. In less cultivated speech the vowel is often nasalized.

The occurrence of /ɑ/ in metropolitan pronunciation is less extensive than that of the corresponding lower low-back,

VOWELS AND DIPHTHONGS OF STRESSED SYLLABLES   61

rounded vowel of Southern British English. As in other types
of American English, /ɔ̆ə/ occurs in several groups of words
that have /ɒ/ in Southern British; but also, in many other
other cases, /ɑ̆ə/ may appear, resulting in homonyms like *cod-
card, lodge-large, bobbed-barbed*. A detailed account of the
distribution, phonetic and lexical, of /ɑ/ and /ɑ̆ə/ is given
later in this study. Here it will suffice merely to state
that in the so-called "short o words," /ɑ/ regularly occurs
before /p/ (*stop, copper, hop-toad*), /t/ (including the /t/
which interchanges with /d/: *got, hotly, rotten, motto*),
/k/ (*box, knock, oxen*),[8] /tʃ/ (*botch, Hotchkiss, watch*), /l/
(except in *doll*, which frequently has /ɑ̆ə/; but /ɑ/ is found
in *collar, Molly, olive, pollen*), and /r/ intervocalic in
words not derived from others in which it is final (*foreign,
horrible, sorry, torrid*).[9] Before other consonants, /ɑ/ occurs in some words, while others have either /ɑ̆ə/ or /ɔ̆ə/.
For the details the reader is referred to the discussion of
those phonemes.

Several words often pronounced with /ɑ/ in New York City
must be specially mentioned. On the lower and intermediate
levels of metropolitan pronunciation, the vowel is almost universal in the final syllable of *paramount*. This pronunciation
is not to be interpreted as an example of the occasional monophthongization of /aŭ/ referred to on page 71, but is probably due to the analogy of *Belmont, Larchmont*, etc. Many
New Yorkers know the word chiefly as the name of two movie-
houses in the city. In the second syllable of *lilacs*, /ɑ/ is
very frequently pronounced, even in the usage of the cultivated. *On*, which is generally recorded in the dictionaries as
having no distinctive weak form, may have /ə/ when unstressed,
/ɑ̆ə/ when stressed, the latter form riming with *barn*. (There
is also an occasional weak form without a vowel.) For *forehead*, a not uncommon pronunciation among uncultivated speakers
is /'fɑˌhed/, which is presumably a blend of /'farəd/ and
/'fɔəˌhed/.

The words in which /ʌ/ has been replaced by /ɑ/ as a result
of spelling-pronunciation are in general the same as in other
types of American English. I cite here only those words in
which I have noted that the usage of some New Yorkers differs
from that recorded in the Kenyon and Knott *Dictionary*. In *compass*, the vowel in cultivated use is /ʌ/, but /ɑ/ is almost
regular on other levels. *Monger* often has /ɑ/ even in educated speech. The distinction between /ɑ/ in *constable* (common noun) and /ʌ/ in *Constable* (family-name) recorded by
Kenyon and Knott I have not observed in metropolitan speech--
the latter also has /ɑ/ (in *Arnold, Constable*, the name of a
well-known store, I have never heard /ʌ/). In *comfort* and *comfortable*, /ɑ/ may sometimes be used by less cultivated speakers.[10]

The use of /ɑ/ instead of /ʌ/ in the negative prefix *un-*

(*unsafe, unsure*, etc.), found in certain American dialects, I have heard a few times in uncultivated speech, but it is quite uncommon. None of my informants pronounce in this fashion.

Particularly on the more cultivated levels of New York pronunciation, a low-back rounded vowel like that of Southern British may sometimes be heard. Its employment is undoubtedly in part a matter of conscious imitation of British or "Eastern" usage. A few speakers pronounce it rather often, not only in place of the more usual /ɑ/ of *rock, stop*, but also of /ɔǝ/ (*broth, loft*) and in those words in which /aǝ/ may appear (*lodge, wash*). This type of pronunciation, although advocated in some manuals of elocution used in New York schools, is not extremely common. Those who pronounce in this manner, moreover, are rather irregular in their usage, not carrying the substitutions through completely. But the imitation of British or "Eastern" practice is hardly the sole cause of the employment of this rounded vowel. Sometimes it is probably a blend, the result of the contamination of /ɑ/ and /ɔǝ/ in words in which both phonemes may occur. For example, before /r/ there is some confusion of the historical classes, *coral, moral*, and a few others often having the /ɔǝ/ of *Dora, storage*, while *Lawrence* is often pronounced with /ɑ/. In my own speech and in that of some others whom I have observed, a vowel like the Southern British one is particularly likely to occur here. It is also common in certain words in which many speakers have come to feel that /ɔǝ/ is inelegant, but in which /ɑ/ or /aǝ/ would seem rather unnatural, for example in *coffee, office, officer; dog; chocolate*. There is no tendency to prefer the rounded vowel in those words in which it is preceded by /w/, such as *wallet, waffles, swamp*.

I am not altogether certain how one should interpret this [ɒ] phonemically. In the speech of some, it probably functions merely as a nondistinctive free variant of /ɑ/; in the pronunciation of others, one can sometimes find oppositions with /ɑ/ and /ɔǝ/, although not minimal contrasting sets (*orange, orator, oral; chock, chocolate, chalk*). In such cases, I suppose, one has to consider [ɒ] as a separate phoneme of rather limited occurrence.

In sections 13.1 and 13.2, I have noted the fact that several of my informants employ this rounded vowel rather frequently.

8.5. /ʌ/. The vowel in *cut, blood, stun* is advanced lower mid-back, unrounded. The direction of variation is chiefly forward: in uncultivated speech one may sometimes hear a vowel that I would describe as lower mid-central, fairly well advanced. Noticeably lowered varieties like those often heard in London English and in some types of Eastern Massachusetts speech do not occur.[11]

There are certain peculiarities in the distribution of the phoneme. Three classes of words must be considered:

VOWELS AND DIPHTHONGS OF STRESSED SYLLABLES   63

a) In less cultivated metropolitan speech, /ʌ/ can occur
in final position before a pause, so that for this type of
pronunciation it really does not belong in this general
class of vowels at all. The words in which /ʌ/ may appear as
a word-final are *blur, her* (stressed), *purr, stir,* all the
words that rime with these in General American and Southern
British, and the stressed form of *for.* In an earlier article,[12] I indicated that the vowel in these words differed
phonetically from that of *cut,* being slightly fronted,
raised, and diphthongal. That is sometimes the case, but in
the usage of many the vowel is identical with the [ʌ] used
elsewhere. It may be quite short and without any glide, so
that the word *stir* in *Stir the soup* sounds exactly like
stuck without the final stop.[13] The same vowel appears in
paradigmatic derivatives before final consonants: *stirs,
blurred.* A blend-form /ʌr/ may also be heard in these words,
which may appear even in the speech of those who do not ordinarily pronounce /r/ before a consonant or a pause.

b) In derivatives before /r/ (*stirring, stirrer, furry,
occurrence, weren't*),[14] /ʌ/ also occurs and may be used by
those who in *stir* and *stirs* pronounce /3ž/ or /r/.

c) Before /r/ in words that are not derivatives of *stir,
spur,* and the like, /ʌ/ is the usual vowel on all levels:
courage, current, hurry, nourish. In general the vowel occurs in the same words here as in Southern British; but it
is frequent also in *stirrup* and *squirrel* (in the former /i/
may also be heard, in the latter I have not observed it);
and it often does not occur, on the other hand, in *Durham,*
which many pronounce with the /už/ of *during.*

Aside from these variations from the practice found in
other regions, the distribution of /ʌ/ exhibits only one or
two peculiarities. For *donkey,* the older /'dʌŋkiĭ/ occurs
far more frequently than it appears to do in other parts of
America. In *pulpit,* I have heard /ʌ/ rather often from undergraduates. In the stressed forms of *from, of, was (wasn't)
what,* in which Kenyon condemns /ʌ/ as not having "attained
to good usage," the vowel is certainly not unknown in the
practice of many of the cultivated in the city.

8.6. /u/. In cultivated pronunciation, the vowel in *full,
foot, stood* is lower high-back, usually only weakly rounded.
Among less cultivated speakers, it is sometimes advanced and
the lip-rounding may disappear completely. The fact that the
interval between the more advanced varieties of /u/ and the
more retracted varieties of /i/ is sometimes very small has
already been mentioned on page 58. Those whom I have observed to use this fronted, unrounded vowel have done so
sporadically: the speaker would first pronounce a vowel identical with my own and then, sometimes in the same word,
would use one that struck my ear as markedly different.

So far as the occurrence of /u/ and /uŭ/ in words of the

group represented by *room* is concerned, the various class-dialects do not exhibit any striking differences from one another. In *broom*, *groom*, and *room*, /uŭ/ is usual and I have observed no tendency to treat *room* differently when it is the second part of compounds. Before /n/ (*noon*, *soon*, *spoon*), I have not heard /u/. Before /p/, /u/ seems to be more common than /uŭ/ in *hoop*; in *coop*, the opposite is decidedly true; /uŭ/ is usual in *Cooper* (several of my older informants pronounced /u/ in *Cooper*, and one of them told me that this pronunciation was common when she was a young girl); in *whooping cough*, both pronunciations are frequent; *whoopee* usually has /u/. Before /t/, /uŭ/ is usual in *root*, uncommon in *soot* (I have not heard /ʌ/). Before /f/, /u/ is preponderantly used in *hoof*, /uŭ/ in *roof*. The slang word *boogie-woogie* usually has /u/ in both stressed syllables. As for words in which the spelling is not *oo*, /u/ alone occurs in *butcher* and is predominantly pronounced in *bosom* (there is also a jocular pronunciation /bə'zuŭmz/, ordinarily plural). In the word *cuckoo* in the sense of "crazy," /uŭ/ is usually heard; the name of the bird is also so pronounced, but many educated speakers use /u/.

The fact has already been mentioned on page 41 that /u/ may occur in a frequent pronunciation of *wurst*. Similarly, the vowel may appear in *frankfurter*, which is very commonly pronounced /'fræŋk‚futə(r, -fudə(r/.

DIPHTHONGS OF THE [ĭ]-SERIES

9.1. /iĭ/. In *see, seed, seat*, a diphthong occurs whose starting-point is lower high-front, often somewhat retracted. The gliding movement is toward a closer position. The glide is a brief one, of course, and completely monophthongal phones occur, but even before voiceless stops, where /iĭ/ is normally shortest, the glide may often be heard. The retraction of the first element is most marked in uncultivated speech. Particularly when it stands in final position before a pause (as in *Give it to me*), one may sometimes hear in uncultivated pronunciation a variety whose starting-point is a lower high-central vowel.[15]

The phonetic distribution of /iĭ/ in high-stressed syllables does not differ from that found in General American and Southern British. In open syllables under secondary stress before a high-stressed vowel (*creative, neologism, piano, Peoria, reaction, reality*), the practice of phoneticians recording other types of English differs, some writing /i/, others /iĭ/. There is no opposition between the two phonemes in this position and the actual phonetic quality may vary. I write these vowels in phonemic transcription as /iĭ/, which is phonetically most accurate for metropolitan pronunciation as a whole.[16]

For the occurrence of /iĭ/ in weak syllables and for

VOWELS AND DIPHTHONGS OF STRESSED SYLLABLES   65

certain variations in the usage of the different class-
dialects, see page 87.
So far as the lexical occurrence of /iĭ/ is concerned, metropolitan pronunciation hardly differs from that of America
generally. In *deaf*, /iĭ/ survives to some extent in old-
fashioned and in uncultivated speech; in *creek*, it is by far
the more frequent pronunciation; in *chic*, both /iĭ/ and /i/
occur; and in *clique* the same variation occurs (/klik/ is the
most common pronunciation among undergraduates). Besides the
usual /iĭ/ in *eagle*, /i/ may occur, although rarely (I have
heard the name of the Brooklyn daily newspaper so pronounced
by several rather well-educated persons). *Negro* is /'niĭˌgroŭ/
and /'nɪgˌroŭ/, the latter being fairly common and in no
sense derogatory. As Thomas notes, /iĭ/ is often pronounced
in the high-stressed syllables of *Patricia* and *initiate*; it
may be added that many who would use it in the former word
would look upon it as extremely uncultivated in the latter.
For *cerebral*, /sə'riĭbrəl/ is far more frequent than the dictionary pronunciation.

9.2. /eĭ/. The starting-point of the diphthong in *say, same,
state* is intermediate or lower mid-front, usually not much
higher than the [e] of *pet* and often identical with it. In
uncultivated speech the first element may sometimes be quite
low. But variation in the first element is chiefly toward a
retracted position, and noticeably retracted varieties may
often be heard from uncultivated speakers. (The occasional
overlapping with the more advanced varieties of the diphthong
in *hurt* and *first* is mentioned below on page 68.) The upward
gliding movement is usually quite perceptible even before
voiceless stops.
The phonetic and lexical distribution of /eĭ/ does not differ except in minor ways from that found in General American
and Southern British. The replacement of /ei/ by /ɛə̆/ before
/l/ in *sail, daily, failure* and the like (actually a suspension of the opposition) in the speech of some New Yorkers is
dealt with under /ɛə̆/ on page 75. As in American English generally, /eĭ/ under secondary stress occurs in *holiday;* the
same pronunciation may frequently be heard in *yesterday* and
the names of the days of the week. For *moire*, /'mɔə̆ˌreĭ,
ˌmɔə̆'reĭ, 'mwɑˌreĭ/ are common, even among educated women,
and I have rarely heard the other pronunciations recorded in
the dictionaries. In *lingerie*, not only is there variation
between [æ̃] and [ɑ̃] in the first syllable, but /eĭ/ may occur
in the final one, even sometimes on the cultivated level. An
old stress-pattern survives in /ˌθiĭ'eĭdə(r/ *theater*, which
is fairly common in less cultivated speech. A number of my
informants pronounced /eĭ/ in *forbade;* this pronunciation is
very frequently used by undergraduates, to whom *forbade*, odd-
ly enough perhaps, is not a very familiar word.
Kenyon's statement that in America generally nouns and

adjectives in -*ative* retain /eɪ̆/ under secondary stress[17] hardly applies to metropolitan pronunciation. In New York City the tendency to drop the secondary stress and reduce the diphthong operates as it has operated in Southern British English, although not quite so many words are affected. Among those in which the loss of stress is common are *appreciative, cooperative, cumulative, decorative, imaginative, initiative, nominative, remunerative*. In some of these words, for example in *cooperative*, I have rarely heard /-ˌeɪ̆təv, -ˌeɪ̆dəv/.

9.3. /aɪ̆/. In cultivated metropolitan speech, the diphthong in *high, ride, white* begins at an advanced low-central position. Its gliding movement is upward and forward to a height lower than that of the end-point of /eɪ̆/. The quality of the first element may vary somewhat from speaker to speaker and from utterance to utterance: it may be advanced a little and raised; it may be retracted as far as the [ɑ] of *pot*; and it may be shifted slightly toward mid-central position (but I have not heard in the speech of the city varieties like those used in Northern England, for example, in some parts of upper New York State or in the Province of Ontario, whose first elements are definitely mid-central).

Very commonly in the less cultivated speech of the city the beginning of the glide is retracted low-back. This retraction of the first element is not striking when the diphthong is followed by voiceless consonants: words like *pipe, kite, knife* may be pronounced about as they are by cultivated speakers. But before voiced consonants and finally, the glide often begins at an extremely low and retracted position, which coincides with that of the retracted monophthongal diaphone of /ɑɜ̆/ (see page 79). Often the upward movement is slow and the first element appears longer than is the case in cultivated pronunciation. Nasalization is frequent.

On the level of less cultivated speech, it is generally true that the strong retraction of the first element of the diphthong in *high* and the use of a retracted vowel or of a, diphthong that begins very far back in *hard* go together. A person who retracts in the one case will normally do it in the other also. Those cultivated speakers, however, mentioned in the section dealing with /ɑɜ̆/ as using a retracted vowel or diphthong in *hard, march*, etc., ordinarily pronounce in *ride* and *high* the diphthong described in the first paragraph of this section.

In monosyllables composed of the first person singular pronoun plus an unstressed verbal form, /aɪ̆/ may be replaced by /ɑ/ (not /ɑɜ̆/). This pronunciation is very common in *I'll* (identical with the first syllable of *olive*), and *I'm* (identical with the first syllable of *omelet*); and it may be heard in *I've* and *I'd*, particularly when these syllables are unstressed.

In the pronunciation of Informants #32 and #33, the second

VOWELS AND DIPHTHONGS OF STRESSED SYLLABLES   67

element of the diphthong when final or followed by a voiced
consonant is often reduced or lost entirely. But their pronunciation, which in this respect resembles that heard in
many parts of the South, is here completely untypical. Nor
does the Southern British substitution of a monophthong for
the sequence /aɪə/ in words like *empire* and *science* have any
counterpart in metropolitan speech.

9.4. /ɔɪ̆/. The diphthong in *joy, join, joint* in cultivated
pronunciation begins at a higher low-back rounded position
and glides upward and forward. The first element is ordinarily identical in quality with the monophthongal variant of
/ɔə̆/. The diphthong occurs in the same words in which the
corresponding one is used in General American and Southern
British English. In addition, it is pronounced in *lawyer* and
the family-name *Sawyer*, which in Southern British are not exact rimes of *employer* and *destroyer*.[18]

The practice of other speakers varies. On a level intermediate between cultivated speech and the extremes of uncultivated pronunciation, a diphthong frequently occurs that is
phonemically equivalent to the one just described, but differs from it phonetically. Its first element is more strongly
rounded, retracted, and slightly higher; the rounding may involve a marked protrusion of the lips. Those who pronounce in
this fashion commonly employ phones of the same kind, that is
retracted and overrounded, in words like *law* and *court*.

But in the pronunciation of many uncultivated speakers the
words in which /ɔɪ̆/ occurs in the standard forms of English
fall into two groups. In one, the smaller, the usual diphthong is the one mentioned in the preceding paragraph. In the
other group, /ɔɪ̆/ may also occur, but alongside it are: (*a*)
diphthongs with a mid-central first element identical with
those which occur in *third* and *turn*; (*b*) /r/, although this
is not as common as the popular spellings *pernt* and *jern*
would suggest; (*c*) a contamination of these two, namely an
[ɪ̆]-diphthong whose first element is [r]. The details are
given in the next section.

9.5. /ɜɪ̆/. Under this rubric, I bring together a rather extensive set of diphthongs which may appear in two large
groups of words represented by *curl* and *coil*, respectively.[19]
The variation exhibited here in metropolitan speech is considerable and the different class-dialects of the city are in
some respects sharply distinguished from one another in their
treatment of these groups. Furthermore, the usage of many
individual speakers is highly irregular, following now one
pattern and now another even in the pronunciation of a single
word.[20]

The classes which we must consider are the following:
Group A. Those words which in Southern British English contain a mid-central stressed vowel followed by any consonant

(except /r/) that does not constitute an inflectional ending: *turpentine, curb, shirt, word, irk, Ferguson, church, urge, surf, serve, berth, further, purse, Jersey, Persia, firm, stern, curl*, etc.[21]

Group B. Those words which in Southern British English contain the diphthong /ɔĭ/, with certain exceptions. These exceptions vary somewhat from speaker to speaker, but always include the words in which the diphthong is final (*boy, joy, toy*, etc.)[22] and usually include the derivatives of such words (*boyish, destroyer, enjoyable, enjoyed, toys*), the words *noise* and *poise* (when the latter is used at all), plus a few others in which the diphthong is followed by a vowel (*loyal, royal, lawyer, Sawyer*). For the details, see below.

As I have indicated, the phonetic quality of the diphthongs that may be heard varies. The first element is ordinarily some kind of mid-central vowel, advanced or retracted, higher or lower, sometimes rounded. But the extremes of variation extend beyond the limits of the mid-central area. On the one hand, the glide may begin farther back; on the other, it sometimes begins at a position that is lower mid-front retracted, in which case there may be an occasional overlapping with /eĭ/.[23] Not infrequently the more advanced and the more retracted types may be used by the same speaker.[24] The extent of the glide and the prominence of the second element may also vary.

As is well known, the occurrence of /3ĭ/ in the words of Group A is not limited to uncultivated usage. On the cultivated level of metropolitan speech, pronunciations like /θ3ĭd/ *third* and /b3ĭst/ *burst* may be heard quite frequently, although younger speakers are likely not to use them. One may often observe that, in a particular family, /3ĭ/ appears in the speech of the older members, while the younger ones pronounce /r/ or /3ə̆/. Mixed patterns are not uncommon on the cultivated and intermediate levels: among my informants, for example, some employ both /3ĭ/ and /3ə̆/, others /3ĭ/ and /r/. The contamination of these last two results in a diphthong [r̩ĭ], which may be heard rather frequently.[25]

The variation in the quality of the diphthongs comprising /3ĭ/ is in part a matter of class-dialect. It would perhaps be dangerous to assert it as a hard-and-fast rule, but in general the starting point is higher and more advanced in the speech of those cultivated persons who employ these diphthongs, and the movement not so pronounced. Sometimes one may hear a mid-central vowel with only a slight upward and forward glide. In uncultivated speech, on the other hand, the starting-point is likely to be lower and farther back and the glide much more prominent.

It should be noted that /3ĭ/ never appears in certain types of words which are pronounced with a stressed mid-central vowel in Southern British English: it does not occur in *fur, stir*, and all rime-words, nor in derivatives of such words

VOWELS AND DIPHTHONGS OF STRESSED SYLLABLES 69

(*furs, furry, occurrence, stirred, stirring,* etc.).[26] For the pronunciation of these types, see pages 63, 85, and 86.

In Group B, the cultivated do not employ the diphthongs discussed in this section, but /ɔɪ̆/.[27] Therefore, even when /3ɪ̆/ appears in their speech in *curl, earl, learn,* such words are not homonyms of *coil, oil,* and *loin.* The distinction between these two classes is also fairly well maintained on the intermediate levels of New York pronunciation and the employment, in words spelled with *oi, oy,* of the diphthong /3ɪ̆/ is thus much less extensive than are certain other characteristics of less cultivated metropolitan speech.[28]

When diphthongs distinct phonetically from [ɔɪ̆] are used in the words of Group B, their exact quality varies just as does the quality of those used by the same speakers in Group A. *Coil-curl, oil-earl, loin-learn* are homonyms. The interchange between /3ɪ̆/ on the one hand, and /r/ (and the blend [r̩ɪ̆]) on the other, which may be observed in Group A, may consequently sometimes appear in the words of Group B also, resulting in pronunciations like [kr̩l] or [dʒr̩ɪ̆n] for *coil* and *join.*[29]

To find a clear pattern in the variation between [3ɪ̆] and [ɔɪ̆] in the *oi*-words is rather difficult. The group of words in which [3ɪ̆] never occurs is not the same in the usage of different speakers. In my earlier discussion of these diphthongs I listed as words always pronounced with [ɔɪ̆] the following: "All words in which the diphthong is final, as for example, *toy, boy, enjoy, destroy, annoy,* and the derivatives of such words; *loyal, royal; poise, noise; exploit, loiter, goiter.*" This list requires some correction. In the first place, the words in which the diphthong is followed by /t/ (interchanging with /d/) should not have been included: I have since observed diphthongs like [3ɪ̆] a number of times in *loiter* and *goiter*[30] and, furthermore, the name *Hoyt* (for example, in *Hoyt Street,* Brooklyn) is sometimes [h3ɪ̆t, hʌɪ̆t]. Secondly, diphthongs like [3ɪ̆] may sometimes be used in *loyal* and *royal,* particularly if the unstressed vowels are syncopated (although I have never heard [r̩] in these words). With the one minor exception mentioned in note 22, page 141, [3ɪ̆] does not occur when the diphthong is a word-final, nor have I heard [r̩] in this position. As for the derivatives, [3ɪ̆] (or [r̩]) does not occur before /z/ in forms like *boys, employs,* or when followed by a vowel that is never syncopated (*boyish, employer*). But in the past tense forms *enjoyed, destroyed,* etc., diphthongs like [3ɪ̆] may occasionally be used. The word *noise* is pronounced [nʌɹɪ̆z] by one of my informants, but this pronunciation is rather unusual.

Behind all the variation in the individual usage of uncultivated speakers, it may be that there is a pattern, usually distorted at one point or another, perhaps by the influence of other class-dialects, according to which [3ɪ̆] and [ɔɪ̆] are merely variants of the same phoneme. In a few instances, the occurrence of [ɔɪ̆] is positionally determined, that is, in word-final position or before an unsyncopated vowel. In most positions, the quality of the diphthong may vary more or less at random. For what it is worth as evidence, I submit the observation that many uncultivated speakers appear unable to hear the difference between these diphthongs--they "sound the same" to them. In working with students who used these uncultivated pronunciations, I have often found that they would for example, say [bɔɾɪ̆] for *boy* and [bɜɪ̆l] for *boil* and think that they were pronouncing the same diphthong in both words. Frequently some rather intensive ear-training is required before such students can be made to hear the diphthongs as different ones.

In a study intended for readers familiar with the history of American English, it seems unnecessary to add that the "Dutch origin" theory of the New York /ɜɪ/ is ridiculous. So far as I know this theory has never been accepted by any competent linguist, but it still crops up every so often in popular articles. Those who entertain it seem unaware that in many parts of the South words like *third* and *burst* are pronounced with an almost identical diphthong. As for words like *coil* and *join*, it is far simpler to assume that uncultivated metropolitan speech preserves in somewhat altered form a distinction that was general in Early Modern English.

DIPHTHONGS OF THE [ŭ]-SERIES

10.1. /aŭ/. The diphthong in *how, sound, house*, varies considerably in metropolitan pronunciation. The starting-point may be any one of a numbe of low vowels in the range approximately set by the [æ] of *hat*[31] and the [ɑ] of *hot*. Variants with a mid-central first element do not occur. The first element may vary noticeably in length; that is, the glide may start quickly or the initial position may be held for a time before the upward movement begins. The lip-modification of the second element rarely involves any real protrusion of the lips; more commonly there is merely a decrease, as the glide progresses, in the distance separating them.

Differences between the class-dialects are in part a matter of the point at which the diphthong begins, the more advanced varieties being uncommon in cultivated speech. But also important are the relative length of the first element and the presence or absence of nasalization. Thus on both the cultivated and the uncultivated level, the starting-point may be about [a], but in the latter type of speech it may be drawn out before the tongue begins its rise and the whole glide may be strongly nasalized.

Writing about this diphthong in the 1890's, Babbitt said that there was "much variation in the first component," but without any fronting of the vowel "to [æ] or a mixed vowel near [æ]" and that "what is heard is generally a regular [ɑ] or something approaching [ɒ]."[32] This is hardly a very good

VOWELS AND DIPHTHONGS OF STRESSED SYLLABLES   71

description of uncultivated usage today, but it is very possible that there has been a change in the quality of the diphthong in the intervening years. While I have not observed anything like [ɒŭ], I have found that, even on the uncultivated level, elderly speakers rarely begin the glide from a markedly fronted position and that their pronunciation in this respect is often the same as my own (in my speech the first element usually lies between [a] and [ɑ]). Among my informants and among New Yorkers generally, diphthongs like [æŭ] occur chiefly in the speech of younger persons.
  The Southern British replacement by a monophthong of the sequence /aŭə/ in words like *power, tower, devouring, now-a-days*³³ is not paralleled in metropolitan pronunciation. Monophthongization may be observed occasionally in a few words, for example in *how* and *now* (Informant #30: [ˌhaˑ dʒə'meɾik iɾt] *How did you make it?*). The substitution of /ɑ/ for /aŭ/ in the last syllable of *paramount*, which is not an instance of monophthongization, is briefly discussed on page 61 above. But in *our* (and *ours*), /ɑə̆/ often occurs, making the word a rime of *car* rather than of *power*. This pronunciation, which appears on all levels, may have developed in unstressed position originally, but it is used under stress also and many speakers do not employ /aŭ/ in this word at all.

10.2. /oŭ/. In *go, rode, boat* a diphthong occurs whose quality varies somewhat, although the variation is not so considerable as that heard in the case of /aŭ/. Most commonly it begins at an intermediate mid-back position, slightly higher and farther back than the [ʌ] of *cut*. Normally the "rounding" of the diphthong does not involve any lip-protrusion: the lips come together at the corner, then as the glide progresses, the space between them narrows. In cultivated speech, one may sometimes hear, especially from women, a diphthong whose starting-point is advanced to a mid-central position, the result being very similar to one Southern British variant, of which it is possibly an imitation. (Such a diphthong is used, for example, by Informant #32.) A third variant, heard in less cultivated pronunciation, has a first element that is also advanced, but at the same time is lowered and without any lip-modification.
  The phonetic distribution does not differ from that found in Southern British English and the lexical distribution only in regard to a few words. Many less cultivated speakers pronounce *forward* as /'foŭwəd/, *almost* as /'oŭˌmoŭst, -ˌmoŭs/, and *always* as /'oŭˌweɪ̆z/. Words like *fellow, marshmallow, piano, window* have /oŭ/ in cultivated speech (the variant used here often being short and with little or no glide);³⁴ in uncultivated pronunciation such words are leveled with *soda, collar*, etc. For /oŭ/ and /uŭ/ in *won't*, see the next section.
  The phoneme does not occur in the group of words represented

by *hoarse, mourning*, although one may occasionally hear /oŭ/ in words like *story* and *oral*, in which it is followed by /r/. For a detailed discussion of this group, see page 83.

10.3. /uŭ/. The diphthong in *shoe, moon, boot* begins at a lower high-back position, somewhat advanced, and glides slightly toward a closer position. The diphthong is rounded in the sense that the lips are closed at the corners and fairly near to each other at the mid-line,·the distance between them decreasing toward the end--there is ordinarily little or no protrusion. When /j/ precedes, as in *pew, acute*, or one pronunciation of *new*, the diphthong begins at a more advanced position; but the extreme fronting heard in some parts of the South does not occur on any level of metropolitan speech.

One may observe two opposing tendencies in the pronunciation of many less cultivated speakers. On the one hand, the first element may be advanced and lowered, the glide starting from an unrounded higher mid-central position. Or one may sometimes hear a fully retracted high-back vowel with little glide and no particular lip-modification,

The distribution, phonetic and lexical, of /uŭ/ is similar to that found in Southern British except in so far as a separate phonemic category must be posited in describing that kind of speech in which /j/ does not occur in *new, tune*, and the like, but in which at the same time such words are not rimes of *do* and *Boone*. (For this matter, see the next section.) In open syllables under secondary stress before a high-stressed vowel (*fluidity, fruition*), I employ /uŭ/ in phonemic transcription; the situation is parallel to that of /iĭ/ in *creative, piano* discussed on page 64. A few words require particular mention. In *won't*, /oŭ/ is used by some educated speakers; others pronounce /uŭ/ and this pronunciation is also generally used by the less cultivated. The diphthong occurs very frequently in *manure*, which then rimes with *doer* and *viewer* rather than with *pure*. *Goal* often has /uŭ/ in uncultivated speech, and this pronunciation may appear in the the speech of children on all levels. The same diphthong is also common in children's speech in the final syllable of *lasso*.

For the pronunciation of words like *roof* and *hoop*, in which both /uŭ/ and /u/ may be heard, see page 64.

10.4. /ɨŭ/. As I have already pointed out in the discussion of the consonant /j/, the practice of many metropolitan speakers in the pronunciation of the classes of words represented by *new, tune, duty, enthusiasm, assume, resume* is irregular. On the completely uncultivated level, the situation is not complicated: /uŭ/, not preceded by /j/, is as regular in these classes as in *noon, tool, doom, zoo, loot*, and the like. Among the cultivated and to some extent on the intermediate levels, such regularity is less commonly found, and usage may be highly variable indeed. Some speakers pronounce the sequence /juǔ/, particularly after /t, d, n/, rather consistently; some do so in certain words but not in others of the same class; and many pronounce the same word now in one way and now in another. In this kind of speech, when /j/ is not pronounced, these words may have /uǔ/ or a diphthong distinct from /uǔ/, that is, with a more advanced first element.

I have observed few speakers who pronounce this diphthong with any regularity in the classes referred to above (none of my informants do). Usually its occurrence is sporadic. After /s/, for example, one of my cultivated informants pronounced /ɨǔ/ in *assume*, but /uǔ/ in *suitable* and *superintendent*. One factor in its use, I think, is the feeling that after certain consonants /juǔ/ is affected and /uǔ/ "not correct," the latter notion often being derived from the Websterian respellings, which only phoneticians understand. In the speech of a person with such attitudes, /ɨǔ/ is likely to appear rather frequently as a conscious or unconscious compromise.

Babbitt, discussing uncultivated speech in the 1890's, described a diphthong that he wrote as [iu], "with stress on the first component."[35] He added that it tended to be replaced by [û] (his symbol for the syllabic of *boot*) after "dentals" in *Tuesday, new, rule*, etc. I assume he meant that such a diphthong, and not the sequence /juǔ/, was common in words like *mute, beauty, cube*. This is certainly not the case today.

DIPHTHONGS OF THE [ə]-SERIES AND THEIR MONOPHTHONGAL VARIANTS

11.1. /iə/. The diphthong in *spear* and *here* begins at a point as high as or usually somewhat higher than the [i] of *pit* and then glides toward a mid-central position, which is normally higher and farther forward than the end-point of the corresponding diphthong in Southern British English. The first element is normally rather long, the second brief. The diphthong is always a falling one: there is no tendency for the second element to become the syllabic peak and pronunciations like those that Jones records as variants ([hjə:*] *hear*, [ʃjə:*] *sheer*, [jə:*] *year*)[36] do not occur. Before consonants the second element is often very short and, if the following consonant is intervocalic, completely monophthongal pronunciations with a fairly long vowel are extremely common (for example in *hearing, piercing, theater, nearly, near it*).

In uncultivated pronunciation, the tendency to monophthongization goes further and affects even those occurrences in which the diphthong is final before a pause. Pronunciations like [biˑ, biː] *beer*, [hiˑ, hiː] *here*, [ˌɑˈɪˈdiˑ, -ˈdiː] *idea* are frequent. Even when monophthongization is not complete, the starting and ending positions may be very close to each other.

For the most part, the diphthong or its monophthongal variant may occur wherever the corresponding diphthong is found in Southern British English. Examples in addition to those already cited are *real, really* (but see below); *leer, sneer; ear, beard, clear, fear; fierce, Pierce; here, mere, austere*.[37] There are certain differences, however, between the Southern British pattern and that of metropolitan speech. In the type of pronunciation exhibited in Jones' *Dictionary* the opposition before /r/ of this phoneme and the lower high-front monophthong /i/ seems to be quite stable. In New York City, on the other hand, the opposition between /i/ in *mirror, spirit* and /iə̆/ in *series, serious, experience* often disappears. As a result, *delirious* and *mysterious* are ordinarily rimes, as are *Syria* and *Algeria, myriad* and *period*. The length of the vowels may vary in both groups but the identification usually arises from a lengthening of the historically short vowel. The coalescence of the two phonemes before /r/, however, is not complete: we are, it would seem, in the midst of a sound-change. Thus a particular speaker who will regularly rime *mysterious* and *delirious* may just as regularly preserve a clear opposition between /iə̆/ and /i/ in *Vera* and *mirror*.

One may at times hear quite short vowels in some words like *series* and *seriously*, which do not have related forms in which /iə̆/ is a word-final. But such pronunciations are very unusual in *clearer, hearing,* and the like.

In the replacement by /iə̆/ of the sequence /iɪə/, New York practice lies between that of General American and that of Southern British, although it is closer to the former. In some words like *Theodore* and *diarrhea*, which Kenyon and Knott record with the equivalent of /iɪə/, metropolitan pronunciation often has /iə̆/. But I have never heard /iə̆/ in many of the words in which Jones records it, for example in *Crimean, European,*[38] *Galilean, lyceum,* and *Medea*.

Certain other words must be mentioned particularly. The "dark" [l] in words like *feel* and *steal* is often preceded by a noticeable glide, particularly in less cultivated speech. The resulting sequence may be replaced by a diphthong phonetically identical with the one in *near*. The diphthong is common, even in cultivated speech, in the forms *he'll, we'll, she'll*. The two words *reel* and *real*, normally kept apart in the careful pronunciation of the cultivated, become homonyms in the speech of others. The word *really* in the speech of most cultivated persons has /iə̆/ (normally monophthongal [iː]) and rimes with the "r-less" pronunciation of *nearly*. In less cultivated speech, it is also pronounced with /iɪ/ and a third pronunciation, which I have occasionally heard, rimes with *silly*.

A large number of New York speakers pronounce /r/ at least sporadically in words like *fears, feared, fierce, clearness,* and in those like *fear, pier* before a pause or a following initial consonant. See pages 48-49.

11.2. /ɛə̆/. The diphthong in *fare* and *hair* ordinarily begins at a point somewhat lower than the position of the [e] in *pet* and then glides to a mid-central position, which as in the case of /iə̆/ is higher and farther forward than in Southern British English. Before consonants that are not intervocalic, the second element may be very slight and before intervocalic consonants, as in *fairer, fairness, fairly, dairy, Sarah, share it*, a completely monophthongal variant is generally used. In uncultivated speech, monophthongs or diphthongs with a very much reduced glide may occur even before a pause: [kɛ·] *care*, [hɛ·] *hair*, etc. The uncultivated diaphones are often produced with a considerable degree of tenseness.

The partial disappearance of the /i/-/iə̆/ opposition before /r/ is not paralleled in the case of /e/ and /ɛə̆/: *ferry-fairy, merry-Mary, very-vary* are always distinguished. (But for the partial loss of the opposition with /æ/ before /r/, see the next section.)

For the pronunciation of /r/ before a pause or a consonant in *fair, fairs, shared, Laird*, etc., see pages 48-49.

The diphthong or its monophthongal variant also occurs rather frequently on the uncultivated and intermediate levels before /l/, in words in which /eĭ/ appears in the standard forms of English: *ale, pale, sail, daily, sailor, failure*. In this type of pronunciation, *daily* and the family-name *Daly* rime with the "r-less" pronunciation of *fairly*. (Actually this is another suspension.)

In a third group of words, far more numerous than either of those so far discussed, /ɛə̆/ (diphthong or monophthong) may also be heard in the speech of many New Yorkers. The existence of vowels higher and longer than [æ] in words like *stand* and *ask* has been noted by a number of writers and the phonetic conditions under which /ɛə̆/ might occur in various types of American English have been set forth by George L. Trager in a series of papers.[39] The pattern described by Trager is found in metropolitan speech very widely, particularly though not exclusively on the lower and intermediate levels. The situation is complicated, however, not only by the analogic changes that he mentions, but also by the deliberate avoidance of /ɛə̆/ on the part of many speakers. Metropolitan usage consequently is extremely variable, differing considerably from one social group to another and differing from person to person within what is roughly the same group. And the practice of a single speaker will often show a great deal of variation in successive utterances of the same word.

Leaving all of these complications out of account for the moment, let us first proceed to define the conditions under which /ɛə̆/ may appear. They are as follows:

Before the voiced stops, voiced affricate, voiceless and voiced fricatives, bilabial and alveolar nasals (/b, d, g, dʒ, f, θ, s, ʃ, v, ð, z, m, n/) when these consonants are final in words or when they are followed by suffixed elements of any sort.[40] Thus in the type of pronunciation here being described, /ɛɚ/ may occur in *drab, drabness, stab, stabs, stabbing; bad* (often a homonym of *bared*), *shad* (often = *shared*), *Dad, Daddy, mad, madly, madder* (adj.), *maddest, sad, sadden; brag, bragging, rag, ragged, bag, three-bagger; badge, badges, Madge; laugh, laughable, laughter, photograph, photographic; bath, baths* (/-θs/), *path; grass, grassy, mass, masses, massing;*[41] *cash, cashable; salve, salves; baths* (/-ðs/); *jazz* (often an exact rime of *shares*), *jazzing; ham, hams, ram, ramming, Sam, Sammy; Ann, Annie,*[42] *fan, fanning, manly, mannish.*

The stressed forms of *have, has, had, hath, an, as, can, and, am* are exceptions to this general rule and have /æ/, although /ɛɚ/ may occasionally be heard in the last two words. Nor does /ɛɚ/ occur before the /d/ that interchanges with /t/ in words like *batter* and *fatter*.

Before these consonants, when they are followed by sequences that do not constitute regular suffixes, the situation is a bit more involved:

a) Before the voiced stops and affricate, /ɛɚ/ does not occur in most words. Some, although not all, of the exceptions are presumably analogical. It would not normally be used in words like *Abbot, Aberdeen, absolutely, cabbage, fabric, habit, rabbit, vocabulary; academy, Addison, advertise,*[43] *caddy, ladder, Madeleine, saddle; aggravate, agony, haggard* (sometimes with /ɛɚ/), *magazine* (/ɛɚ/ occurs rather often in *wagon*); *adjective, gadget, exaggerate* (the frequent occurrence of /ɛɚ/ in a few words like *imagine* can hardly be analogical).

b) Before the voiceless fricatives:

1) In the case of /f/, /ɛɚ/ may appear before the medial and final sequence /ft/ (*after, graft, rafters*) and does not normally occur in other cases. It would not be heard in *affectation, Africa, raffle, sapphire* (but *taffy* is often /ˈtɛɚfiː/).

2) In the case of /θ/, /ɛɚ/ does not appear: /æ/ is usual in *Athens, athlete, Catherine, mathematics* (but note that the short form, *math*, is a word that may have /ɛɚ/).

3) In the case of /s/ and /ʃ/, /ɛɚ/ may occur, no matter what follows: *acid, ask, asphalt, Astor, cascade, castle, fasten, gasoline, gasp, gasping, Massachusetts, mast, plastic, sarsaparilla; Cashman, cashier, fashion, passionate.*

c) Before the voiced fricatives, /ɛɚ/ does not usually appear, /æ/ being regular in words like *gravel, savage, Savarin* (although /ɛɚ/ is frequent in *avenue*); *gather, lather* (of soap); *hazard, Lazerus, plasma, spasm.* Nor does /ɛɚ/ occur before /ʒ/ in *azure, casual.*

VOWELS AND DIPHTHONGS OF STRESSED SYLLABLES 77

d) Before the nasals /m/ and /n/, when they are followed by vowels, syllabic consonants or /j/, /ɛə̆/ does not occur, except as it may be sporadically introduced by analogy. Words like the following normally have /æ/: *Amityville, camel, damage, grammar;*[44] *banner* (flag), *Canada, channel, Indiana, manual.* But /ɛə̆/ may occur in all other cases: *ampere, camp, family* (/ɛə̆/ arises here in the disyllabic pronunciation, where the nasal is not followed by a vowel), *ramble, stampede; band, bandage, candy, commandment, dandruff, circumstance, dancing, fancy, Francis, Mansfield, transfer, pansy, slant, Atlantic, Stanley, mansion, branch.*

In the preceding paragraphs a number of words have been mentioned which belong structurally to the /æ/-group but in which /ɛə̆/ rather frequently occurs. It is probable that in some of these cases the substitution is analogical, under the influence of words of similar appearance. Thus the oppositions found in *manning* (participle) and *Manning* or in *fanning* and *Fanning* may not occur in the speech of many who learn the family-names from the written form and pronounce them with /ɛə̆/ because they look like the participles. (There is no conscious reasoning about the matter, of course.) So also a word like *dagger*, which is not a derivative but which is sometimes pronounced with /ɛə̆/, may be influenced in some obscure fashion by words like *nagger* and *three-bagger*.

A second factor adduced by Trager as a further explanation of the occasional irregular occurrences of /ɛə̆/ is that of dialect borrowing. It may be noted, for instance, that in the pronunciation of certain other areas of New York State there appears to be only one vowel-phoneme, not very different in quality from the New York City /ɛə̆/, in all the "short *a*" words. Speakers from these areas use this higher vowel in *hammer* as well as in *ham* and in *cap* as well as in *cab*. A word that would normally have /æ/ in metropolitan speech might first be learned by a New Yorker from such a speaker. If the following consonant were one before which both vowels were possible in his own speech, he might then pronounce the word with /ɛə̆/. It seems to me unlikely, however, that dialect borrowing from areas outside the city is a very frequent cause of these irregularities.

For other patterns in the pronunciation of the words under consideration, see the next section.

11.3. /æə̆/. (In this section, as the reader will see, I am actually dealing with two cases, that of /æə̆/ as a phoneme distinct from /ɛə̆/ and that of [æə̆, æ·] as free variants of /ɛə̆/.)

The diphthong begins approximately at the position of the [æ] of *hat* and glides toward mid-central. Diphthongal and monophthongal variants appear under conditions similar to those described in the discussion of /ɛə̆/. The occurrences are as follows:

a) In words like *flare* and *stairs*, [æɜ̆, æ·] appears sporadically alongside [ɛɜ̆, ɛ·]; it is quite common before /r/ in *Cary, Gary, parent, Sarah, vary, variation,* and *various*. In these latter cases, the length-difference between the vowel and the [æ] of *carry* often disappears, so that *Cary* and *carry* are pronounced as homonyms. This type of pronunciation is not heard in the more cultivated forms of New York speech.[45]

b) Where cultivated English has /eɪ̆/ before /l/ in words like *ale, sail, sailor, daily, failure,* [æɜ̆, æ·] may occasionally appear beside [ɛɜ̆, ɛ·] in uncultivated pronunciation.

c) In words of the type of *glad, stand, jazz,* which have been discussed above, [æɜ̆, æ·] is also very common. Here several types of pronunciation may be distinguished. In the usage of many cultivated speakers, [ɛɜ̆, ɛ·] does not occur in these words at all, or occurs only in rare instances.[46] In their speech [æɜ̆, æ·] normally appears before /b, d, g, dʒ, f, θ, s, ʃ, v, ð, z, m, n/ when these consonants are word-finals or the first members of final clusters. (The stressed forms of *have, has,* etc. are exceptional because their vowels are shorter, although of the same quality.) Elsewhere, for example in *baggage, Daddy, ragged, passing, ransom, stampede,* /æ/ appears ordinarily, It would certainly make a neater formulation to classify [æɜ̆, æ·] in this kind of pronunciation merely as a positional variant of /æ/; but since as a result of this difference in length *had* and *sad, has* and *jazz* (or *has* [hæs] and *mass*), and *am* and *ham* are not rimes, such a classification seems hardly possible.

Many New Yorkers--and this is perhaps the commonest pattern of all, especially on the intermediate levels of metropolitan speech--pronounce [ɛɜ̆, ɛ·, æɜ̆, æ·] in words like *glad, stand, jazz*, in an extremely haphazard fashion.[47] Often they will pronounce the higher and the lower varieties in successive utterances of the same word, and "compromise" pronunciations of all possible in-between qualities are also common in their speech.[48] This kind of variation is no doubt in part due to a not wholly successful attempt to avoid [ɛɜ̆, ɛ·], as being "ugly" and "incorrect"; but it may also be observed very frequently in the speech of those to whom such notions are not likely to have occurred.

Of those whose usage varies in this fashion, many also pronounce, at least occasionally, diphthongs whose starting-point is lower low-front retracted (or the corresponding monophthong). As Thomas has suggested,[49] such pronunciations are probably due to the "over-correction" of [ɛɜ̆, ɛ·]. The highly irregular pronunciation of many speakers might perhaps best be described as exhibiting free variation, in all the words in question, throughout the entire range of low-front quality.

11.4. /aɜ̆/. One of the matters dealt with in the preceding section was a common type of metropolitan pronunciation in which the syllabics of words like *ask, flag, glad, stand* varied widely and at random between the limits of [ɛɜ̆, ɛˑ] and [aɜ̆, aˑ]. We may distinguish from this another type in which [aɜ̆, aˑ] does not appear in words like *flag, glad, stand*, but is restricted to the *ask*-group, that is, to those words not containing orthographic *r* that are frequently pronounced in similar fashion by speakers in Eastern New England. As in New England, the group so pronounced by any individual speaker often does not include all the words respelled with the symbol for the "intermediate vowel" in our dictionaries. Among my informants, #32 is the one who pronounces in this fashion with the nearest approach to consistency.

In those parts of New England where this kind of pronunciation is indigenous, it may be heard on all levels. In New York City, on the other hand, such pronunciations are employed only by a minority of more or less cultivated speakers. In my observation, they are far more frequent in the speech of women than of men. There can be no doubt that they are not part of the inherited speech-ways of the area.

11.5. /ɑɜ̆/. It is necessary to describe two varieties of the diphthong that occurs in *hard* and *far*. One has as its first element an advanced low-back unrounded vowel, more or less identical in quality with the most usual vowel in *hot*, from which point it glides, often only slightly, toward mid-central position. The first element may vary to some extent toward a still more advanced position and a few speakers occasionally pronounce words like *far* in a fashion which approximates that of Eastern New England speech. But these extremely fronted variants are rare, and I have never observed any New Yorker who used them regularly.[50]

The second type of the diphthong that is common in metropolitan speech differs from the first in that it begins at a much retracted low-back position. Sometimes, although not in most cases, it is accompanied by a slight rounding of the lips.

It cannot be said without qualification that the first of these is the more cultivated, and the second the less cultivated type. To be sure, the retracted variety is frequently heard from uncultivated speakers and is also very common on the intermediate levels. It is not unknown, however, in the speech of persons of cultivation, as may be seen from my comments in sections 13.1 and 13.2. The pronunciation of some speakers, it might be added, often varies noticeably between the more advanced and the more retracted positions.

Alongside the diphthong a monophthongal type [ɑˑ, ɑː], occurs. The monophthong is rare in final position before a pause, but is usual before intervocalic consonants; in monosyllables before final consonants both types vary at random.

The classes of words in which /ɑ̆/ may occur are the following:

a) Words with orthographic r that are pronounced with the corresponding low-back unrounded vowel in Southern British English: car, sharp, cart, lark, card, argue, harsh, and the like.[51]

b) A fairly large group of words that do not contain orthographic r, but which have the spellings a, ah, al: almond,[52] Bali, calm, Chicago, khaki,[53] Nevada,[54] Omaha, pajamas,[55] Shah, tomato,[56] Utah are examples.

c) Words of the ask-group that are pronounced according to the pattern of Southern British English by a small minority of speakers, most of them women. Frequently /ɑ̆/ occurs in only a few words of the sort, the rest being pronounced with the more usual low-front vowels.[57] Some speakers (Informant #4 is an example) pronounce both [ɑ̆, ɑ·] and [æ̆, æ·] in these words.

In rather /ɑ̆/ occurs rather often in the speech of those who do not employ it in other words of this group. To a lesser extent this is also true of the word aunt.

d) Words that in Southern British English contain the low-back rounded vowel (/ɒ/) before certain consonants and consonant clusters. The occurrence in American English of rather long vowels in words like job, god, and doll, which has been noted by several writers, seems in the type of General American recorded by Kenyon not to involve any phonemic disturbances, the longer vowel being merely a positional variant of /ɑ/. In New York City, on the contrary, the long vowels or diphthongs that may occur in such words cannot be assigned to /ɑ/, since both [ɑ] and [ɑ̆, ɑ·] may occur contrastingly under the same phonetic conditions, as will be seen below. The use of this longer vowel, or diphthong, together with the absence of /r/ in the preconsonantal position brings about an extensive homonymy in the speech of many persons (gob-garb, god-guard, lodge-large, doll-Dahl, etc.) which is one of the striking characteristics of metropolitan pronunciation.

The conditions under which /ɑ̆/ may occur are as follows:

1. Before the voiced stops when they are final in words or are followed by regularly suffixed sequences (with the qualifications noted below). Thus /ɑ̆/ may appear in bob (often = barb), Bob, bobbed, gob (often = garb), job, jobber, cod (often = card), god (often = guard), ungodly, pod; eggnog, hog, hoggish, log, logging, togs. The occurrence of /ɑ̆/ is complicated, however, in several ways. In the first place, /ɑ̆/ may or may not appear in the derived forms of more than one syllable. A speaker who pronounces /ɑ̆/ in job, hog, fog may use a shorter vowel in jobber, hoggish, and foggy. In some extended forms, for example in Bobbie, /ɑ/ is regular. Furthermore, some of the monosyllables may have /ɑ/ when they are the first elements of compounds. Thus a speaker to whom cod and card are homonyms may nevertheless pronounce codfish

VOWELS AND DIPHTHONGS OF STRESSED SYLLABLES 81

as /ˈkɑdˌfiʃ/ and *card-trick* as /ˈkɑɚdˌtrik/. Similarly, the high-stressed vowels in *bobcat*, *hod carrier*, and *cogwheel* are normally /ɑ/.[58]

Words in which the stops are followed by sequences that do not constitute regular suffixes are normally pronounced with /ɑ/: *cobbler, gobble* (contrasts with *garble*), *lobster, lobby, Robert; body, modern, toddy* (contrasts with *tardy*), *toddle; goggles* (contrasts with *gargles*), *geography, photographer.* But an irregular pronunciation with /ɑɚ/ occurs in *toboggan*, making the word homonymous with the "r-less" pronunciation of *to bargain*.

2. Before /dʒ/ when it is final or followed by regularly suffixed elements: *lodge* (often = *large*), *dodge, dodged, Dodgers, dodging.* But as in the case of the voiced stops, /ɑ/ may also occur in the derivatives even when the speaker pronounces the underlying form with /ɑɚ/: *Dodgers* may or may not rime with *enlargers.* When the affricate is followed by sequences that are not regular suffixes, /ɑ/ is usual: *Blodgett, homogenize, Rogers.*

3. Before /ʃ/ in a few words under the same conditions: *gosh, squash, wash* (riming with *harsh*); but a speaker who says /wɑɚʃ/ may pronounce /ɑ/ in the compound *washcloth*. In the words *bosh* and *josh* and in the place-name *Oshkosh*, I have heard only /ɑ/. In *Mosholu* (a street-name in the Bronx), /ɑ/ is regular, and it is usual in *Washington*.

4. Before voiced fricatives, /ɑɚ/ may occur in *bother* (riming with *father*), but elsewhere /ɑ/ is usual: *novel, Ovid,* and one pronunciation of *grovel, hovel, hover; Boswell, Moslem, Oswald, rosin,* and one pronunciation of *wasn't*.

5. Before /l/, /ɑɚ/ may occur in *doll*, making it a homonym of the family-name *Dahl*, but /ɑ/ is usual elsewhere, even in the monosyllables: *loll, Sol (Solomon), dissolve; dolphin, revolver, solvent; Bollard, collie, demolish, dolly, folly* (contrasts with *Farley*), *hollow, jollity, lollipop, olive, Oliver, policy, solid.*

6. Before the nasals /m/ and /n/, when they are final or followed by suffixed elements, /ɑɚ/ may appear, but there is a good deal of irregularity: *bomb* (often a homonym of *balm* and a rime for *harm*), *bombed, bomber, Tom* (but *Tommie* always has /ɑ/), *John* (but *Johnnie* has /ɑ/), *on* (when stressed; the unstressed form has /ɑ/), *swan, wan.* The shorter vowel occurs in *Don* (like *Donald*, but occasionally lengthened), *don, bonbon, bonfire, Conn* (usually contrasts with *Kahn;* but there are some who pronounce these names alike). Elsewhere, /ɑɚ/ does not usually occur. /ɑ/ is regular in *atomic, comical, comma, Dominic, hominy;*[59] *pomp, romp, rompers, swamp* (I have heard /ɑɚ/ a few times in this word); *pompadour, compass* (usually pronounced with /ɑ/ rather than with /ʌ/ in less cultivated speech); *honest, monotone, tonic; bond, bondage, fond; Constance, continent.*

7. Before /r/, /ɑɚ/ does not usually occur in the "short

82 VOWELS AND DIPHTHONGS OF STRESSED SYLLABLES

o" words, but sporadic lengthening may appear in less cultivated speech, as a result of which *sorry* and *starry* sometimes rime. In *authority, borrow, Florence, foreign, forest, horrible, horrid, Morrill, Morris, Oregon, origin, quarantine, quarrel, quarry, sorrow, tomorrow, Warren, warrant,* the most usual vowel is /ɑ/. For the frequent occurrence of /ɔə̆/ in some words (*coral, moral, orator*), see page 62 and page 84; for [ɒ], see page 62.

The observant reader will perhaps have noticed that in the preceding paragraphs I have always been careful to say that /ɑə̆/ *may* occur under the conditions described. For in truth there is a great deal of variation. The long vowel or diphthong is very common and is heard on all levels of metropolitan speech--/lɑə̆dʒ/ *lodge* and /bɑə̆m/ *bomb* are not pronunciations that are confined to uncultivated use.[60] But often in such words one will hear phones that are rather short and definitely monophthongal. The consistent use of vowels distinctly shorter than /ɑə̆/ is not common;[61] but very frequently a speaker will pronounce *bobbed*, for example, as a homonym of *barbed* and then pronounce *job* with a much shorter vowel. Or he will pronounce the same word first with what is indubitably /ɑə̆/, and then with what is presumably /ɑ/. And, as one might expect, all sorts of intermediate phones may also be heard. Particularly when the speaker's /ɑ/ and /ɑə̆/ are qualitatively the same (so that *shop* and *sharp* are distinguished by vowel length alone), the observer is often left in considerable doubt whether the speaker is riming *wash-harsh, Tom-harm,* etc., or not. (I have encountered this difficulty even when transcribing from records, where the words could be repeated again and again.) It is probable that the frequent or regular occurrence of the shorter vowel in extended forms, compounds, and related words (*bombing, Johnnie, hog-tied, washcloth, goddess*) operates to distort a pattern which might otherwise exhibit more regularity.

11.6. /ɔə̆/. In cultivated metropolitan speech, the diphthong in *law* and *fraud* begins at a higher low-back position, with the lips somewhat rounded, and moves toward mid-central. The first element is not quite so high as the corresponding Southern British type, but at the same time is higher than the varieties heard in many regions of the United States. The gliding movement is normally slight and the monophthongal variant is very common, occurring regularly before intervocalic consonants and frequently in all other positions except finally before a pause.

A phonetically different variety is very common in the less cultivated speech of the city. The first element, made at a position that is somewhat higher[62] than that described in the preceding paragraph, is very much retracted, practically to a point beyond which it is no longer possible to produce a vowel of this height.[63] The lips are well rounded, often with

considerable protrusion. In the speech of many persons, the
diphthongal glide is very marked, even before voiceless
stops. It may be noted that the greater frequency of the
diphthongal type in uncultivated speech is at variance with
the more extensive use of monophthongal allophones of /iə̆/
and /ɛə̆/ in the same type of pronunciation.
  This variation in the phonetic quality of /ɔə̆/ in the usage
of different metropolitan speakers is more striking than the
differences in its lexical distribution. To some extent in
more cultivated speech the lower low-back rounded vowel [ɒ]
occurs in some of the groups discussed below. (For the question of how this vowel should be classified phonemically, see
page 62.) Furthermore, there are certain words in which usage
varies markedly, chiefly between /ɑ/ and /ɔə̆/. But on the
whole there is a good deal of unanimity regarding the particular words and the word-classes in which /ɔə̆/ appears.
  The lexical distribution of the phoneme is as follows:
  a) It is regularly employed in those words containing orthographic au, aw, al, ough in which General American normally has the corresponding vowel: almost, always,[64] August,
Austria, author, auto, because,[65] bought, caught, daub, daunt,
false, faucet,[66] gaunt, haunted, launch, laundry, Laura,
laurel,[67] law, paunch, paw, salt, sauce, saunter, sausage,
small, Waldorf, walnut, Walsh, Walter, waltz. In cauliflower,
/ɑ/ is more frequent than /ɔə̆/. Maurice may have /ɑ/ or [ɒ],
but is also very commonly pronounced in a Frenchified fashion
as /məˈriːs/.
  b) It is regularly employed in words that in General American contain the corresponding vowel followed by /r/ in the
preconsonantal or final position: absorbent, border, born,
California, corner, for, forty, Gordon, horse, Mormon, morning, Norma, north, orchestra, ordered, orphan, quart, short,
Waldorf, war, warbler,[68] ward.
  c) It is regularly employed in words in which many General
American speakers pronounce /oŭ/ followed by /r/: boarder,
chorus, door, Dora, force, four, hoarse, lavatory, more,
porch, pork, sore, worn.
  The distinction preserved in some regions of the United
States and of the British Isles between the two preceding
groups does not exist in metropolitan pronunciation. A small
number of cultivated speakers pronounce /oŭ/ before /r/ in
a few wòrds of the type of chorus, oral, and story, but even
such pronunciations are not common, and I have yet to discover a single native New Yorker who consistently distinguished
between words of the two types. In the pronunciation of the
overwhelming majority of metropolitan speakers on all levels,
for (stressed) and four, horse and hoarse, morning and mourning are exact homonyms.
  d) It occurs in many of the words with orthographic o or wa
that in the prevailing type of Southern British pronunciation
have /ɒ/. The lexical distribution of /ɔə̆/ in these words

differs in some respects from that found in other types of American English.

1) Before stops, /ɔ̌/ occurs only in *chocolate, dog,* and *water,* /ɑ/ or /ɑ̌/ appearing elsewhere. But many persons consider /ɔ̌/ inelegant in the first two of these words and replace it with [ɒ]. In *doggerel,* a less common word, /ɔ̌/ may occur, but /ɑ/ and [ɒ] are also frequent.

2) Before the voiceless fricatives /f, θ, s/, both /ɔ̌/ and /ɑ/ occur, the former being used in the monosyllables, with a few exceptions, and in a not very large number of the other words. Examples with /ɔ̌/: *off, cough, loft, soft, offer, office, officer, often, coffee, coffin; boss, loss, moss, Ross, toss, cost, frost, lost, Boston, Foster; broth, cloth, froth, moth.* With /ɑ/: *doff, scoff, profit, waffles; apostle, costume, docile, fossil, gospel, hospital, McCloskey, possible, prosecutor, Wasserman; apothecary, Goth, Gothic, Gotham.* Some words vary in pronunciation between /ɔ̌/ and /ɑ/, for example, *glossy, ostrich,* and *wasp.* In such words and in a few like *coffee* and *office,* where /ɔ̌/ has come to seem uncultivated to many speakers, the use of [ɒ] is rather common.

3) Before the nasal /ŋ/, /ɔ̌/ occurs in *along, belong, elongate, long, song, strong, wrong,* but /ɑ/ is usual in *Bronx, Congo, ding-dong, gong, prong, thong, throng, tongs.* Before /n/, the usual vowels are /ɑ/ and /ɑ̌/ (see page 81). The pronunciation of *gone* varies: /ɔ̌/ predominates, but /ɑ̌/ is also frequent, particularly in less cultivated speech, and some uncultivated speakers pronounce a rather anomalous long vowel, which differs from their /ɑ̌/ because of its more advanced placement. *Shone* has only /oǔ/. Before /m/, /ɔ̌/ does not occur; see page 81.

4) Before /r/ in the intervocalic position /ɔ̌/ is not normally heard in the "short *o*" words, but a few (*coral, moral, oracle, orator*) have in the usage of many speakers gone over into the group represented by *chorus* and *Dora. Warrior* is more often than not pronounced according to the analogy of *war*. In such words of varying pronunciation, [ɒ] is especially common.

In the still predominating "*r*-less" type of metropolitan pronunciation, the homonyms *morning-mourning* are exact rimes of *awning* and *dawning,* and *horse-hoarse* are exact rimes of *cross* and *loss*. *Sought* and *sort, sauce* and *source, laud* and *lord* are homonymous. It should be understood that there is no greater tendency to employ the diphthongal variant in words containing orthographic *r* than in those that lack it. In both groups the diphthongal and the monophthongal types appear in a variation that is partly free and partly determined by position. For this reason, the practice followed in Kenyon and Knott's *Dictionary* of indicating a diphthong in the "Eastern" pronunciation of words like *horse* and *source,* but not in those like *cross* and *sauce* is not valid in so far as it applies to metropolitan speech.

VOWELS AND DIPHTHONGS OF STRESSED SYLLABLES 85

The sequence /oŭ/ plus unstressed vowel in words like *blower, lower* (adj.), *rower, sower, Samoa* is normally not leveled under /ɔə̆/, as it sometimes is in Southern British English.[69] An exceptional case is *Noah*, which is very commonly pronounced as a homonym of *gnaw*.[70]

11.7. /uə̆/. The diphthong in *poor* and *sure* begins at a lower high-back position, at the height of the [u] in *book* or somewhat higher, and glides toward mid-central. Ordinarily the glide does not end at so low a point as it does in the case of the corresponding diphthong of Southern British English. The lip-modification of the first element is accompanied in the pronunciation of some uncultivated speakers by an exaggerated protrusion.

Before intervocalic consonants in the same word (*Moorish, poorly, sureness, curious*), monophthongs occur rather regularly on all levels of metropolitan pronunciation. They also appear within phrases in cases like *poor example* and *sure indication*. Before final consonants, for instance in *cures* and *cured*, the glide may be much slighter than in Southern British, but completely monophthongal variants are uncommon. Nor does the monophthongal variant occur in final position before a pause, even in uncultivated speech. In this respect, /uə̆/ is not on all fours with /iə̆/ and /ɛə̆/.

Before /r/, for historical reasons, a clear /u/-/uə̆/ opposition does not exist. The phonetic situation is as follows: in *surer, poorer, curing*, and the like, which are paradigmatic derivatives of words in which /r/ may appear as a word-final, rather long vowels are normal: a pronunciation like ['kjurɪŋ] would sound unnatural to a New Yorker's ear. In other cases, in *curiosity, durable, insurance, Muriel, purity, security*, etc., the vowel length varies between [u] and [u· (u⁺)].

Certain other variations from the practice found in Southern British English may be noted. In the first place, the sequence /uŭ/ plus unstressed vowel is leveled under /uə̆/ only in the case of *you're*; this diphthong does not occur in *bluer, brewer, chewer, doer, fewer, truer*.[71] Nor is it employed in *Stewart, steward*, or in *cruel, jewel*,[72] and their derivatives. Secondly, there is no tendency in New York pronunciation to replace /uə̆/ by other diphthongs whose first elements are mid-back or higher low-back. In *poor, sure, curious*, and the like, /ɔə̆/ does not occur.

On page 63 above the fact is noted that the name *Durham* is often pronounced, not with /ʌ/, but with the vowel of *during*.

11.8. /ɜə̆/. In words of the type represented by *stir, stern, birth*, a not inconsiderable number of cultivated New Yorkers[73] pronounce a diphthong with a mid-central starting-point and a minimal glide to a more open position. (In my observation, women are more likely to pronounce in this fashion than men; the latter, if they do not employ the ancestral /ɜɪ̆/ in *stern* and *birth*, are more likely to pronounce /r/.) The gliding movement is most apparent when words like *stir* and *fur* are final before a pause; the monophthongal variant is common elsewhere. The quality may be about that of the most usual Southern British type or may have a more advanced and somewhat higher tongue-position. The lips are sometimes slightly rounded. I have not heard from New Yorkers those markedly retracted varieties (practically in the back-vowel range) that are employed by some speakers in Eastern New England.

The occurrence of /ɜə̆/ is often rather irregular: it may appear beside /ɜɪ̆/ in the speech of the same person, the two types interchanging at random; or it may interchange with /r/. One might venture the comment at this point that in metropolitan speech reasonably "consistent" dialects are found chiefly on the extremely uncultivated level. Those to whom questions of propriety and "correctness" have any meaning at all are likely to be rather susceptible to the influence of other regional types. As examples in addition to the present one, I would cite the often very irregular occurrence of /r/ in the preconsonantal position, the frequent variation in the speech of many between /juŭ/, /ɨŭ/, and /uŭ/ in words like *new* and *duty*, and the disturbed patterns in the low-front vowel range that is discussed in section 11.3.

In the speech of those who employ /ɜə̆/, its phonetic and lexical distribution is practically the same as in Southern British. But there are a few deviations. Included in the group, of course, are those words, *Berkeley, Berkshire, clerk, derby, Jervis, Kerr*, in which the British pronunciations with the equivalent of /ɑə̆/ either do not occur at all or are merely occasional affectations. Furthermore, it may be noted that some of those who pronounce /ɜə̆/ in *stir, fur*, and *spur* employ /ʌ/ in the derivatives in which /r/ is intervocalic, so that *furry* and *hurry* are rimes, as is not the case in Southern British.

11.9. /ʌə̆/. As is noted below on page 141, note 13, it is necessary to set up a separate category to describe adequately the pronunciation of those who have a threefold opposition in *a curd, a cud*, and *occurred*. Some of my informants, for example, pronounce /ɜɪ̆/ in the first of these, /ʌ/ in the second, and in the third a diphthong with a slight glide (or a monophthong longer than [ʌ]). The first element may be slightly higher and farther forward than the [ʌ] of *cut*, but the diphthong does not resemble phonetically the one discussed in the first paragraph of the preceding section. Its occurrence is restricted to word-final position (*stir, occur*) and to paradigmatic forms with /z/ and /d/ (*stirs, stirred*).

THE VOWELS OF WEAK SYLLABLES

12.1. /iĭ/. In the initial syllables of the groups of words represented by *election, eternal, evasive; because, believe, betray; declare, defend, department; prefer, prepare, pretend; reduce, regret, report; seduce, selective,* /iĭ/ may occur, alternating with /ə/. (For the phonetic quality of the vowels brought together under the rubric /ə/, see the next section.) Every speaker seems to vary, to some degree at least, in his pronunciation of these syllables, but in general it may be said that /ə/ is more common in cultivated than in uncultivated speech. The very frequent occurrence of /iĭ/, with the syllable pronounced so that a slight secondary stress often seems to rest on it, is a rather noticeable feature of the pronunciation of many less cultivated speakers.

Occasionally /iĭ/ may appear in the initial syllables of certain other words which are not historically members of the groups represented above. As examples one might cite *effective, efficient, essential; divine, neglect*.

In final syllables, either open, or closed by paradigmatic /z, d/, /ii/ occurs: *carry, valley; carries, Lucy's; carried*. The vowel in these syllables is rarely diphthongal (though if a word like *carry* or *valley* is followed by an initial vowel, one may often hear a slight [j]-glide); and the height may vary. But although a vowel resembling the stressed one in *pit* may sometimes be heard in connected speech, /iĭ/ is nevertheless the proper rubric for New York English as a whole. As is indicated on page 141, note 16, New Yorkers are often puzzled by the usual dictionary practice of using the same symbol in both syllables of words like *city* and *silly*. In metropolitan pronunciation, *bandied, Lucy's, posies* are ordinarily not homonymous with *banded, looses, poses*, even when the latter are pronounced with [i].

Similarly, /iĭ/ appears in the final syllable of classical names like *Circe, Melpomene, Thucydides*; and in words like *aborigine, acme, species, crises*.

In medial syllables immediately before another vowel, weak or stressed, /iĭ/ is usual: *carrier, chariot, dreariest, dubious, hurrying, radium; periodic, radiator, variation*.

In medial syllables before certain suffixes beginning with consonants, the /iĭ/ of an underlying form is retained: *penniless, happiness, loneliness*. Before the suffix *-ly*, /ə/ replaces /iĭ/ in *easily, happily, luckily*, and the like. Before the suffix *-ful*, the /iĭ/ of an underlying form is replaced by /ə/ in cultivated speech: *beautiful, pitiful*. In these words uncultivated speakers very frequently pronounce /iĭ/: /'bjuŭdiĭfəl/.

The unstressed forms of *be, he, me, she, we,* and of *the* before a vowel fall into the same category. The vowels of these forms differ from those of the stressed forms chiefly in length. Before following vowels a slight [j]-glide may often be observed.

12.2. /ə/. In English pronunciation generally, there is a good deal of variation in syllables that are completely unstressed between lower high-front vowels, mid-central vowels, and vowels of intermediate quality. Jones often indicates such variants in Southern British,[1] and other writers dealing with that form of English make comments of a like nature.[2] American pronunciation as a whole exhibits even more variations of this sort, which are frequently referred to in the Kenyon and Knott *Dictionary*.[3] With a few exceptions, the variations discussed by these writers involve the occurrence of central vowels in cases where [i] is more frequent, or is for some other reason thought to be the norm.

The variation in the vowels of completely unstressed syllables which may be observed in metropolitan speech goes far beyond anything that I have found in the descriptions of other forms of English. In New York pronunciation not only do vowels of central quality very commonly occur in such unstressed syllables as those referred to in note 3;[4] but contrariwise, [i] may often be heard in place of vowels of central quality in syllables in which it is rarely or never recorded by writers describing other dialects.[5] The most striking instance of this latter phenomenon is the frequent appearance of [i] or of vowels approaching [i] in quality in syllables that in General American contain unstressed syllabic [r̩].

The range through which the vowels of completely unstressed syllables may vary in metropolitan speech is somewhat restricted. A New Yorker, listening intently to Southern British English, is likely to be struck by two facts: first, that the unstressed [i] is, in terms of his own pronunciation, often "clearer," that is, more distinctly advanced; and second, that the Southern British [ə], especially in final open syllables, is often noticeably lower. The New York unstressed vowels all lie closer together. Even the most open vowels do not have any suggestion of that [ɑ]-like quality that Americans sometimes hear in the Southern British [ə] of words like *over, sofa,* and *picture*.[6]

Within this range variation is sometimes free, sometimes more or less determined by the phonetic surroundings. There is free variation, for example, in final closed syllables before /t, d, θ, s, z, dʒ/. Here let us consider two groups of words. The first comprise those in whose final syllables Jones records [i] as the usual Southern British vowel: *closet, gadget, graduate* (noun), *hatchet, profit, wallet; appointed, arrested, hoisted, planted, torrid; walketh; careless,* duchess, Francis; dentist, greatest; cabbages, molasses, offices, raises; average, college, damage, Talmadge. The second group is made up of those words that in Southern British have [ə] and in General American have [ə] or [ɨ]: Charlotte, Connecticut, desert (noun),[7] anchored, captured, custard, fractured, Leonard; mammoth; anxious, boisterous, compass; ancestors, feathers, officers, prisoners. These two groups are not systematically distinguished from each other by any recurrent difference in their unstressed vowels. As in many other parts of America, the vowels in the first group include all possible variants between [i] and [ə]. But so do the vowels in the second group of words. The occurrence of [i] or of vowels close to [i] in the final syllables of Connecticut, captured, August, boisterous, officers, and the like seems to me, in fact, to be one of the most interesting characteristics of metropolitan English.

In certain situations this kind of variation does not appear, [i] or [ə] alone being found or at least overwhelmingly favored. Thus [ə] does not occur before /ŋ/ and [i] does not ordinarily appear before /m/ or /l/: reading, knowing; system, album; pencil, projectile, seasonal.

Before /k/, the pronunciation of some speakers shows an opposition of a sort, but it is a fleeting and unsubstantial one. In this position [i] is the favored vowel and predominates in atomic, music, tonic, and the like. It is also very frequent in words like barracks, hammock, Lenox, and stomach. The use of [i] in some of these words is occasionally ridiculed by spellings like stummick, and some educated speakers may consciously avoid [i] in certain cases. But when the question of propriety has never been raised, these words and those like atomic form a single group.

In initial unstressed syllables, the situation is the same. In certain surroundings [i], [ə], and intermediate vowels occur in free variation; in other circumstances, either [i] or [ə] is decidedly favored. In an initial syllable closed by /k/, there is the same preference for [i] as in final syllables; and this vowel is as likely to appear in accept as in except, in accessory as in excessive.[8] In an open syllable before a following /m/, [ə] is the favored vowel, as well in imagine as in among.[9]

In medial syllables also, [i] and [ə] are not opposed to each other. The following consonant may have some effect on the occurrence of variants: for example, the higher, more advanced vowels may sometimes be heard in hurricane, but are quite unusual or nonexistent in easily. In general, [ə] is the more common vowel.

Nor is the situation any different when we consider the weak forms of prepositions, pronouns, and the like. It-at, in-an, is-as, for example, whose weak forms constitute minimal contrasting pairs in some types of English, are not so kept apart in metropolitan pronunciation. Their vowels may vary through the same range from [i] to [ə]; and both *in* and *an* may be pronounced [n̩] after certain consonants.

The nature of the following consonant is not the only factor that may affect the occurrence of variants. A preceding palatal, for instance, seems to favor the higher, more advanced vowels. Thus [i] and [iʰ] are quite common in words like *genius* and *Australian*, where the preceding consonant is /j/. Again, in uncultivated speech, [ʃid] may be heard for *should*, but I have never heard any similar pronunciation of *would* and *could*. Contrariwise, the central vowels are favored when the "dark" allophone of /l/ precedes, as in *valid* and *salad*.

In the foregoing paragraphs I have not dealt with all the phonetic situations in which these vowels may occur. But an examination of every separate case would result in the same conclusion which has already been indicated: The differing vowels that may be observed in completely unstressed syllables--ranging in quality from [i] to [ə]--are nondistinctive variants, their variation being partly free and partly determined by the phonetic surroundings. They are not significantly opposed to each other, but are members of the same phoneme, which I have labeled /ə/.

I say "phoneme" because I think that /ə/ is best conceived as a separate category, distinct from the vowel-phonemes of stressed syllables. The contrary view, first advanced by Bloomfield and adopted by some other writers, is that all the vowels of unstressed syllables are merely positional variants of stressed vowels. This conception, however, requires one to assign identical phones occurring in the same surroundings now to this phoneme, now to that--which is a rather dubious procedure. Actually the situation here resembles that of the stops after /s/ or of the alveolar stops in the type of pronunciation that does not distinguish *bitter* from *bidder*. The difference is that in those cases an opposition between two phonemes is suspended, whereas here the suspension is a multiple one. On page 21 it was stated that assigning the stops in *spill*, *still*, and *skill* to /p/, /t/, and /k/ was legitimate enough if one made it perfectly clear that the procedure was an arbitrary one. In this case, where so many oppositions are suspended, it seems to me more reasonable to set up a distinct category.

APPENDIX A

13.1. PRIMARY INFORMANTS[1]

#1. Woman, age about 65. Born in Brooklyn, educated at Packer Collegiate Institute. Active in local women's clubs. Has spent a number of summers in New England. Husband a teacher. F born in Brooklyn, spent two years in early life in upper New York State and five in Connecticut; a businessman. Paternal grandparents born in upper New York State; PGF a lawyer. MGF born in Washington, D.C.; an inventor. MGM born in Manhattan. Part of material recorded: *Rat* selection, extempore conversation.

The informant's speech is completely consistent in the absence of /r/ in the preconsonantal position. The consonant is not infrequently omitted finally before a following vowel, in which case the vowel is lightly glottalized; but /r/ occurs several times in words like *Panama* and *law*. Words like *when* and *whistle* have /hw/; /hj/ is regular in those like *huge*. Her practice in the matter of words like *duty, new, tube, studio* is not consistent: /j/ sometimes appears, sometimes is absent. There is no blade-articulation of the alveolars, nor is there any tendency to affricate [t-] and [d-]. The intervocalic consonant in words like *elevated* and *later* is voiceless more often than not. /θ, ð/ have only fricative allophones. The articulation is in general crisp and firm; final stops are frequently exploded before a pause.

Only in one or two words like *thirty* is there any suggestion of the /ɜĭ/-type, and even in these the glide toward high-front is barely perceptible. Ordinarily words of this group are pronounced with /ɜə̆/, as are those like *occur, preferred*. Words like *choice* and *ointment* have /ɔĭ/, with a rather high and well-rounded first element. There is no retraction of the first element of the diphthong in *ride, time,* etc. The diphthong /ɛə̆/ is restricted to words like *care* and *square*. *Rather* has /aə̆/, but other words of the *ask*-group are not distinguished from those like *flag* and *stand:* they all have vowels of the quality of [æ], with some lengthening and diphthongization in final syllables (phonemically /æ/ and /æə̆/). The quality of the allophones of /aə̆/ varies somewhat, but is never markedly retracted. Similarly, there is no retraction in the case of /ɔə̆/ (*hall, off, thought, warm*, etc.) The pronunciation of *long, strong, wrong* is unusual in that they have what appears to be /aə̆/. In *down, house, town*, etc. the diphthong begins well back and the first element often coincides with the [ɑ] of *hot*. There is no tendency to centralize the starting-point of /oŭ/ in *home, pole, road,* etc.;

here, as in *school, too*, etc., the lip-rounding is rather strong, in keeping with her rather vigorous articulation. Centralized varieties of /i/ and /e/ do not occur. In *foggy, trolley, watched*, and the like, the vowel is normally unrounded, although there are a few occurrences of [ɒ].

#2. Woman, age 50-55. Born in Manhattan, now lives there. Wadleigh High School, New York Training School for Teachers; a teacher of art in the city schools. F born in Manhattan of a well-to-do family, educated in the city (the informant was uncértain about the details); lost most of his wealth as the result of unfortunate investments. PCF born in Manhattan, lived upstate for some years; his father was born in Massachusetts. PGM born either in New York City or upstate of a family also originally from New England; an unusually welleducated woman for her generation. M born in Manhattan of a socially prominent family, which had been here in the city since about 1700. MCF, a businessman, and MCM were from different branches of this family; both were born in Manhattan. Part of material recorded: all sentences, the *Rat* story, extempore conversation.

The "*r-less*" pattern predominates, though there are some occurrences of the consonant in words like *barge, Calvert, shared, tardy*, and also those like *third* and *blurred*. The consonant does not occur in *Panama, law*, etc. /hw/ appears in one word; the others have /w/. The cluster /hj/ is regular except in *humor*. /j/ is common but not regular after /n, t, d/ (*new, tube*, etc.). There is no tendency toward bladearticulation, nor is there any affrication of [t-, d-]. /θ, ð/ have only fricative allophones. Despite the occasional reduction of final clusters, the articulation is generally clear and distinct.

There are no retractions in the front-vowel range. In the the *third*-group, no regular pattern occurs: /ɜɪ/ occurs in a few cases, usually with a minimal glide, /r/ is common, and /ɜɚ/ also appears. Similarly, words like *blurred* and *preferred* vary between /r/ and /ɜɚ/. Words such as *dared, fairly, Sarah* have only [ɛɚ, ɛ·] (sometimes [ɛɪɚ]); those like *aunt, crab, dam, fast* vary considerably: [ɛɚ, ɛ·, æɚ, æ·, æː]. Lengthening in the "short *o*" words is irregular: for example, *bomb, hog, rod* have /ɑɚ/, while *god, squash, Tom* have /ɑ/. Occasional retractions may be observed in the case of /ɑɚ/ (*harbor, hog*) and /ɔɚ/ (*bought*), but they are not very marked. There is no retraction of the first element of the diphthong in *five, pie*, etc. In *choice, ointment*, and the like, the quality varies somewhat, but there is no suggestion of the /ɜɪ/-type. The starting-point of the diphthong in words like *pound* and *house* is usually about [a]; varieties like [æʊ̆, æ̃ʊ̆] do not occur. In words like *collie, got, profit, Scotch*, the vowel is regularly unrounded.

#3. Man, age 68. Born in Brooklyn, educated at a private
academy, a public elementary school, City College, and the
Columbia School of Mines. After graduation he spent about
four years away from the city, chiefly in the Far West. The
rest of his adult life has been spent as an editor on the
staff of an engineering journal published in New York. In recent
years he has lived in a suburban town in Nassau County,
but he commutes to his office in Manhattan. F born in Brooklyn,
secondary school education, a businessman. PGF born in
Bridgeport, Connecticut; a Methodist clergyman with charges
in Suffolk County and Brooklyn; the author of several books
describing his travels to the Holy Land. PGM born in Brooklyn.
M is Informant #7; see below. Part of material recorded: all
sentences, the *Rat* story, extempore conversation.

The informant's conversational speech is generally of the
"*r*-less" type, with the exception that there are rare occurrences
of the consonant in words like *hair* and *hard* and that
[r̩] is common in *Germans, turnips*, etc. (but see below). In
the test sentences the frequency of the consonant in the preconsonantal
position shows a marked increase. (This is a
matter of conscious alteration--the speaker believes that one
"should pronounce the *r*'s.") There are no occurrences on
these records of /r/ in words like *law* and *Panama*. The cluster
/hw/ appears several times in reading, but is not part of
his natural pattern; /hj/ is regular. In *Dewey, enthusiastic,
new, studio*, and the like, /j/ is frequent, particularly in
conscious speech. The /ɨu̯/-type appears in a few words. There
is no affrication of the alveolar stops and no occurrence of
[ʔ] in *Seattle*, etc. The intervocalic consonant in *gratifying,
sort of*, etc. is commonly voiced in conversation. /θ, ð/ have
only fricative allophones.

The diphthong /3ɪ̯/, which is regular in the *third*-group in
the speech of his mother, appears in a few words beside the
more common /r/; the glide toward high-front is rather slight.
There are several occurrences of the contamination [r̩ɪ̯]. In
choice, ointment, etc., /3ɪ̯/ never appears. The first element
of /aɪ̯/ is never retracted, nor is there any noticeable retraction
in the case of /aə̯/ and /ɔə̯/. In some of the "short
o" words /aə̯/ appears, but there is no regular pattern: *hog*,
for example, has the diphthong, while *bobbed* has a short vowel
and is not homonymous with *barbed*. In a number of words
like *avenue, drastic, glass, handle*, the quality of the vowel
or diphthong coincides with that heard in *cares* and *scarce*,
but the lower varieties are very frequent: [græ̯əs] *grass*,
[ˈpæntrɪ̯] *pantry*, [ˈθræʃɪŋ] *thrashing*. There are no occurrences
of /aə̯/ in the *ask*-group, nor does /aə̯/ appear in his
speech. The diphthong in *pounds, now*, etc. is often [au̯] and
the starting-point is never markedly fronted. There is no
tendency to centralize the first element of /ou̯/ and /uu̯/. In
college, Donald, popular, tonic, wandered, etc., the vowel is
unrounded; *thongs* is [θɐŋz], but this is unusual.

#4. Woman, age 50-55. Born in Manhattan. Attended public school, Horace Mann, New York Training School for Teachers. Now a teacher in the public schools. F born in Manhattan, educated in the public schools, in business as an importer. Paternal grandparents both born and educated in the city; PGF a businessman. Family has lived in the city at least since the beginning of the nineteenth century, having come here originally from northern New England. M born and educated in the city. Maternal grandparents both born in England, came to New York before the Civil War. MGF a physician. Part of material recorded: all sentences, the *Rat* story, extempore conversation.

The informant's pattern in regard to the appearance of /r/ in the preconsonantal position is mixed: in the *Rat* story, for example, it is pronounced in about two-fifths of the possible occurrences, and it occurs not infrequently in her conversational speech. As a result of this mixture, the consonant is introduced into the word *cob*. Words like *church* and *sunburn* rather regularly have /r/ (although in a small number of words /ɜ̆/ appears). In word-final position before an initial vowel, the consonant is very frequently lost and the vowel is preceded by the glottal stop. Words like *wheel* and *whistle* vary between /hw/ and /w/; the cluster /hj/ is regular in *huge, humor,* and the like. In *due, enthusiastic, news, studio, tubes, Tuesday,* etc., /j/ regularly appears. There are no affricate allophones of /t, d/; in words like *better* and *city*, the consonant is usually voiceless. In *Seattle*, but not in other words of the type, [ʔ] is substituted for [t]; in some other cases, final [t] is accompanied by a simultaneous glottal stop. Only fricative allophones of /θ, ð/ occur. The informant's speech is in general moderately rapid, the articulation careful and precise. Consonant clusters are very rarely simplified, stops in absolute final position usually exploded. There are a few examples of rather unnatural "over-articulation," such as the open juncture between stop and affricate in *grand jury* and oral plosion in *saddened*.

The diphthong /ɜɪ̆/ does not occur. There is no retraction of the first element of /aɪ̆/. The diphthong in *house, pound,* etc. sometimes begins at a slightly advanced position, but never varies as far as [æŭ]. The occurrence of /ɛɜ̆/ is in general restricted to words like *square* and *scarce;* such words as *mantle, thrashing; lamb, plaid* ordinarily have definitely lower vowels or diphthongs which begin at a lower point (phonemic situation: /æɜ̆/ in final syllables, /æ/ elsewhere). The informant's pronunciation of words of the *ask*-group is not consistent: in many, but by no means all of them, the /aɜ̆/- and /ɑɜ̆/-types appear. In words such as *atomic, college, got, sorry, squash, warrant,* both rounded and unrounded vowels appear; in *hog, John, wash,* etc., the vowels are usually quite short and there are only one or two cases which should probably be assigned to /ɑɜ̆/.

#5. Young man, age 22. Born in Brooklyn. St. Francis Xavier, Polp Prep, one and a half years at a private school in New Haven; two years in the Navy; summer session at Brown University; now a premedical student at Columbia. F born in Brooklyn. St. Augustine's, Fordham Law School; a tax consultant. PGF born in Brooklyn. Poly Prep, Rensselaer; an engineer with offices in Brooklyn. PGM born in Brooklyn. Secondary school education. M born in Brooklyn. St. Francis, Adelphi College, Columbia Graduate School. MGF born in Brooklyn. Grammar school education; a businessman. MGM born in Brooklyn. Secondary school education. Informant believes that all his great-grandparents were born in Ireland. Part of material recorded: all sentences, the *Rat* story, extempore conversation.

So far as the occurrence of /r/ is concerned, the speaker's usage is of the type described on page 49: the consonant occurs regularly as the syllabic in words like *church* and *heard* but is otherwise absent, with insignificant exceptions in reading, from the preconsonantal position. The cluster /hw/ does not occur; /hj/ is regular. In words like *tubes*, *Dewey*, *new*, /j/ does not occur (see the next paragraph). In some occurrences the voiceless stops in initial position are rather heavily aspirated and there is some affrication of [t-];[2] intervocalically, in words like *forty* and *university*, the consonant is normally voiced. /θ, ð/ have only fricative allophones. The informant's speech is "defective" in two respects: [-f] is very frequently substituted for [-θ] (*bath*, *with*),[3] and a front-palatal nasal is substituted for [-ŋ] in unstressed syllables (see page 139, note 62).

The diphthong /ɜɪ/ does not occur: words like *church* have only /r/, those like *coil* only /ɔɪ/. There is no retraction of the first element of /aɪ/. The diphthong in *out*, *pound*, etc. ordinarily begins at about [a]; markedly advanced varieties do not occur. In words like *road*, the starting-point is often centralized. Words like *new*, *Dewey* and those like *coop*, *zoo* form a single group; in both cases the first element of the diphthong is often advanced, sometimes to the high-central position. In the low-front range the following phonemes occur: /ɛə̆/ (*scarce*, *square*). /æə̆/ (*fast*, *jazz*, *plaid*). /æ/ (*after*, *master*, *pantry*, *thrashing; cat*, *Catholic*, *fragile*, *hammer*, *has*, *hatchet*). This pattern is distorted in a few cases by lowering in the first group: [hæə̆] *hair*, [stæə̆z] *stairs*.[4] The category /aə̆/ does not appear in his speech. There is often a strong retraction observable in the case of /aə̆/, not only in words like *part* and *barge*, but also in many monosyllables of the type of *bombed* and *John*, in which this phoneme frequently occurs. In words like *continent*, *dollars*, *popular*, *sorry*, *waffles*, *wallet;* rounded vowels do not appear.

#6. Man, age about 60. Born in the Bronx, attended public

school there, graduated from City College. A teacher of art in a New York City high school. Father's family of New York Dutch descent. F born in Brooklyn, attended public elementary school, then a private academy in Manhattan; a salesman for Scribner's publishing house. PGF born in Brooklyn or Manhattan; an inventor and photographer (one of the first in the city). PGM, of French and English descent, spent her childhood in New Rochelle, then moved to the city. M born in Mamaroneck, as a small child taken to Wisconsin, where family stayed for about a year. Educated at a private school in the Bronx. MGF, born in Manhattan, an artist, member of the National Academy of Design. MGM's birthplace not known. Part of material recorded: all sentences, the *Rat* story, extempore conversation.

With insignificant exceptions, /r/ does not occur before consonants or pauses. It is pronounced in *law* and *saw* before a following vowel (though in other instances of a similar sort it is absent). The cluster /hw/ does not occur. *Humor* is /'juŭmə(r/ but all other words of this group have /hj/. /j/ appears in *new, knew, studio,* but otherwise does not occur on these records after alveolars. The alveolar stops are not affricated; in *auto, city, loitering,* etc., the intervocalic consonant is normally voiced. /θ, ð/ are always fricatives.

In the *third*-group /ɜĭ/ is regular, but this diphthong never appears in *choice, foil,* etc. There is no retraction of the first element of /aĭ/, an occasional slight retraction in the case of /ɔĭ/ (*boiled, Boyd,* etc.). Words like *crab, grass, lamb, plaid; master, tamper, pantry* vary considerably: [ɛə̆, ɛ·] (very common), [æə̆, æ·] in the monosyllables, and usually shorter monophthongs with the same qualitative variations in the longer words. Excessively low vowels do not occur in these words. The category /aə̆/ does not appear, nor does /ɑə̆/ occur in the *ask*-group. There is some retraction in many words like *guard* and *party* (/ɑə̆/), while in those like *lobster* and *toddy* the vowel is often advanced. In words of the latter group (*Scotch, Molly, orator, atomic, waffles*), there is no rounding. The vowel or first diphthongal element in *cost, corner, hoarse,* etc. (/ɔə̆/) often has a somethat retracted position. Lengthening in the "short *o*" words is variable: *bomb, god, hog,* for example, have rather short vowels (/ɑ/), while *dodge, squash, Tom* have longer vowels or diphthongs.

There is a good deal of nasalization.

#7. Woman, age 89. Born in Brooklyn, educated at a private academy. Of English, Irish, French, and Dutch descent. Formerly active in Protestant church work. Husband was a businessman. F born in Manhattan; a theatrical manager. PGF born either in Brooklyn or in Massachusetts; a businessman in Brooklyn. PGM's birthplace not known, but she grew up in Brooklyn. MGF, a well-known figure in Brooklyn a hundred

years ago, born in Newburgh, came to Brooklyn as a young man
in 1826; a private banker, reformer, writer for the old
Brooklyn *Star*. MGM born in Brooklyn. Part of material recorded: the *Rat* story, readings from the Psalms, and a selection of sentences.

The informant's speech is completely consistent in the absence of /r/ from the preconsonantal position. It is very
frequently omitted at the end of words before an initial vowel, which is preceded by the glottal stop; *Anna, law, Panama,
Utah* are pronounced in similar fashion before vowels, but
there is one occurrence of /r/ in *idea*. The cluster /hw/ does
not occur: both in words like *whisper* and those like *went*,
she usually pronounces a voiced, velarized bilabial fricative
(see page 52). The cluster /hj/ is regular. /j/ does not occur in words like *Dewey, new, tubes*. There is no tendency to
affricate [t-, d-]: the voiceless stops in final position are
frequently accompanied by a glottal closure and [-ʔ] is often
substituted for [-t]. Only fricative allophones of /θ, ð/ occur.

All words of the *third*-group are pronounced with /ɜɪ̆/, but
this diphthong never appears in those like *coil* and *ointment*.
There is no retraction of the first element of /aɪ̆/. The
starting-point of /ɔɪ̆/ varies to a certain degree and is
sometimes quite low; in several occurrences the diphthong resembles the Southern British diaphone [ɒɪ̆]. The diphthong in
house, pound starts at [a] or farther back. In *cold, hopeless*, etc., there is no tendency to centralize the first element. A few words like *Dewey* and *knew* contain diphthongs with
a starting-point more advanced than that heard in words like
cool; in others this fronting does not appear. The syllabics
in words like *hand, handle, pad, task* vary in height, the
higher ones coinciding with those in *hair* and *stairs* (*glass*
and *scarce*, for example, are rimes). The category /aə̆/ does
not occur, nor the /ɑə̆/-type appear in any words of the *ask*-
group. In many occurrences of /aə̆/ there is a marked fronting
of a sort unusual in the New York area (see page 79). The
diphthong occurs occasionally in words like *hog*, but short
vowels are more common. The vowel or first diphthongal element in words like *board, north, walk* varies in quality: it
is never retracted and overrounded, but is sometimes lower
than is usual in the city. The category /ʌə̆/ appears regularly in words like *fur* and *stirred;* the latter word, for example, has a vowel not very different in quality from the [ʌ]
of *stud* and *blood*, but longer. The vowels in words like *borrow, lock, novel, shopping, swallow, waffles* are normally not
rounded; but strongly rounded vowels occur in *watch, wash*.

A number of pronunciations occur that are old-fashioned in
New York English. As I have stated on page 52, the bilabial
fricative in *went, whispered*, etc. is perhaps a survival.
There are also pronunciations like /kup/ *coop*, /ˈkupə(r/
Cooper, /ˈfæsət/ *faucet* (corrected to /ˈfɔə̆sət/), /hɜɪ̆θ/

hearth (this she volunteered, saying that she used it as a girl but now said /hɑɹθ/), /'sɔɚspən/ *saucepan*, and /ˌðɛɚrˈɑf/ *thereof*.

#8. Woman, age about 50. Born in Manhattan, educated at public schools, Teachers College, Fordham. Principal of a girls' junior high school. F born in Manhattan, secondary school education, owner of a restaurant. Paternal grandparents born in Ireland, came to New York before the age of 20; PGF a sugar dealer. M born in Manhattan, attended the public schools, graduated from what is now Hunter College. MGF born in Manhattan. Informant knows nothing of his schooling and occupation; he died shortly after the birth of her mother. MGM born in Manhattan, elementary school education. Maternal great-grandparents apparently all born in Ireland. Part of material recorded: all sentences, the *Rat* story, extempore conversation.

The informant's speech is generally of the "r-less" type with the exception that the consonant occurs regularly as the syllabic in words like *third*, and sometimes occurs (along with /ʌɚ/) in those like *fur* and *preferred*. There are in addition a few other instances of /r/ in the preconsonantal position. In words like *idea, law, Utah*, /r/ does not occur. In many cases the consonant is noticeably labialized.[5] *Wheel, which, whisper*, etc. all have /hw/ (this speaker, #1, and #34 are the only ones among my informants who employ this pronunciation consistently). The cluster /hj/ is regular in *huge, humor*, etc. There are no affricate allophones of /t, d/; between vowels in words like *matter* and *gravity*, the consonant is very frequently voiceless. /θ, ð/ have only fricative allophones, with the exception that a voiceless dental stop twice occurs in final position when followed by [ð-] (*with the calf, Al Smith the Happy Warrior*). The unvoicing before a pause of the final consonant in *matches, thongs, feathers, woods*, and many similar words is fortis, rather than lenis, as is also the case in *college* and *Dodge*. In general the articulation is consciously precise and careful.

The diphthong /ɜɪ/ does not appear in her speech. There is no retraction of the first elements of /aɪ/ and /ɔɪ/. In a few words the starting-point of the diphthong /aʊ/ approaches [æ], but this is unusual. The first element of /oʊ/ in *road, zone*, etc. is often advanced to central position and there is a parallel fronting in the case of words like *afternoon* and *do, new* and *student* (some of the latter words have /j/). Words like *fast* and *plaid* rather regularly have long vowels or diphthongs (/æɚ/) distinct from those of *scarce* and *square*; in words of more than one syllable (*plaster, thrashing*), the vowel is /æ/. The /aɚ/-type occurs in a few words of the *ask*-group but is unusual. The quality of the vowel or first diphthongal element in words like *part* and *barn* varies, being quite retracted in some occurrences. Some of the "short *o*"

monosyllables contain this same phoneme (for example *job* and
Tom), others have rather short vowels. In words like *atomic,
Lawrence* (see page 145, note 67), *popular, quarantine*, the
vowel is normally unrounded.

#9. Young man, age 19. Born in Queens, educated in the public
schools there, now a Columbia undergraduate. F born in Manhattan, public schools, New York University; an auditor. M born
in Queens; parochial elementary school, public high school.
PGF born in Manhattan; an assistant to a theatrical producer.
PGM born in Pennsylvania, came to the city at the age of 18.
MGF born in Germany, was brought here as a small child; the
owner of a pickling factory. MGM born in Manhattan. The informant was uncertain as to how many of his grandparents had
had a high school education; none of them went to college.
Part of material recorded: all sentences, the *Rat* story, extempore conversation.

The consonant /r/ occurs regularly as the syllabic in the
third-group and the *stir*-group, but is otherwise absent in
the preconsonantal position; there are two exceptional occurrences (*mother, years*) in the conversational passage, a few
more in reading. There are no instances of its appearance in
Anna, idea, law, Panama, saw, Utah. The cluster /hw/ occurs
in *wheat* and *whistled*, but not in the other words of this
group; /hj/ is regular. After /n, t, d/, /j/ appears in most
of the words like *news, Tuesday, due*, and there are several
occurrences of the /ɨŭ/-type; in one way or the other, these
words seem always to be distinguished from those like *noon,
two, doom*; the /ɨŭ/-type also appears in *suit*. There is no
blade-articulation, no affrication of [t-, d-]; before the
syllabic allophone of /l/, [-ʔ] is substituted for [-t] in
bottle, but in the other words of this group the stop is oral,
voiced or voiceless. Intervocalically the cases like *shutters*
(= *shudders*), the consonant is usually voiced. Only fricative
allophones of /θ, ð/ occur (the word *through* in *right through
the rock* is exceptional).

The diphthong /3ɪ̆/ does not appear at all; there is no retraction of the first elements of /aɪ̆/ and /ɔɪ̆/. The starting-point of the diphthong in *around, house*, etc. is in most
cases markedly advanced and [æŭ] is frequent; particularly
before /n/ (*around, pounds*), the diphthong is often nasalized.
Varieties of /oŭ/ and /uŭ/ with a centralized first element
do not occur. There is a rather stable pattern in the low-front range: /ɛə̆/ in *fair, fairly, scarce*, etc.; /æə̆/ in monosyllables like *grass, lamb, plaid*; and /æ/ elsewhere. Pronunciations like [dɛɾəm] *dam* are very unusual. The words of the
ask-group are never distinguished from those like *lamb*. The
quality of /ɑə̆/ varies, being sometimes retracted; the diphthong often appears in monosyllables like *hog, job, Tom*; derivatives like *bombing, foggy, robber* have short vowels.
There is no retraction or overrounding in the case of /ɔə̆/.

In words like *collie, population, tonic, waffles*, the vowel is not rounded; vowels approaching [ɒ] occur in a few words before /r/ (for example in *torrid*) and also appear a number of times before voiceless fricatives in words like *Boston, faucet, Ross, sausage, wasp; coffin, office*, where the speaker is perhaps consciously avoiding /ɔə̆/.

#10. Woman, age 70-75. Born in Manhattan. Attended public schools, and went to normal school for two years, but did not become a teacher. Husband a real-estate broker and insurance agent. F born in Manhattan, educated in the public schools; a wholesale liquor dealer. Paternal grandparents born in Austria. M born in Manhattan; public school education. Maternal grandparents born in Germany. Part of material recorded: the *Rat* story, extempore conversation, and a selection of sentences.

The consonant /r/ occurs in words of the *third*-group a few times beside the usual /3ɪ̆/ and appears in the *stir*-group in the contamination [ʌr, ʌ·r]. With these minor exceptions, her conversational speech is consistently of the "r-less" type; in reading there are a few more instances of /r/ in the preconsonantal position. The consonant sometimes occurs in words like *Anna* and *law*, although there are no examples in the read material. The cluster /hw/ appears in a few words in reading, but is otherwise absent; /hj/ is regular. In words like *new, tubes, Dewey*, /j/ occurs almost regularly in reading, but is rare in her conversation. There is no tendency to affricate [t-, d-]; both voiceless and voiced consonants occur in words like *city* and *later*. Only fricative allophones of /θ, ð/ occur.

The diphthong /3ɪ̆/ appears rather regularly in the *third*-group, the glide towards high-front sometimes being rather slight. It never occurs in *coil, ointment*, etc. In words like *dime* and *five*, there is no retraction of the first element. The long vowels and diphthongs in words like *can* (sb.), *gas, grass, lamb* ([æ·, æə̆, æᵀ, æᵀə]) are distinct from those of *fair* and *scarce*; words of more than one syllable like *master, pantry, thrashing* have the vowel of *hat*. There is occasionally some slight retraction observable in the case of /aə̆/, none in the case of /ɔə̆/. The former phoneme appears in some of the monosyllables like *doll* and *John*. In some words (*anchored, Danny, drastic, had, rat*) very low and retracted variants of /æ/ occur. The vowel in *college, congress, quarry, Vermont, Warren*, etc. is normally not rounded; vowels like [ɒ] appear chiefly before /r/ (*Lawrence, Oregon, warrior*).

#11. Young man, age 24. Born in Manhattan, now lives in Queens. Parochial schools; one year at Fordham, then at Columbia in the Navy's V-12 program, graduated from Columbia. F born in Jersey City, where he went to the public schools;

graduate of a technical school in Newark; moved to the city, where he is now an engineer at the Bell Telephone Laboratories. PGF born in Hoboken, attended schools there and in Jersey City; a jeweler. His parents were French-speaking immigrants from Alsace-Lorraine. PGM born in Switzerland, brought to New York at the age of 7. M born in Manhattan, parochial high school graduate. MGF born in Boston, attended school there, came to the city at the age of 21, where he was in the produce business. His parents were born in Ireland. MGM born in the city. Material recorded: all sentences, the *Rat* story, extempore conversation.

The occurrence of /r/ before consonants and pauses is quite irregular: in the conversational passage, it appears in slightly more than one-quarter of the possible occurrences; in reading it is pronounced more than one-half the time. It is regular in the *third*-group and the *stir*-group. In *Panama*, *law*, and the like, it does not appear on these records. The cluster /hw/ does not occur; /hj/ is pronounced in all words like *huge* with the exception of *humor*. In *new*, *tube*, *Dewey*, *enthusiastic*, etc., /j/ does not appear. The alveolars are point-articulated and there is no affrication of [t-, d-]. In words like *city*, *theater*, *credits*, the voiced intervocalic consonant sometimes practically disappears, although his articulation in general is reasonably distinct. The glottal stop does not occur in words like *bottle*, although he told me that he once pronounced in this fashion. /θ, ð/ have only fricative allophones.

The diphthong /3ĭ/ does not occur at all. There is no retraction of the first elements of /aĭ/ and /ɔĭ/. The starting-point of the diphthong in *house* and *pounds* is sometimes fronted, but not so far as to reach the position of the vowel in *hat*. The first elements of /oŭ/ and /uŭ/ (both in words like *room* and those like *tube*) are not advanced. The pattern in words like *grass*, *lamb*, *sash*; *master*, *planning* is fairly regular: in monosyllables and final syllables [æɜ, æ·], elsewhere the vowel of *hat*. In *daily*, *nailed*, *tale*, the syllabics are identical with those in *fair* and *hair*. In words like *bomb* and *job*, /aɜ/ occurs quite frequently; a moderate retraction is sometimes observable. There is no retraction in the case of /ɔɜ/; often, as the result of a conscious change, the tongue-position is lower than is usual in New York. Words like *horrible*, *popular*, *waffles* have vowels that are not rounded.

#12. Young man, age 19. Born in the Bronx. Parochial elementary school, Bronx High School of Science, now an undergraduate at Columbia. F born in the Bronx. Public elementary school, parochial high school, Fordham, Fordham Law School; a lawyer in the office of the City Comptroller. PGF born in the Bronx, high school education; a painting contractor. PGM born in the Bronx, schooling not known. M born in Manhattan;

parochial elementary and high schools, then a teachers' training school; a teacher of remedial reading. MGF born in Germany, brought to New York as a small child; high school education; a hardware dealer. MGM born in Jersey City, went to school there, came to the Bronx before her marriage. Part of material recorded: all sentences, the *Rat* story, extempore conversation.

In the informant's conversational speech, /r/ occurs regularly as the syllabic in the *third*-group (words like *her* and *preferred* show the contamination [ʌr, ʌ·r]) and appears in *tours* on one record, but is not otherwise pronounced before consonants and pauses; in reading, the consonant occurs in the preconsonantal position a number of times. It is pronounced in *law* and in one utterance of *saw*. The clusters /hw/ and /hj/ do not occur. /j/ does not appear in words like *news, tubes, due,* whose syllabics are not distinguished from those of *noon, two, do.* There is no affrication of [t-, d-], but the initial voiceless stops are often rather heavily aspirated before stressed vowels. Words like *little* vary: [ˈbɑtɬ] *bottle,* [ˈbæʔɬ] *battle.* A dental stop occurs in one of three utterances of *Arthur,* but except for this, /θ, ð/ have only fricative allophones.[6]

The words *coin* and *Hoyt* are pronounced with diphthongs that seem to be contaminations of the /ɔɪ/- and /3ɪ/-types; other words of the group have /ɔɪ/. In several words the first element of /aɪ/ is retracted, but this is unusual. The startingpoint of the diphthong in *house, pounds,* etc. is never markedly advanced; varieties of /oʊ/ and /uʊ/ with a centralized first element do not occur. In words like *bad, grass, land; jamboree, master, pantry,* the vowels or first diphthongal elements vary a good deal in height, the higher ones coinciding with those in *fair* and *shares;* the lower varieties are more common. There is little tendency to retract in the case of /aɜ/ and /ɔɜ/. The phoneme /aɜ/ appears in some but not all of the words like *hog* and *squash.* In *block, horrible, not, profit, rosin, wandered* and the like, the vowels are not rounded and are often rather advanced.

#13. Woman, age 70. Born on Staten Island, family moved back to Manhattan when she was a small child. Educated in public schools and a private academy to the age of 16. Active in Protestant church work. Husband was an actuary. F born in Manhattan, went to a private academy; the owner of a furniture store. PGF born in Manhattan; a cabinetmaker. PGM, of Dutch descent, born in Brooklyn. M born in Manhattan; elementary schooling at a private academy. MGF born in Manhattan; a ship's chandler. His parents were German. MGM born in Manhattan. Part of material recorded: the *Rat* story, extempore conversation, and a selection of sentences.

The speaker's usage is completely consistent in the absence of /r/ from the preconsonantal position; in reading at least,

the consonant is also very frequently omitted at the end of
words before a following vowel. I did not observe any occurrences of the consonant in words like *Anna, law,* and *Utah.*
The cluster /hw/ does not occur; /hj/ is regular. /j/ does
not appear in words like *news, tubes, Dewey, suit, enthusiastic,* in which the syllabics are not distinguished from those
of *cool* and *noon.* In one or two instances [t-] is affricated
in high-stressed syllables, but this is unusual; there is no
blade-articulation. Words like *little* vary: [-tl̝] *Seattle,*
[-dl̝] *little,* and [-ʔl̝] *petals.* There are no affricate or
stop allophones of /θ, ð/.
The diphthong /ɜɪ̆/ is regularly employed in the *third*-group;
the first element is sometimes placed rather far back, for
example in [ˈsʌnˌbʌin] *sunburn.* In words like *boil* and *ointment,* /ɜɪ̆/ never appears. The first element of /aɪ̆/ is not retracted. The diphthong in *house, pounds,* etc. varies between
the limits of [aŭ] and [ɑŭ]; nothing resembling [æŭ] occurs.
There is no tendency to centralize the first elements of /oŭ/
and /uŭ/. Raised vowels or diphthongs with a raised first element are common in words like *grass, lamb, master, pantry;*
the higher ones coincide with those in *fair* and *stairs.* The
quality of /aə̆/ varies somewhat, being in some cases rather
strongly retracted. In monosyllables (*bobbed, bomb, cod, doll,
John, on, Tom*), /aə̆/ is frequent. (It might be noted that the
occurrence of /aə̆/ in such words and the more or less parallel occurrence of /ɛə̆/ in words like *man, plaid, rag* do not
seem to be particularly recent innovations in metropolitan
speech.) There is no retraction observable in the case of
/ɔə̆/. The category /ʌə̆/ appears in words like *her* (stressed)
and *preferred.* In words like *block, foreign, novel, profit,
wallet, Warren,* rounded vowels do not occur.

#14. Woman, age 73. Born in Manhattan (Greenwich Village sec-
tion). Went to a public school for a short time; then sent to
a private tutor. Has lived in Manhattan and in the Bronx. The
early death of her father left the family in difficult cir-
cusstances, and she has supported herself during most of her
adult life as a practical nurse. Parents both born in downtown Manhattan; elementary school education; F a designer and
printer of cloth. Paternal grandparents born in the North of
Ireland, maternal grandparents in Scotland; all came to New
York after marriage. Part of material recorded: the *Rat* story,
extempore conversation, and a selection of sentences.
The speaker's usage in regard to the occurrence of /r/ is
in general of the type mentioned on page 49: the consonant appears regularly as the syllabic in the *third*-group and monosyllables of the *stir*-group (*purring, stirring* have /ʌ/), but
is otherwise absent, with some exceptions, from the preconsonantal position. It is pronounced in the words *Anna, law,
Panama, saw* before vowels. The cluster /hw/ occurs a few
times in reading, but is rare; /hj/ is regular. Words like

new, tubes, due are pronounced in irregular fashion, with and without /j/. There is no affrication of [t-, d-], no occurrence of the glottal allophone of /t/ in words like *bottle*. Intervocalically in words like *city*, both voiceless and voiced consonants appear. /θ, ð/ have only fricative allophones.

The category /ɜɪ/ does not occur. There is no retraction of the first element of /aɪ/. In words like *boy* and *choice* the first element is often rather high and well-rounded, without retraction, approaching [oɪ̈]. Raising occurs in many words like *branch, crab, dam, grass, pasture*, but ordinarily is slight so that there is no coalescence with the group represented by *fair* and *scarce*. The /aə̆/-type occurs in a few words of the *ask*-group. There is no retraction in the case of /ɑə̆/ and /ɔə̆/; the variants of the former in a few cases, in fact, are rather fronted. /ɑə̆/ occurs in a number of monosyllables like *doll, fob, John*. In general, her vowels in the lower back range are often uncharacteristic of the city and not easily arranged in any system of orderly categories: to choose a few examples out of many, I transcribed [ɑ·] in *belongs, wrong,* [ɔˑ] in *Austria, chorus, floor, loft, long, song,* [ɔᴧə̆] in *door, hoarse, horse*. Perhaps her pronunciation here has been distorted by the influence of her grandparents' speech, or perhaps this is merely an instance of that sort of personal idiosyncrasy which appears every so often to bedevil the dialect geographer.

#15. Woman, age 55. Born in Brooklyn, grew up in Manhattan. Public schools through high school, then attended a business school. Secretary to the president of a shipping company. F born in Brooklyn; public school education; an executive in a drug manufacturing company. PGF born in Manhattan of German-born parents; the owner of a grocery store. PGM born in Germany, brought here as a child. M born in Manhattan; elementary school education. Maternal grandparents both born in Germany; MGF was a building contractor. Part of material recorded: all sentences, the *Rat* story, extempore conversation.

Both in conversation and in reading, the speaker's usage is consistently of the "r-less" type. The only exceptions are that the consonant sometimes occurs as the syllabic in the *third*-group beside the more usual /ɜɪ/ and sometimes in the *stir*-group (but *preferred* rimes with *cud*). The consonant occurs in *law* and *saw*; in other words of a similar sort which occurred in the test material, /r/ did not appear and the following vowel was preceded by the glottal stop. The cluster /hw/ occurs sporadically; the informant volunteered that she tried to pronounce in this fashion because she had been taught to do so in school. /hj/ is regular except in *humor*. In words like *new, tubes, due*, /j/ appears irregularly. There is no affrication of [t-, d-], only [-t] before /l/ in *little, Scotland*, etc.; in words like *pretty* and *senator*, the conso-

nant is often voiceless. In about half a dozen utterances /θ, ð/ are represented by dental stops and affricates (*through, at the, with*); in all other cases fricatives occur. The articulation is generally rather precise.
The diphthong /ɜĭ/ occurs as the most usual pronunciation in words like *third* and appears in one utterance of the word *choice*. There is no retraction of the first element of /aĭ/. The diphthong in *house, pounds*, etc. is often [aŭ], and allophones with any marked fronting of the first element do not occur. There is no tendency to centralize the starting-points of /oŭ/ and /uŭ/. Words like *bag, fast, planning, plastic* have syllabics of varying height; the higher ones coincide with those in *fair* and *scarce*, but [æə̆, æ·] are common in the monosyllables, [æ] in the longer words. The category /aə̆/ does not occur and /ɑə̆/ does not appear in any word like *ask*. There is no retraction in the case of /ɑə̆/ and /ɔə̆/. Some of the monosyllables like *bombed* and *John* have /ɑə̆/, but the short vowel is also frequent and is regular in derived forms of more than one syllable. In words like *collie, orator, popular*, the vowels ordinarily are not rounded; vowels like [ɒ] occur in a few words (for example in *off, sorry, waffles*).

#16. Young man, age 20. Born in Flushing, in the borough of Queens. Attended parochial school there, then Fordham Preparatory in the Bronx; an undergraduate at Columbia. F born in Yonkers, went to elementary school there; Manhattan Preparatory, Columbia College, Columbia School of Engineering; a civil engineer. Paternal grandparents both born in Yonkers; elementary education; PGF a shoe salesman. M born in Brooklyn; parochial schools, a teachers' training school; was a teacher before her marriage. Maternal grandparents both born in Brooklyn; elementary school education; MGF a printer. Most of great-grandparents were born in Ireland. Part of material recorded: all sentences, the *Rat* story, extempore conversation.
The speaker's usage is generally of the "*r*-less" type with the exception that words of the *third*-group are regularly pronounced with [r̩] (in several cases there is a slight glide toward high-front). In the *stir*-group, *preferred* rimes with *cud, her* stressed before a pause is [hʌr]. In the read material there are a few other instances of /r/ in the preconsonantal position. The consonant is rather frequently pronounced in words like *law* and *Panama*. The clusters /hw/ and /hj/ do not occur. /j/ is not pronounced in *new, tubes, due, enthusiastic, suit*, and the like. The alveolar stops are not affricated; [-ʔ] is frequently pronounced in words like *bottle* and *Seattle* (but *little* has [-d̩]); intervocalically in words like *city*, the consonant is rather regularly voiced. /θ, ð/ have only fricative allophones. The voiceless fricative occurs in plurals like *baths, mouths*.
In one or two words of the *coil*-group, a diphthong occurs

that seems to be a contamination of the /3ĭ/- and /ɔĭ/-types. The first element of /aĭ/ is somewhat retracted before voiced consonants. In words like *house* and *pounds*, the starting-point of the diphthong is advanced, often as far as [æ]; particularly in the neighborhood of nasal consonants, the diphthong is strongly nasalized. (There is a good deal of nasalization in his speech generally.) The first elements of /oŭ/ and /uŭ/ are not centralized. In words like *glass, sand; master, pantry*, the pattern of raising is carried through with a high degree of regularity. (The informant speaks a very consistent dialect, on the whole; after listening to a hundred or so sentences, the observer can practically predict what he will say in any succeeding one.) There is some retraction in the case of /aə̆/ and /ɔə̆/. In words like *bombed, fog, John, lodge,* /aə̆/ is very frequent. Rounded vowels do not occur in *college, popular, waffles,* and the like.

#17. Young man, age 23. Born in Brooklyn, where he attended parochial schools. Columbia graduate. During the war, he was in the Navy for a short time as an ensign. F born in Brooklyn, graduate of New York University; a lawyer. Paternal grandparents probably born in Germany, brought to New York as small children; PGF a carpenter at the Brooklyn Navy Yard. M born in Brooklyn; high school education. Maternal grandparents born in Ireland, brought here as children; MGF a machinist. Part of material recorded: all sentences, extempore conversation.

The consonant /r/ occurs regularly as the syllabic in the *third*-group; words like *her* (stressed) and *preferred* are pronounced with [ʌr]; there are in addition rare occurrences of /r/ in the preconsonantal position in other words. At the end of words before an initial vowel, the consonant is often omitted; and there are no examples of it in words like *law* and *Utah* on these records. The clusters /hw/ and /hj/ are absent; /j/ does not occur in words like *new, tubes, due*. There is no affrication of [t-, d-]; a glottalized voiceless stop appears in *Seattle*, but in most words of this group the stop is voiced. Only fricative allophones of /θ, ð/ occur.

The diphthong /3ĭ/ does not appear. The first element of the diphthong in words like *five* and *pie* is sometimes moderately retracted. The starting-point of the diphthong in *house, pounds,* etc. varies to a certain extent, but [æŭ] does not occur. There is no tendency to centralize the first elements of /oŭ/ and /uŭ/. Raised vowels or diphthongs with a raised first element occur with considerable regularity in words like *glass, land; Astor, pantry;* the raising is not always sufficient to make them coincide with those of the *fair, scarce*-group. Moderate retraction is observable in some of the words like *harm* and *pork.* /aə̆/ is quite common in the "short *o*" monosyllables and sometimes appears in derivatives of more than one syllable. /ɔə̆/ occurs before /r/ in *coral*,

PRIMARY INFORMANTS   107

immoral, orator, Oregon. There is no tendency to round the
vowels in words like *continent, horrible, lobster, waffles*.

#13. Young man, age 21. Born in Brooklyn, educated in the
public schools, now a Columbia undergraduate. F born in
Queens, high school education; an officer in the Fire Department.
Paternal grandparents both born in the city; PGF had a
high school education, a minor executive in a publishing
house. This side of the family originally from Ireland. M
born in Brooklyn, high school education. MGF born in Connecticut,
came to New York when he was about 20; an industrial
chemist (the informant was uncertain as to whether he had
gone to college). MCM born in Maine, came here before marriage.
Part of material recorded: all sentences, extempore
conversation.
    The informant's usage is rather consistently "r-less" with
the regular exception of the words in the *third*-group; as
for the *stir*-group, *preferred* has [ʌr], *her* stressed before
a pause is [hʌ]. The consonant is frequently omitted as a
word-final before a following vowel, in which case the vowel
is usually preceded by a light glottal stop; nor is it pronounced
on these records in *Asia, law, Panama, Utah*, etc. The
cluster /hw/ does not occur; /hj/ appears only in *Hughes*, not
in the other words of this group. In words like *new, tubes,
due*, /j/ does not occur. Initially in stressed syllables the
voiceless stops have a fairly heavy aspiration; [t-] is often
somewhat affricated, although this is not very marked. In intervocalic
position in words like *auto* and *heating* both
voiced and voiceless consonants occur; *Seattle* and *bottle*
have voiceless oral stops. Only fricative allophones of /θ,
ð/ occur.
    The diphthong /ɜɪ/ does not occur. The first element of the
diphthong in words like *buy* and *dime* is sometimes slightly
retracted. The first element of the diphthong in *house,
pounds*, etc. is often advanced. There is no tendency to centralize
the first element of the diphthong in words like
road. The vowels or first diphthongal elements in words like
flag, glass, pantry, thrashing, although often raised somewhat,
are usually distinct from those in *careless, fair,
scarce*. *Daily* rimes with *fairly*. There is sometimes some retraction
in the case of /aɚ/, but not of /ɔɚ/; /aɚ/ occurs in
many of the "short *o*" monosyllables. In *foreign, Johnny, popular,
profit, wandered, warrant*, etc., the vowel is not
rounded.

#19. Young man, age 20. Born on Staten Island and has always
lived there. Public schools, now an undergraduate at Columbia.
F born on Staten Island, attended public schools there, Columbia
graduate, a wholesaler of plumbing supplies. PGF born
in Ireland, came to Staten Island as a young man, probably
had no more than elementary education; a plumber. PGM born on

Staten Island, elementary education. M born on Staten Island; high school graduate, attended a business school in Manhattan. MGF born on Staten Island (his parents were born in Germany); a clerical worker for a utility company (as a young man had been a butcher). MGM born on Staten Island (of her parents one was born there, the other probably in Ireland); elementary school education. Part of material recorded: all sentences, the *Rat* story, extempore conversation.

In the informant's conversational speech, /r/ occurs occasionally in the preconsonantal position; in reading, the frequency increases to about one-quarter of the possible cases. The consonant appears in *law* and *saw* before a following vowel and in *asthma* before a pause. The cluster /hw/ is absent, but /hj/ is regular. In *new, tubes, due,* etc., /j/ is never pronounced. The alveolar stops are not affricated; in the intervocalic position in cases like *bought a barge, butter,* the consonant rather regularly is voiced, as it is in words like *Seattle.* Beside the more usual fricative varieties of /θ, ð/, there are occasional occurrences of dental stops and affricates. The informant's speech is rapid; the articulation is often rather lax, and the loss of consonants is very frequent.

Words like *Curtis, first, terminal* vary: /ɜɪ̆/ is frequent, /r/ occasional; often the contamination [ɼɪ̆] appears. In words like *choice, foil,* his pronunciation is similarly variable, some words being pronounced with a contamination of the /ɜɪ̆/- and /ɔɪ̆/-types. The first element of /aɪ̆/ is sometimes retracted, although not markedly so. In *down, pounds,* and a few other words, the starting-point of the diphthong approximates [æ]; in other words it begins lower and farther back. There is no fronting in the case of /oŭ/ and /uŭ/. The informant's speech is extremely consistent in its distribution of /ɛə̆/ and /æ/ in words like *ask, crash, pantry* on the one hand; *habit, hammer* on the other. It is rather interesting to note that in the sentence "An adder is a poisonous snake," he first pronounced /'ɛə̆dər/ (that is, "one who adds"), then when he had grasped the meaning of the whole sentence, corrected it to /'ædər/. In the *ask*-group, the /aə̆/- and /ɑə̆/-types do not occur. In *large, part,* etc., a retracted vowel or a diphthong with a retracted starting-point is common. Monosyllables like *bomb, god, hog* normally have /ɑə̆/; in *atomic bomb,* for example, the stressed syllabics differ markedly not only in length, but in quality. The vowel in *Bobby, foggy, foreign, horrible, want,* etc. is regularly unrounded. There is a good deal of nasalization.

#20. Young man, age 20. Born in Manhattan, now lives in the Bronx. Parochial schools; at present a Columbia undergraduate. F born in Manhattan, parochial schools, two years at Fordham; the superintendent of an omnibus company. Paternal grandparents both born in Manhattan, parochial elementary school education; PGF an employee of a street railway company. Great-

grandparents also born in New York of Irish families. M born
in Manhattan, parochial schools; also attended school for a
short time in Nyack, where her family lived briefly. Maternal
grandparents born in Manhattan; their parents were Irish immigrants. Part of material recorded: all sentences, extempore
conversation.

There are a few occurrences of /r/ in the preconsonantal
position in words like *Gordon, shared, tardy* and the consonant also appears occasionally in the *third*-group beside /3ĭ/
(the contamination of the two types also occurs). The consonant is pronounced as a word-final before vowels in *Asia,
law, Panama, Patricia, saw*. Often the [r]-articulation has a
strong lip-modification (of the dialectal, not the speech-
defective sort); intervocalically in words like *very* and *carry*, it is quite striking. The clusters /hw/ and /hj/ do not
occur, and /j/ is absent from *Dewey, enthusiastic, news,
studio, suit*, and the like. In many words [t-] is noticeably
affricated, as is [d-] in several cases; intervocalically in
words like *better* and *forty*, the consonant is regularly
voiced; before /l/, [-ʔ] occurs in *battle, bottle, Seattle,
Scotland*, [-d] in *hospital* and *little*. Only fricative varieties of /θ, ð/ occur. All plurals like *baths* and *wreaths* have
the voiceless fricative. The fricative component of the affricate in words like *college* and *barge* is a voiceless fortis
before a pause.

The occurrence of /3ĭ/ in the *third*-group has already been
mentioned. In words like *oil* and *join*, the diphthong varies:
the first element is sometimes a somewhat retracted and
strongly rounded [ɔ], sometimes lies between [ɔ] and [ʌ]. In
some cases the starting-point of the diphthong in *time* and
buy is retracted, and there is some tendency to centralize
the first elements of /iĭ/ and /eĭ/. The diphthong in *house,
pounds*, etc. varies towards [æŭ]; the first element of /oŭ/
is sometimes completely unrounded. Neither in words like *news*
nor in those like *room* is the starting-point of /uŭ/ centralized; on the contrary, retraction is observable in certain
occurrences. Words like *glass, flag, planning* have vowels or
diphthongs that vary considerably, between the limits of
[ɛə̆, ɛ·] and [æ˞ə̆, æ·]. No words of the *ask*-group are treated
differently from those like *flag*. Retraction appears in some,
but by no means all the occurrences of /aə̆/ and /ɔə̆/. In
words like *bog and rod*, /aə̆/ is frequent. Of the *stir*-group,
her (stressed) has [ʌə̆], *preferred* rimes with *cud, occurred*
has [ɹ̩]. In some words, for example in *back*, very low and
centralized varieties of /æ/ appear. *Hospital, popular, quarry, waffles*, and the like have unrounded vowels; in some instances I have transcribed [ɑ˦]

#21. Young man, age 19. Born on Staten Island and attended
public schools there; now an undergraduate at Columbia. F
born in Elizabeth, brought to Manhattan at the age of 10; did

not complete high school; a stationary engineer. Paternal
grandparents born in Ireland and were married there, came to
this country in adult life. PGF'S occupation not known; PGM
a cook in a convent. M born on Staten Island, did not complete high school. Maternal grandparents born on Staten
Island; MGF died when informant's mother was a small child
and he knows very little about him. Preceding generation born
in Ireland. Part of material recorded: all sentences, the *Rat*
story, extempore conversation.

The consonant /r/ occurs rather regularly in words like
heard and *Hearst* (there are several exceptional instances of
/ɜɪ/ and words of the *stir*-group usually have the contamination [ʌr]). Except for this, the informant's conversational
speech is of the "*r*-less" type. In reading, there are a number of occurrences of the consonant in words like *garment* and
yours. In *saw* /r/ appears as a word-final, but in the test
sentences words of this type were ordinarily pronounced without the consonant and with the following vowel preceded by
the glottal stop. The clusters /hw/ and /hj/ are absent; /j/
is never pronounced in *news*, *tubes*, *due*, and the like. There
is no noticeable affrication of [t-, d-]; intervocalically in
city, *theater*, etc., the consonant is rather regularly voiced;
[-ʔ] and a less frequent [-d] occur in words like *battle* and
catalog. Only fricative allophones of /θ, ð/ appear.

The diphthong /ɜɪ/ rarely occurs in the *third*-group. In the
group exemplified by *oil* and *ointment* there is a mixture of
types: [ɔi] ([ɔ˩ɪ]), [ʌɪ], and contaminations, the first being most common. The starting-point of the diphthong in *buy*,
mind, etc. is often strongly retracted. In words like *me* and
day, the first element of the diphthongs tends to be centralized; the centralization is most noticeable in open syllables before a pause. The starting-point of /aŭ/ varies in the
direction of [æ]; there is no tendency to centralize in the
case of /oŭ/, or of /uŭ/ (either in words like *tubes* or those
like *room*). The varying quality of the vowels and diphthongs
in *bad*, *grass*, *pantry*, etc. may be indicated briefly by noting that in the phrase *half in and half out*, the first *half*
is [hæːf], the second [hɛ˩f]. Marked retraction and a strong
diphthongal glide is often observable in the case of /ɑə̆/ and
/ɔə̆/. The phoneme /ɑə̆/ occurs in a greater number of monosyllables like *bomb* and *hog*, and sometimes appears in derivatives like *Bobbie* and *foggy*. Before /r/, /ɔə̆/ occurs in *coral*,
immoral, *orator*, *Oregon*. In *popular*, *Wanamaker*, and the like,
the vowel is not rounded.

#22. Boy, age 15. Born in Manhattan; now a student in a public high school. F born in Manhattan; high school education;
a department store clerk. Paternal grandparents born in the
city; elementary education; PGF a building superintendent.
Most of great-grandparents on this side were born in Ireland.
M born in Manhattan; high school education. MGF born in

Brooklyn, of German descent; an employee of a milk company. MGM born in Norway, brought to Brooklyn as a child. Both grandparents probably had no more than elementary education. Part of material recorded: all sentences, the *Rat* story, extempore conversation.

The consonant /r/ occurs regularly as the syllabic in the *third*-group (occasionally there is a slight off-glide toward high-front) and words like *preferred* may exhibit the contamination [ʌr]; in addition, in a very small number of cases /r/ appears in words like *carton*, and in those like *summer* before a pause. Otherwise, his speech is "*r*-less." In *Asia, law*, etc., the consonant often occurs. The cluster /hw/ and /hj/ are absent; /j/ does not appear in *news, tubes, due*, etc. The initial voiceless stops sometimes have a rather heavy aspiration and there is some tendency to affricate [t-], although not very strongly. In *water, theater*, and the like, the consonant is ordinarily voiced; [-ʔ] appears in *battle, bottle, Seattle*. In rare cases a dental stop occurs for [ð-] (*to the laundry*). In *college* and *garage* before pauses, there is a fortis unvoicing of the fricative component of the affricate.

The diphthong /3ĭ/ does not occur. The first element of /aĭ/ and of /ɔĭ/ is often retracted. In *house, pounds*, etc., the starting-point of the diphthong is advanced toward [æ]. There is no tendency to centralize in the case of /oŭ/ and /uŭ/. The vowels or first diphthongal elements in *Dad, glass, lamb; avenue, mantle*, etc. are sometimes low, but the occurrence of the higher varieties, coinciding with those in *fair* and *scarce*, approaches regularity. Retraction is common in the case of /aǒ/ and /ɔǒ/. The phoneme /aǒ/ appears very frequently in the monosyllables like *hog* and also in derivatives like *robber*. Before /r/, it is doubtful if an /ɑ/-/aǒ/ opposition exists, for the vowels in words like *borrow* and *forest* are quite long. *Coral* and *immoral* have /ɔǒ/. In *popular, waffles*, etc., there is no tendency to round the vowel.

#23. Man, age 27. Born in Brooklyn and now lives there. Attended public schools; served in the Coast Guard for two years. Now a student at Columbia. F born in Manhattan, attended public schools, did not complete high school; a stock exchange clerk. PGF an Alsatian by birth, came to New York as a young man; a baker. PCM born in Germany, came here as a young girl. M born in Brooklyn, did not complete high school. MGF born in Ireland, came to New York at the age of 28; a transport worker. MGM born on the Isle of Man, came here as a young woman. Part of material recorded: all sentences, the *Rat* story, extempore conversation.

Words of the *third*-group vary between /r/, /3ĭ/, and the contamination [rĭ]; his pronunciation is otherwise consistently "*r*-less." On these records there are no occurrences of /r/ in words like *Anna* and *law*. The dialectal lip-modification of the consonant is sometimes observable, although not regular. The clusters /hw/ and /hj/ do not appear in his speech; /j/ is regularly absent from *news, tubes, due, enthusiastic*, and the like. There is an irregular affrication of [t-]; in *getting, photographic*, etc., the consonant is rather regularly voiced; *Seattle* and *bottle* have [-ʔ] but *hospital* has [-d]; the glottal allophone of /t/ also occurs not infrequently in words like *hat* before a following consonant. The articulation of [s] and [z] is of the sort described on pages 38-39. /θ, ð/ are regularly represented by fricatives. In the participles and similar words /n/ occurs beside /ŋ/ rather frequently in conversation and appears in the test sentences occasionally.

The words of the *coil*-group vary, and the speaker's usage here is self-conscious: for example, he pronounced *Hoyt* as [hṛɪt], then corrected it to [hɔᵊɪt]. He is one of those many New Yorkers who find it difficult to say or read without stumbling sentences like *This ointment's good for sunburn* or *He would always shirk making a choice*. The first element of the diphthong in words like *buy* and *dime* is often retracted. In *house, pounds*, etc., the starting-point of the diphthong is somewhat advanced, but not as far as [æ]; there is no centralization in the case of /oʊ̆/ and /uʊ̆/. The vowels or first diphthongal elements in *bag, grass; Astor, mantle*, etc. vary considerably in height; the higher variants, which are very common, are identical with those in *flares* and *scarce*. Variants of /aə̆/ and /ɔə̆/ showing retraction are common, and the glide is often very marked. In words like *hog*, /aə̆/ is frequent. *Her* (stressed) has [ʌə̆], *occurred* the contamination [ʌr]. Unrounded vowels regularly occur in words like *goggles, omelet, popular, wallet*.

#24. Young man, age 23. Born in Manhattan on the lower West Side. Attended public schools, spent several years in the Army; now a student at Columbia. F born in Manhattan, did not complete high school; a telephone company repairman. Paternal grandparents both born in New York City; PCF a telephone repairman. M born in Manhattan, elementary school education. Maternal grandparents both born in Germany, came here in adult life. MGF a service-man for an elevator company. Part of material recorded: all sentences, extempore conversation.

The consonant /r/ occurs regularly as the syllabic in words like *heard* and *German* (there is sometimes a glide toward high-front) and words like *her* and *preferred* show the contamination [ʌr]. With these exceptions, the informant's speech is consistently "r-less." On these records there are no occurrences of /r/ in *Anna, law*, etc. There is a noticeable speech-defective labialization of the consonant. The clusters /hw/ and /hj/ do not occur; /j/ does not appear in words like *new, tubes, due, enthusiastic, suit*. Not infrequently [t-] is affricated; intervocalically in words like *forty* and *later* and before the syllabic allophone of /l/

(*bottle*, etc.), the consonant is voiced. In a small number of
cases the dental stop and affricate allophones of /ð/ occur.
In the word *joint* a diphthong occurs that suggests the
/ɜɪ/-type; the other words of the *coil*-group are pronounced
with [ɔɪ, ɔʱɪ]. The first element of /aɪ/ shows no particular
retraction. In words like *house* and *pounds* the starting-point
of the diphthong is sometimes advanced, but never as far as
[æ]. There is no fronting in the case of /oŭ/. A few words
like *suit* and *Tuesday* have a diphthong that begins farther
forward than that in *room*, but ordinarily the two groups are
not distinguished. Words like *bag*, *bath*, *jazz* commonly have
long vowels or diphthongs distinct from those in *flares* and
scarce, being much lower; in a few instances (for example in
avenue, *dam*, *family*), the higher variants appear. The vowels
or diphthongs in many words like *card*, *tardy*, *Tom* often exhibit extreme retraction; before /r/, certain words like
Doris and *quarry* have long vowels that are presumably /aə̆/
also. Retraction is much less marked in the case of /ɔə̆/. In
atomic, *gong*, *Gothic*, *Molly*, *polished*, etc., the vowels are
not rounded.

#25. Woman, age about 70. Born in Manhattan on the site of
the present General Post Office. Elementary education. Has
always lived at home. F born on the lower East Side; elementary education; kept a shop in which he repaired gas-meters.
Paternal grandparents born in London, came here after their
marriage; PGF a maker of straw hats. M born in downtown Manhattan, elementary education. Maternal grandparents born in
Ireland, probably brought here as children. MGF's occupation
not known. Part of material recorded: the *Rat* story, a selection of sentences.

With the exception that [r̩] and [r̩ɪ] occasionally appear
both in the *third*-group and in words like *boisterous* and *Boyd*,
the informant's speech is regularly "r-less." The consonant
occurs as a word-final before initial vowels in *Anna*, *Asia*,
law, *Panama*, *saw*, *Utah*. The cluster /hw/ is absent; /hj/ occurs only in *humors*. /j/ is never pronounced in *news*, *tubes*,
Dewey, *enthusiastic*, *suit*, and the like, whose syllabics are
identical with those in *room* and *two*. There is occasionally
a slight affrication of [t-]; before /l/, her usage is variable, with [-t] in *Seattle*, [-d] in *little*, and [-ʔ] in *petals*; [-ʔ] appears in *rotten*, *satin*. In a few cases dental
stops and affricates occur in place of [ð-], but /θ/ has only
fricative allophones. In participles and similar words /n/ is
fairly frequent in her conversation, rare in reading.

The diphthong /ɜɪ/ ordinarily occurs in the *third*-group and
the *coil*-group (see above). Its appearance in *boy's* is irregular. The first element of /aɪ/ is occasionally somewhat retracted, but not markedly so. There is no fronting of the
starting-point of /aŭ/, which varies between the limits of
[a] and [ɑ]. The first elements of /oŭ/ and /uŭ/ are not cen-

tralized (the occurrence of /oŭ/ in the third syllable of *California* I have also noted a few times in the speech of other less cultivated speakers). Raised vowels or diphthongs with a raised first element, identical with those in *fair* and *scarce*, are rather regularly pronounced in *ask, bag, glass, jazz; acid, answer, mantle, planning*, etc., although lower ones sometimes occur (*pantry, rafters* with the vowel of *hat*). Strongly retracted varieties of /aə̆/ and /ɔə̆/ are not uncommon. In monosyllables such as *bomb, doll, fob, wash*, /aə̆/ is frequent, but it is not extended to derivatives of more than one syllable: *bombing, robber* have /a/. In *popular, robber, Washington*, etc., the vowel is not rounded.

#26. Woman, age over 70. Born in Manhattan on the West Side. Parochial elementary education. Husband was a clerk for an insurance company. F born in Manhattan in the Greenwich Village section; elementary education; a plumber. Paternal grandparents born in France, came to New York as children. M born in Greenwich Village section; elementary education. Maternal grandparents born in Ireland, came here before marriage. Occupations of grandfathers not known. Part of material recorded: the *Rat* story and a selection of sentences.

The informant's usage is very consistently of the "r-less" type. The only exceptions are the occasional appearance of the contaminations [ṛɪ] (*heard*) and [ʌr] (*her*). In *Anna, law, Utah*, and the like, /r/ occurs very frequently. The cluster /hw/ is absent; /hj/ occurs only in the name *Hughes*. In words like *news, Tuesday, Dewey, enthusiastic, suit*, /j/ never appears; these words have the same syllabic as *room* and *two*. Occasionally a slight affrication of [t-] is observable; intervocalically in cases like *city* and *go tomorrow*, the consonant is normally voiced; before the syllabic allophone of /l/ in *little, Seattle*, etc., [-t] and [-d] occur, but not [-ʔ]. A dental affricate allophone of /θ/ occurs in the initial cluster /θr/ (*three, thrashing*), but otherwise only the fricative varieties of /θ, ð/ appear. Fortis unvoicing before a pause is almost regular in *matches, Mormons, thongs; college, garage*, etc. Final clusters are frequently simplified.

The diphthong /3ɪ/ occurs in *Germans, third*, etc. and in *Hoyt, ointment*, etc. (There is some irregularity: before /l/ in *boil, coil, foil*, etc. the diphthong is often [ɔɪ], while this variant does not occur in the *third*-group.) The first element of /aɪ/ is never markedly retracted. The starting-point of the diphthong in *house, pounds*, etc. is never advanced toward [æ]; [aŭ] is frequent. There is no tendency to centralize the first elements of /oŭ/ and /uŭ/; in the latter case, in fact, the glide often begins quite far back. Vowels or diphthongs coinciding with those in *fair, scarce* occur with considerable frequency in *clams, Dad, grass; answer, molasses*, etc.; but the lower varieties also appear. The

quality of the vowels or first diphthongal elements in words
like *barge, park, rod, Tom* varies; some I have marked as retracted, others have a rather advanced position. Some occurrences of /ɔ̆/ also show retraction. In *popular, tomorrow,
waffles*, etc., the vowel is not rounded.

#27. Man, age 25. Born in Brooklyn and now lives there. At-
tended parochial schools, spent three years in the Air Force,
now a student at Columbia. F born in Brooklyn, did not complete grammar school; a motion-picture electrician. Paternal
grandparents both born in Brooklyn; neither completed elementary school; PGF a worker in the municipal street-cleaning
department. M born in Brooklyn, graduated from parochial elementary school. MGF born in Brooklyn, graduated from parochial elementary school; a coal and ice dealer. MGM born in
Jersey City, moved to Brooklyn at the age of 19; educated at
a parochial elementary school in Jersey City. Informant believes that all his great-grandparents were born in Ireland.
Part of material recorded: all sentences, the *Rat* story, extempore conversation.

With the exceptions of words like *third* and *curtain*, the
informant's speech is consistently of the "r-less" type:
these words vary between /3ĭ/, /r/, and the contamination
[r̩ĭ]. In *Anna, law, saw*, etc., the consonant frequently occurs. The clusters /hw/ and /hj/ do not appear; in *news,
tubes, due*, and the like, /j/ is not pronounced. The voiceless stops are often rather heavily aspirated and [t-] frequently affricated. The alveolars are blade-articulated. In
conversation, dental stop and affricate allophones of /θ/ and
/ð/ are fairly common; they do not appear so often in reading.
Frequently [ð-] is assimilated to a preceding final consonant.
The articulation in general lacks precision: losses and weak-
enings, particularly of the alveolars, are very numerous, not
only from final clusters, but also in many other cases too
varied to reduce to any formula.

The diphthong /3ĭ/ in a few words, for example in *certainly*,
begins so far forward that it probably overlaps on /eĭ/. It
does not appear in *oil, join*, and the like, whose syllabics
usually begin with a somewhat retracted and strongly rounded
[ɔ]. The starting-point of /iĭ/ and /eĭ/ is in some cases
noticeably centralized. There is often some retraction of the
first element of the diphthong in *dime* and *five*, but it is
not very marked. In *barge, barn*, etc. there may be a similar
retraction and in *soft, draw*, etc. it is quite pronounced.
Long vowels or diphthongs (/aŏ/) are frequent in words like
bog and *bomb* and even in the first part of compounds like
codfish and *hod carrier*. There is no tendency to round the
vowels of *popular, Scotch, wander*, and the like.

#28. Woman, age 50-55. Born in the Bronx, elementary school
education; an unemployed needle-trades worker on home relief.

F born in Czechoslovakia, brought to New York as an infant; attended an elementary school in the Bronx; a saloon-keeper. M born in Manhattan, moved to the Bronx in 1869, attended a public elementary school there. Maternal grandparents born in Ireland; MGF a patrolman on the old Central Park police force. Part of material recorded: the Rat story, extempore conversation, and a selection of sentences.

The informant is extremely conscious of certain matters of pronunciation, and as a result there is a considerable disparity between her more unguarded conversation and her careful speaking and reading. For example, in ordinary conversation the participles are rather regularly pronounced with /n/; in reading /ŋ/ is usual. In conversation but not in reading, with before /ð/ (with them, etc.) is regularly pronounced with a voiceless dental stop. In the third-group the occurrence of /ɜ̆ɪ/ is more frequent in her ordinary conversation than in reading.

Both in speaking and in reading, the occurrence of /r/ in the preconsonantal position is very irregular; in one short passage of extemporaneous conversation, it appeared in about two-fifths of the possible cases. (When the consonant is pronounced in this position, the vigor with which it is frequently articulated would be approved in Peoria.) In Anna, Jamaica, law, saw, seesaw, /r/ occurred as a word-final. The cluster /hw/ appeared twice in reading, but was otherwise absent; /hj/ is regular in her speech. Words like new, tubes, suit were variously pronounced in reading: /j/ occurred in several, several were pronounced with a diphthong distinct from /uŭ/, in most /uŭ/ occurred; the last, I think, is her most natural usage. There is some affrication of [t-] and [d-]; in words like city and elevated the consonant is normally voiced in conversation, but the voiceless stop is frequent in read material; before the syllabic allophone of /l/, [-t], [-d], and [-ʔ] all appear. Scotland has [-ʔ]. With the exception mentioned in the preceding paragraph, I noted only fricative allophones of /θ, ð/. All nouns like mouth and path have regular plurals.

In the third-group, both /ɜ̆ɪ/ and /r/ appear (occasionally there is a contamination of the two types). The diphthong in coil, doily, join, ointment, etc. varies considerably: it sometimes begins with an [ɔ] identical with that of cultivated speech, sometimes with [ʌ], and sometimes with an intermediate phone. The first element of the diphthong in line is strongly retracted and similar retractions occur in some other words, but ordinarily the starting-point of /aɪ̆/ is farther forward. In house, pounds, etc., the diphthong never begins at a markedly advanced position and may begin at [ɑ]. The syllabics of words like ask, flag; candy, fasten are often identical with those in fair and scarce, but lower varieties are also frequent. On the Rat record, the /aə̆/-type appears in aunt and half, but one doubts that this is her

natural usage. In some occurrences of /aə̆/ (for example, in
harm and *Tom*), there is strong retraction; in others the vowels or first diphthongal elements are placed well forward.
/aə̆/ is common in the "short *o*" monosyllables, but short vowels also occur. There is no marked retraction or overrounding
in the case of /ɔə̆/. In *block, hospital, novel, prospect,
wallet*, and the like, the vowels are normally unrounded; in a
few words I transcribed [ɒ], chiefly before /r/ (*foreign, forest*). A lower high-central vowel appears in *building* and
Smith.

#29. Man, age 81. Born in Brooklyn, has lived most of his
life in Manhattan. His parents died when he was a small child,
and he was educated to the age of 11 in a Brooklyn orphan
asylum. Worked at different times as a bookbinder, stonecutter, restaurant worker. Now on home relief. Though it seems
scarcely necessary to record these facts, his parents were
both born in Brooklyn and his father was a carriage-painter.
Part of material recorded: the *Rat* story, extempore conversation, and a selection of sentences.

The informant's usage is completely consistent in its "*r*-less" pattern. In *Anna, Asia, law, Nassau, Panama, window*,
etc., /r/ occurs before vowels as frequently as in words like
dollar and *wore*. The clusters /hw/ and /hj/ do not occur; /j/
is regularly absent from *news, tubes, due, enthusiastic*, and
the like--such words form a single group with those like *room*
and *two*. There is no affrication of [t-, d-]; voiced consonants occur very often in words like *city* and *elevator*; before /l/, I recorded no instances of [-ʔ]. /θ, ð/ are represented quite frequently by dental stops and affricates, and
in a number of words phones occur that must be assigned to
/t̪/ or /d̪/: for example, in *thrashing* and *with fear* I heard
the stops as alveolar; and the informant himself volunteered
that *oaths* and *oats* were homonymous. In the participles, and
in similar words like *morning*, /ŋ/ sometimes occurs, but /n/
is more frequent. On the recording of his extempore conversation, there are three participles in which /ŋ/ is followed
by a rather weakly articulated voiced stop. The articulation
is often not very distinct and the reduction of clusters is
frequent.

The diphthong /3ɪ̆/ is regular in the *third-* and *coil*-groups;
in both the first element of the diphthong varies through the
same range from [3] to [ɔ]. There is rarely any marked retraction of the starting-point of /aɪ̆/. In *house, pounds,
scouts*, and the like, the diphthong always starts well back,
about at [ɑ]; nor is there any advancing of the first elements of /oŭ/ and /uŭ/. The occurrence of raised vowels or
diphthongs with a raised first element in words like *ask,
dam, gas; answer, Massachusetts* approaches regularity, although lower varieties also occur. Retraction is observable
in some occurrences of /aə̆/ and /ɔə̆/. In the "short *o*" mono-

syllables /aɞ/ appears in some cases, but other words have
vowels that are quite short (his pronunciation /bʌm/ bomb is
unusual in New York City, so far as I have observed). In *foreign, popular, Wanamaker*, etc., the vowels are not rounded.

#30. Man, age 31. Born in Manhattan, in the Hell's Kitchen
district; has always lived in Manhattan except during his
Army service. Did not finish elementary school. An elevator
operator. F born in Manhattan, attended elementary school,
worked in a slaughterhouse, later as a garage attendant. PGF
either born in Manhattan or born in Germany and brought here
as a small child; a slaughterhouse worker. PGM born in the
city. M born in Brooklyn, later moved to Manhattan; elementary education. MGF born in Ireland, brought to the city as
a boy; occupation not known. MGM born in the city. No recording was made of this informant; he made several appointments
with me, but failed to appear each time.

The usage of this speaker, like that of the preceding one,
exhibits a completely consistent "r-less" pattern. The consonant is frequent as a word-final in words like *Anna* and *saw*.
All allophones of /r/ are accompanied by a strong lip-modification of the dialectal sort. The clusters /hw/ and /hj/ do
not occur; /j/ is never pronounced in words like *new, tubes,
due*. Blade-articulation of the alveolar consonants is regular.
There is a rather noticeable "low" [s]. The initial allophones of /t/ and /d/ are strongly affricated; in *bottle,
Seattle, Scotland*, and the like, [-ʔ] occurs, as it does in
Catholic. Dental stop and affricate allophones of /θ, ð/ are
more common than in the speech of any other informant. [ð-]
is rather regularly assimilated to /s, z, n, l, ŋ/⁷ when
these are final in the preceding word. In some cases phones
occur that must be assigned to /t/ or /d/: *Catholic* has already been mentioned; *three* and *tree* seem to be identical;
with followed by a vowel is pronounced with the same voiced
tap that occurs in *city* and *bidder; with you* (sing.) is
[ˈwiᴜtʃə]. Fortis unvoicing before a pause may occur in cases
like *college* and *matches*. In participial forms, /n/ is regular. Assimilatory changes are common (for example, [iᴜd
ˌɔːliɪˈpenz] *It all depends*) and consonant losses are very
frequent (for example,[ˈdiᴜsriᴜk] *district*).

The diphthong /ɜɪ/ is regular in the *third*-group and the
coil-group. The first element of /aɪ/, /eɪ/, /iɪ/ are commonly retracted. The diphthong in words like *house* and *pounds*
begins at about [a]; [æu̯] does not occur. The first element
of the diphthong in *don't, go*, etc. is completely unrounded.
In words like *grass* and *pantry*, /ɛɞ/ is fairly regular. Monophthongal variants of /iɞ/ and /ɛɞ/ may occur in absolute
final position. Retraction is frequent in the case of /aɞ/
and /ɔɞ/. There is the usual mixture of short vowels and long
vowels or diphthongs in the "short *o*" monosyllables like *fog*
and *John*. In *novel, shopping, wallet*, and the like the vowels
are never rounded. The vowels /i/ and /e/ have variants that
are very much retracted toward the central position.

APPENDIX B

13.2. SUPPLEMENTARY INFORMANTS[1]

#31. Woman. "Manhattan. Age 78. Descendant of a former president of Columbia College (actually of two presidents--AFH); sister of -------(a well-known novelist and poetess--AFH). Rather precise, aggressive speech, modeled after that of aunts, uncles, and governesses. Tries--not always successfully--to avoid local pronunciations. Somewhat hard of hearing." The Rat selection, extempore conversation, and a selection of sentences.

The mixture of dialects to which Dr. Lowman refers--specifically of metropolitan and Southern British--is very striking. In most words of the ask-group, /aə̆/ occurs, the quality often being rather retracted; but there is /æ/ in answer and /ɛə̆/ in aunt. Into one utterance of grand, /aə̆/ is introduced In the third-group both /ɜə̆/ and /ɜɪ̆/ appear. The informant is unaware that she employs the latter type; in fact, she refers to it as uncultivated, adding that "the well-brought up ones were always scolded for using that sort of expression."[2] Purring, stirred, etc. have only /ɜə̆/. Words of the group represented by rotten and probably have both rounded and unrounded vowels. Among other characteristics that seem due to British influence are the very vigorous articulation of stops, the use of a voiceless somewhat aspirated [t] intervocalically in all but a few cases, the frequent occurrence of tapped [r] intervocalically, the advanced position of [i] and [e], the strongly gliding varieties of /iə̆/ and /ɛə̆/ (although the monophthongal allophones also occur), and the low [ə] in absolute final position in words like brother. The intonation patterns are also suggestive of the same influence.

There are no occurrences of /r/ in the preconsonantal position. The consonant is sometimes omitted at the end of words before a following vowel and the vowel is preceded by the glottal stop; /r/ does not occur in idea, Ida before vowels. The cluster /hw/ does not occur: when, whistle, etc. have /w/. In due, tune /j/ occurs, but not in new. Word-final [l] is sometimes very "clear."

A noticeably lowered [æ] occurs in some words: Alice, carry, charity, family, malice. There seem to be no occurrences of /aə̆/ in the "short o" words: John, log, odd have fairly short vowels. The first element of the diphthong in hour, about is usually well back; in one utterance of the word house it is centralized and suggests the Tidewater type.

#32. Woman. "Manhattan. Age 63. Social Register. Slight, delicate. Precise speech. Summers spent on Long Island." The Rat story, extempore conversation, and a selection of sentences.

There are no preconsonantal occurrences of /r/. The consonant is often absent in word-final position before a following vowel (for example, in *Astor estate*), but contrariwise is pronounced in *idea*. The cluster /hw/ does not occur. /j/ does not appear in *new, due, tune, Stewart*. In words like *heating, theater, eighty*, the intervocalic consonant is usually voiceless. In general, the consonants are firmly and distinctly articulated.

The vowels are placed well forward: there are no centralizations in the front-vowel range, nor noticeably retracted allophones of /aə̆/ and /ɔə̆/. The first element of /oŭ/ in *most, snow, locomotive*, etc. is commonly advanced to the midcentral position and a similar fronting occurs in some words like *school* and *noon* (and also *new* and *Stewart*). In many words like *stern* and *stirred* [ɜ:] appears, its position being farther forward than that of the corresponding Southern British vowel. The word *up* is pronounced a number of times with a very advanced vowel.

Both /ɜə̆/ and /ɜɪ̆/ occur in the *third*-group, both sometimes being used in successive utterances of the same word; the former is more frequent. In *fur, stirred*, and the like, /ɜə̆/ is regular. The *ask*-group rather regularly has /aə̆/, distinct from the syllabics both of *stand* and of *farm*, but there are occasional variations: /æ/ appears in one utterance of *answered* and of *rafters*. /ɛə̆/ is restricted to words like *bared* and *scarce:* words like *ambulance, Astor, handsome* have /æ/, those like *crash* and *pad* longer vowels of the same quality (see page 78). In *doctors, forehead, impossible, want, watch*, the vowel is regularly unrounded. Before voiced consonants in *wise, arrived, behind*, and many other words, the second element of the diphthong is reduced or entirely lost, as it is in many parts of the Southern states. A similar reduction may be observed in the pronunciation of #33.

#33. Man. "Age 55-60. Old Flushing family. Man of leisure. somewhat hard of hearing. Has traveled a good deal." The Rat story, extempore conversation, and a selection of sentences.

There are certain personal idiosyncrasies in the pronunciation of this speaker that are as striking as any regional characteristics. In *Ida, lines, widening, wise*, and some other words the second element of the diphthong is reduced or lost before voiced consonants (this also occurs in the speech of #32). In a number of words (*attractive, back, Lebanon, yes*), the "checked" vowels are drawled under stress in a fashion that is unusual in the metropolitan area.

There is no pattern in the pronunciation of /r/ in the preconsonantal position: it occurs haphazardly somewhat more than one-third of the time. The syllabic allophone of /r/ is

generally used in the *third*-group, although there are several
words in which the /ɜə̆/-type appears, while /ɜɪ̆/ occurs in
German (with only a slight glide). The consonant is pronounced
in *idea*. In *whistle, wheel, anywhere,* /hw/ occurs, but the
other words of this group have /w/. /j/ is pronounced in *due,
new, tune.* There is no affrication of [t-, d-]. The intervocalic consonant in such cases as *gave it up, charity, theater*
is usually voiced, and there are certain other voicings of a
rather odd sort: [ð] in *I think,* [v] in *different.* /θ, ð/
have only fricative allophones.

Raised vowels or diphthongs with a raised first element,
sometimes coinciding with the syllabic of *scarce,* are common
in words like *ask, aunt, crash, glass, half, hand, pad,* and
task; in another occurrence of *aunt* the /aə̆/-type appears.
Both retracted and unretracted varieties of /aə̆/ occur and in
one or two words, although not usually, there is a similar
retraction of /ɔə̆/. In words like *no, over, slowly,* there is
no fronting of the first element of the diphthong. The diphthong in *plows* has a rather advanced first element, but in
most other cases begins at about [a⁺]. In words like *foggy*
and *watched* the vowel is normally unrounded; in *log* and *odd*
it is rather long and presumably /aə̆/.

#34. Man. "Manhattan. Age 85. Excitable and loquacious. Mid-
dle class. Lower Manhattan. After running a drapery warehouse,
he retired and has lived in White Plains in recent years."
Extempore conversation.

There are rare examples of /r/ in the preconsonantal position, but his speech is generally of the "*r*-less" type. The
consonant does not occur in *I saw it.* In *which, why, White-
hall,* and the like, /hw/ is regular--the informant is one of
the few New Yorkers whom I have observed to pronounce consistently in this fashion. In *during, new, substitute,* /j/
does not appear. The alveolar stops are not affricated; /θ,
ð/ have only fricative allophones. The articulation is generally distinct.

Person, service, Turnbull, work, etc. regularly have /ɜɪ̆/.
There is no retraction of the first element of /aɪ̆/, nor any
marked retraction in words like *Armory* and *farms.* In *body,
Bronx, college, doctor, Thomas, want, Washington,* the vowel
is never rounded. Higher low-front vowels (/ɛə̆/) occur in *bad,
draft, fast, half, man, passes, ran, shanty,* and a number of
other words of similar structure. There is no fronting of the
first elements of /oŭ/ and /uŭ/, and the diphthong in words
like *ground* and *bounty* also begins well back. *Fourteenth,
therefore,* and *northern, war* have the same syllabic phoneme,
/ɔə̆/. (This is of course general in the city; I mention it
merely to indicate that the falling together of the two types
is not particularly recent.)

#35. Woman, sister of #36. "Born and raised in Brooklyn, now

lives in Queens. Middle class. Age 55 or a little more." The
Rat story, a short extempore passage, and a selection of sentences.
   The informant's speech is consistently of the "r-less" type
with the exceptions that [ɻ] occurs in some words like *fur*
and *stirred* and appears several times in those like *turned* in
place of the more usual /3Ĭ/. The lip-modification of the consonant is rather marked. In word-final position before a following initial vowel, it is frequently lost and the vowel is
preceded by the glottal stop. The cluster /hw/ does not occur:
whistle, when, etc. have /w/. *New* is /njuŭ/, but /j/ does not
appear in *due, during, tune.* There is some affrication of [t-]
in a few words but it is not very noticeable. In words like
hitting and *little* the consonant is usually voiced; in *theater*
there is a fully articulated voiced stop. At the end of the
syllable before an initial consonant, the voiceless alveolar
stop is often glottalized or the glottal stop is substituted
for it; this appears to be regular before the syllabic allophone of /n/, as in *Martin, rotten, satin.* /θ, ð/ have only
fricative allophones.
   The diphthong /3Ĭ/ occurs in most of the words like *desert*
(vb.), *search, shirk, turnips* (see above). Words like *boisterous, choice, joists, pointed* have only /ɔĬ/. There is no
retraction of the first element of /aĬ/. In *about, ground,
hour, plows,* etc., the diphthong begins rather far forward
and is sometimes nasalized. The monophthongal allophone of
/ɛə̃/ occurs in word-final position in *bear, care, hair.* In
aunt, crash, grass, pad, rafters, scabs, and the like, higher
low-front vowels (/ɛə̃/) are frequent but not regular: pronunciations like [hæ·f] *half,* ['ænsə] *answer* also occur. The
syllabic in *barn, cars,* etc. varies somewhat, being quite retracted in *march* but not in *scars.* There is no noticeable retraction in the case of /ɔə̃/ in *board, called, forth.* In
foggy, lots, rotten, want, etc., the vowel is never rounded.

#36. Man. "Born and raised in Brooklyn, now lives in Queens.
Cashier in a restaurant. Age 60 or a little less." The *Rat*
story, extempore conversation, and a selection of sentences.
   With one or two exceptions, the speaker's pronunciation is
consistently of the "r-less" type. The consonant occurs in
Alabama and *idea,* but is also frequently lost in word-final
position before a following vowel. The noticeable labialization that occurs in his sister's speech is absent. In *whatever, wheel, whether,* etc., /hw/ never occurs. /j/ does not
appear in *due, new, tune.* There are no dental stop or affricate allophones of /θ, ð/. The alveolar stops are not affricated; in *whatever, get off,* and the like, the intervocalic
consonant is rather regularly voiced. Participial forms have
both /ŋ/ and /n/. The tempo is generally rather slow, the articulation much more vigorous in reading than in the conversational passages.

In *hurling, persons,* and all similar words, /ɜɪ̆/ alone occurs; it also appears in *joists,* but the other words of this group on the records have /ɔɪ̆/. There is no retraction of the first element of /aɪ̆/ in *line, primary,* etc., nor are there retracted allophones of /aə̆/ and /ɔə̆/. In *account, crowded,* etc., the diphthong begins somewhat farther back than in his sister's speech. Monophthongal allophones of /iə̆/ and /ɛə̆/ are frequent; [ɛ·] occurs a number of times in absolute final position. Raised vowels or diphthongs with a raised first element, coinciding with the syllabic of *scarce,* are frequent in words like *crash, half, last, pad, rafters, Sands, transportation,* but lower varieties also occur. In one occurrence of *aunt,* the New England /aə̆/-type appears. In *forehead, hot, stop, want, watched,* etc., the vowel is regularly unrounded, and often has a rather advanced position.

#37. Woman. "Manhattan. Age 79. Old Greenwich Village stock. Middle class. Voice normally loud; here subdued at times." Extempore conversation.

There are no occurrences of /r/ before consonants or pauses --her speech is completely consistent in this respect. The cluster /hw/ does not appear: *what, when, where, while* have /w/. /j/ does not occur in *new, knew.* There are no affricated allophones of /t, d/. In cases like *intoxicated, not at all,* the intervocalic consonant is usually voiced. /θ, ð/ are always fricatives.

In *church, concerned, first, girl,* etc., /ɜɪ̆/ is regular; no words like *choice* appear on these records. In *weren't* (disyllabic) the vowel is /ʌ/. In *time* the first element is rather far back, but in the other occurrences of this diphthong there is no retraction. Nor is there any retraction in the case of /aə̆/; on the contrary, in a few words (for example, in *artists*) the Eastern New England type is approximated. In several occurrences of /ɔə̆/ (*all, called, force*), the vowel is somewhat lower than is usual in New York City. The first element of /aʊ̆/ (*Houston, south, county*) varies back to [ɑ˄]; no markedly fronted variants occur. In *not, democracy, Washington,* and the like, the vowel is regularly unrounded. In *after, ask, avenue, can't, classes, fashion,* the vowels are higher low-front.

#38. Woman. "Age about 55. Irish descent. Parents born in lower Manhattan. Grew up in Greenwich Village. Limited education. Strong voice and careful speech. Some speech defects, of which the most noticeable is a labial r." The *Rat* story, a short passage of extempore conversation, and a selection of sentences.

The speaker's usage is quite consistent with regard to the regular absence of /r/ before consonants and pauses; the only exceptions are two occurrences of the word *fur.* The consonant is pronounced in *idea of it.* The cluster /hw/ does not occur:

whistle, wheel, why, etc. have /w/. In one utterance of the word *new,* /j/ appears, but it does not occur in the other words of the same group. The voiceless alveolar stop is sometimes slightly affricated after /n/, but not in other positions. /θ, ð/ have only fricative allophones.

In *girl, certainly, church, shirk,* etc., /3ĭ/ is regular; the diphthong sometimes begins quite far back, [ʌˡĭ]. In *avoid, boisterous, choice, joists, pointed,* /3ĭ/ also occurs. In *stirred* the vowel is somewhat long and advanced, not identical with that of *Hudson, hurried,* and *purring*. The first element of /aŭ/ varies somewhat, once or twice approaching [æ], but is usually farther back. In *forehead, horror, on, opposite, rotten, want, watched,* the vowel is not rounded. There is no noticeable retraction in the case of /ɑə̆/ and /ɔə̆/; the latter occurs in *florist,* which is more commonly pronounced with /ɑ/ in the city. High low-front vowels (/ɛə̆/) appear in a number of words like *answer, candy, crash, stamping,* but there is a good deal of mixture: [æ] occurs in *answered* and *rafters* and a longer vowel of similar quality in *glass* and *task*.

#39. Woman. "Manhattan. Age 60-65. Humble origin. Became a street-singer and evangelist at 16. Speech becomes very unnatural when she puts her preaching manner on." The *Rat* story, extempore conversation, and a selection of sentences.

The occurrence of /r/ in the preconsonantal position is irregular: it appears in somewhat less than one-third of the cases. Usually it is pronounced in *work, service,* and the like, although /3ĭ/ occurs several times. Between vowels, the consonant is often a reduced trill (an affectation) and a similar articulation sometimes occurs after consonants, for example, in *broom* and *Abraham*. It is omitted from the unstressed initial syllables of *prepared* and *prescription;* it appears in *idea*. The cluster /hw/ occurs in one word but is usually absent. There are no affricated allophones of /t, d/; /θ, ð/ are always fricatives. The articulation in general is rather vigorous.

In words like *Amsterdam, aunt, glad,* etc., there is wide variation throughout the entire low-front range. In *happen, matter, palace,* and a number of other words, vowels that are excessively low and retracted occur: [a], [aˡ], and even [ɑ˧] (see pages 59-60). /3ĭ/ appears in *avoid, boisterous, join*. There are affected frontings in *move, spoon, stoop, through* and /j/ actually occurs in *afternoon*. In *doctor, orange, tonic, watch,* etc., the vowel is usually unrounded, but a rounded vowel appears in *gospel* and an exaggerated one in *God*. In *born, called, coarsely, horse, loft,* etc., the vowel is sometimes unusually low.

APPENDIX C

13.3. *TEST SENTENCES*

1. Keep off the grass.
2. He eats like a hog.
3. It belongs to her.
4. She hasn't got whooping-cough.
5. His father gave him a thrashing.
6. I told Mrs. Walsh I was sorry.
7. You're going too fast.
8. They heard the donkey bray.
9. The cat was purring.
10. He whistled to the collie.
11. The Germans thought they were a master race.
12. They collected eight pounds of tin foil.
13. He put the humidor on the mantle.
14. We only make a small profit.
15. It's a very choice cut of lamb.
16. Mrs. Williams made some currant jelly.
17. It's a Scotch plaid.
18. My Dad came here from California.
19. This tonic ought to strengthen him.
20. He raises cabbages and turnips.
21. She swept the floor with a broom.
22. He's a graduate of City College.
23. The song was very popular.
24. The hatchet's in the garage.
25. Norma Talmadge was a movie queen.
26. Donald still goes to grammar school.
27. Take the Eighth Avenue subway.
28. He preferred to buy them by the carton.
29. They put an ad in the *Mirror*.
30. She made him a Waldorf salad.
31. They read about the atomic bomb.
32. Molly wore a satin evening dress.
33. They put molasses syrup on the waffles.
34. Old Mr. Hughes fell down the stairs.
35. The orator made a stirring speech.
36. They rent a loft in the garment district.
37. Which of these is yours?
38. I'd rather live in a chicken coop.
39. She had to buy another curtain-rod.
40. Good Humors now cost a dime.
41. Johnny's a good athlete.
42. It costs twenty-five dollars and seventy cents.

43. Mary made some almond cookies.
44. Look out for the barbed wire.
45. The boy's name was Tom.
46. He hit through short-stop for a three-bagger.
47. They anchored in the harbor.
48. We grow cauliflowers and squash.
49. Get off at the Hoyt Street station.
50. The glass is very fragile.
51. We're not harming them.
52. The answer he gave was wrong.
53. Utah is the home of the Mormons.
54. His average was over three hundred.
55. They've got camels at the Bronx Zoo.
56. He left the ice-tongs in the pantry.
57. Don't be so careless with matches.
58. I don't like this gargle.
59. The compass always points north.
60. It only lasts for an hour.
61. She made a plug of absorbent cotton.
62. He picked a card.
63. Mr. Calvert sells auto accessories.
64. They bound his arms with leather thongs.
65. He hammered it into the soft wood.
66. It was a horrible tragedy.
67. Give him a dollar.
68. The hat was trimmed with ostrich feathers.
69. There's a Catholic church on the corner.
70. The heating coil is damaged.
71. They followed the track through the woods.
72. He bought a barge.
73. His family comes from Oregon.
74. Panama is in the Torrid Zone.
75. He bent one of the prongs of the fork.
76. His aunt forbade him to go.
77. He's always lived here in the borough.
78. Patrick was a very nervous bridegroom.
79. Asia is a big continent.
80. Thursday was a very foggy day.
81. He fractured the bones of his upper arm.
82. I like lobster better than crab.
83. My voice is getting very hoarse.
84. They advertise in the *Daily News*.
85. Some dentists don't like to use gas.
86. She's out with John.
87. Mr. Warren was appointed postmaster.
88. He behaved in a peculiar manner.
89. He cut the roots with an axe.
90. She sent the clothes to the laundry.
91. The width of the street is forty-nine feet.
92. Your father won't argue.
93. The suit's made of good fabric.

94. They took Francis to the hospital.
95. He spoke to Goldfarb.
96. The wax melted in the fire.
97. The pupils were not tardy.
98. It's a branch of the St. Lawrence River.
99. He almost lost his mind.
100. There's a dam at the end of the reservoir.
101. No loitering in this block.
102. They were guarding the prisoners along the road.
103. She bought a can of salmon.
104. The two youths were arrested.
105. He fought with Billy Conn.
106. This ointment's good for sunburn.
107. Everything they had was shared.
108. Somebody sent Barbara a valentine.
109. The Congo River is in Africa.
110. He's the author of this novel.
111. I didn't lose my wallet.
112. I left the magazine in the living-room.
113. The hurricane wrecked the telegraph lines.
114. They put the wreaths behind the coffin.
115. They called Al Smith "The Happy Warrior."
116. They heard the gong in the fire-house.
117. The children played with the calf.
118. Dora was very enthusiastic about it.
119. They wandered along the Palisades.
120. The school is built in the Gothic style.
121. Rosin is made from turpentine.
122. The house wasn't bombed.
123. She heated the broth until it boiled.
124. It was covered with marshmallow sauce.
125. The magistrate issued a warrant.
126. They held a rally in Prospect Park.
127. A lot of foreign ships dock in Brooklyn.
128. You'll find a hanger in the closet.
129. I spoke to Bobby.
130. They knew the words of the chorus.
131. He's reading the memoirs of General Grant.
132. He planted a laurel bush in the back-yard.
133. They took their baths one after the other.
134. They hoisted the piano through the window.
135. Mr. Rogers is on the Grand Jury.
136. The Mayor said burlesque was immoral.
137. He took part in a pageant.
138. There was a throng of people at the door.
139. We believe in only one God.
140. His ancestors came here from Austria.
141. Did you ever see a gadget like this?
142. Mr. Allen will have to withdraw.
143. Let's toss a coin for it.
144. Tomorrow will be August tenth.

145. Seattle's in the state of Washington.
146. He polished his shoes until they were glossy.
147. Danny had a boil on his neck.
148. They were held in quarantine for half a day.
149. He couldn't speak above a whisper.
150. We don't often go on excursions.
151. The wagon got stuck in the bog.
152. He worked up a good lather.
153. The Paramount Theater's in Times Square.
154. Take the Hudson Tubes to Jersey City.
155. He bought some milk at the dairy.
156. I had four cavities in my teeth.
157. The child wasn't harmed.
158. The soap was too harsh.
159. He rubbed the salve into his scalp.
160. She wouldn't marry him.
161. He was born in Athens.
162. That's nothing but a fairy-tale.
163. Don't tamper with the lock.
164. His name is Gordon Babcock.
165. We're planning to leave on Tuesday.
166. His parents were very cross.
167. The manager is Mr. Schwab.
168. Moss grows in damp places.
169. They keep the acid in a special bottle.
170. They dropped flares on the water.
171. I'll tell you as much as I can.
172. Mr. Hamilton lives near Forest Park.
173. The cows are in the pasture.
174. The orchestra never plays jazz.
175. If he has the book, you can borrow it.
176. We'll have to take drastic steps.
177. Robert gave her some candy.
178. She had bobbed hair.
179. There were five telephone booths at the back.
180. The handle of the faucet is loose.
181. Olive oil is very scarce.
182. January has thirty-one days.
183. He gave Madge a coral necklace.
184. The bank has only one guard.
185. I'll give you a written guarantee.
186. He bought a Dodge.
187. Mr. Foster spoke to him casually.
188. He swallowed the aspirin.
189. The moths were dazzled by the light.
190. She's a Hollywood glamor girl.
191. He sold his banjo to Freddie Boyd.
192. I don't like corn on the cob.
193. I need a breath of fresh air.
194. Boston is in eastern Massachusetts.
195. He has to buy the furniture.

TEST SENTENCES

196. They live in Gary, Indiana.
197. He shouldn't have the authority.
198. He was on MacArthur's staff.
199. The quarry is up in Vermont.
200. Laura's dress had a red sash.
201. I'll meet you in the Astor lobby.
202. He took Doris to the Senior Prom.
203. Harold doffed his hat politely.
204. What made Sammy do it?
205. He joined the Officers' Club.
206. I only asked a simple question.
207. The blond girl didn't like the band.
208. Mr. Doyle is our Congressman.
209. The motor was clogged with sand.
210. Mr. Ashley voted for Dewey.
211. We dared him to go into the haunted house.
212. The party was getting pretty boisterous.
213. The class was working on a new project.
214. Mrs. Cooper makes fine apple pie.
215. There was an accident on Fulton Street.
216. They sell them at Namm's Department Store.
217. Radishes don't always agree with me.
218. He won't make any more noise.
219. She put the heating pad on her sore arm.
220. I'm going to buy sóme chairs.
221. We aren't too glad to hear it.
222. They measured the length of the shadow.
223. Sarah gave the boy a quarter.
224. She nearly drove her mother frantic.
225. Amityville is on the South Shore.
226. He's a robber.
227. They blasted right through the rock.
228. The quarrel ended in a stabbing.
229. His forehead was hot and feverish.
230. I think they're giving him blood plasma.
231. This is first quality sausage.
232. The plaster is coming off the walls.
233. They thought it was too much bother.
234. The animals were very little.
235. Tabby was sleeping in the Morris chair.
236. The fair is held annually.
237. We hold these truths to be self-evident.
238. The blow broke his jaw.
239. He was captured at the Mexican border.
240. She's a famous gun-moll.
241. Mathematics is very hard this year.
242. She took a taxicab to the ferry.
243. They tried to camouflage the fort.
244. The four paths all lead to the river.
245. It threw the crowd into a panic.
246. Please reply promptly to this offer.

247. They caught the rabbit in the snare.
248. She sang at Castle Garden.
249. It was Chicago's worst disaster.
250. The fight occurred on Saturday.
251. He got a job running a launch.
252. Mr. Ross examined his record.
253. The photographer bought an enlarger.
254. I'll take a Spanish omelet.
255. It won't do any harm.
256. Nancy was stung by a wasp.
257. They listened to the warblers.
258. They grow a lot of wheat in Kansas.
259. He's in the barn.
260. This is a card-trick.
261. He runs a photographic studio.
262. It was an old paddle-wheel steamer.
263. What's going on?
264. They danced a waltz together.
265. Catherine made a chocolate layer cake.
266. The barrel has three hoops.
267. She's out with Don.
268. He glanced at the picture.
269. He took his shoes to the cobblers.
270. Uncle Sam won't let you.
271. He ordered roast loin of pork.
272. He hurried to the laboratory.
273. His right arm was bad.
274. It hasn't varied for ten years.
275. She laughed but it wasn't very funny.
276. He wrote for a Sears-Roebuck catalog.
277. The only fish they sold was shad.
278. He was initiated into the lodge.
279. They weren't home this afternoon.
280. It's the law of the land.
281. I won the coffeepot in a raffle.
282. The jacket was trimmed with fur.
283. The sheath knife was almost like a dagger.
284. Absence makes the heart grow fonder.
285. The boys scared the daylights out of him.
286. Lard is made from pork fat.
287. They caught a cod.
288. They put some brandy in the hot toddy.
289. She stuck them into her shopping bag.
290. They went to see the Dodgers.
291. They hung the hammock on the porch.
292. Mr. Todd got madder and madder.
293. They calculated the height of the building.
294. There's a huge cavern under the cliff.
295. Our flag was still there.
296. He got some stamps at the post office.
297. I took a cold bath this morning.

298. An adder is a poisonous snake.
299. They staged a mock air battle.
300. He's in the hod-carriers' union.
301. He was saddened by his mother's death.
302. This whiskey comes from Scotland.
303. Tadpoles grow up to be frogs.
304. They nailed down all the laths.
305. His right arm was bared.
306. He deals in clams and oysters.
307. He certainly looked worn and haggard.
308. Agnes was an orphan.
309. The girl's nickname was Barbie.
310. This is a codfish.
311. The tablecloths were soiled.
312. They saw the horse's hoofprints.
313. I don't like these goggles.
314. Patricia aggravated the teacher.
315. He got a room at the Hotel Taft.
316. February 12th is Lincoln's Birthday.
317. Mrs. Savage takes in boarders.
318. He split the log into two halves.
319. They're dragging the pond for the trunk.
320. They caught some mackerel and some sea bass.
321. She read about Goldilocks and the Three Bears.
322. It's a cure for asthma.
323. There are too many mouths to feed.
324. The gangster had a tommy-gun.
325. He owned a big shaggy dog.
326. We're not bombing them.
327. It's pulled down by the force of gravity.
328. It's a passionate love story.
329. Look at the doll.
330. The Kentucky Derby is a racing classic.
331. They grappled for his body.
332. He's a barber.
333. They sent her a basket of oranges.
334. Give it to Carl.
335. She couldn't unravel the yarn.
336. Anna is afraid she has goiter.
337. It's made of a new kind of plastic.
338. He was an honor student at Erasmus Hall.
339. He's not as strong as Daniel.
340. They soaked the roof with gasoline.
341. Let him try it if he dares.
342. He gave Florence a vanity case.
343. His hands were covered with soot.
344. It's an old-fashioned watch.
345. She did a big wash.
346. The plane vanished into the fog.
347. Fasten it very firmly.
348. Your father will flog you.

349. He's gone to London.
350. She's a cashier at Wanamaker's.
351. Passengers must not talk to the driver.
352. They were prodding the prisoners along the road.
353. They made a bronze casting.
354. There's a lavatory on the fifth floor.
355. This is the parlor.
356. We've got halibut and red snapper.
357. The raspberry sherbet made him sick.
358. He bought a watch-fob.
359. The clasp was bent and broken.
360. His speech was full of oaths.
361. Do you want some mashed potatoes?
362. They went into a long passageway.
363. The girl was drowned in the surf.
364. She put some chopped walnuts into the taffy.
365. I did it because Mr. Murray told me to.

NOTES

GENERAL OBSERVATIONS

1. *American Speech*, XVII (1942), 30-41, 149-157; *Quarterly Journal of Speech*, XXXIII (1947), 314-320; *An Introduction to the Phonetics of American English*. (For full bibliographical information regarding books and articles cited in this study see the Selective Bibliography.)
2. The same point is made by Hans Kurath in his review (*Language*, XX [1944], 150-155) of the Kenyon and Knott *Dictionary*.
3. *Quarterly Journal of Speech*, XXXIII (1947), 319-320.
4. *American Speech*, XVII (1942), 33.
5. For the symbols used in this study, see pp. 15-16, 18-19.
6. *Quarterly Journal*, XXXIII (1947), 318.
7. Classifications arrived at in this way will often not coincide with those found in books of another sort, whose purpose is to inculcate an artificial standard as being alone "correct." We have had a plethora of such books in New York and the end of them is not yet in sight. Their authors have a pronounced bias in favor of Southern British English and their standard might be called a Mid-Atlantic one, having its local habitation about fifteen hundred miles north-east-by-north of Ambrose Light. "General American" is in their eyes a provincial dialect, barbarous and uncouth. So far as the speech of the city itself is concerned, they find little to praise except their own bizarre way of speaking. In their books, consequently, pronunciations which are common in the cultivated usage of the city are very frequently condemned.
8. *Language*, p. 81.
9. All my informants are monoglot speakers of English and the children of such speakers (for one minor exception, see the biographical notes on Informant #28, p. 116). In most instances English has been the only language spoken in the family for a number of generations. In a few cases, however, the first language of one or more members of the grandparental generation was German or French (the details are given in section 13.1). For the reasons suggested below, I have not used anyone as an informant in whose family Yiddish or Italian was once employed. Many New Yorkers, of course, whose grandparents spoke one of these languages speak English in a fashion which is quite free from foreignisms; but so many do not that I thought it wise to exclude such persons entirely.
10. The notion that dentalization and the affrication of certain allophones of /t/ and /d/ are due to the influence of Yiddish is discussed on pp. 25-26.

11. I must mention here the three exceptional cases which
I have come upon. Two were students whose parents were born
in Liverpool; in their speech the occurrence of the stop in
singer and the like was rather obviously not a foreignism,
but a survival of Lancashire dialect. The third case I simply have no explanation for: on the records made by Informant
#29 a weakly articulated stop appears in a few words like
running. But I would stress how completely unusual the informant's usage is in this respect.

INFORMANTS, METHODS, AND SYMBOLS

1. See George L. Trager and Bernard Bloch, *Language*, XVII
(1941), 223-246.
2. *Language*, XVIII (1942), 228-237.

THE CONSONANTS

1. In this study the terms "initial" and "final," when applied to phones, refer to position in syllables. When it is
necessary to refer to word-initial or word-final position,
these terms will be qualified.
2. Positional variants of other consonants (/b, k, s/,
etc.) with similar lip-modifications may also occur; in the
following sections the existence of such variants will be
taken for granted and not specially mentioned in each case.
3. The sequence: stressed vowel plus /f/ plus alveolar
stop plus unstressed vowel (*lifting, lift it*) is similar.
4. The assertion is made by Charles F. Hockett (*Language*,
XVIII (1942), 10, n. 11) that this problem really does not
exist. He says that "if a phone *a* in a certain position is
in complementary distribution with two other phones *b* and
c," either it resembles one of the two more than it does the
other and should be classified accordingly; or it is "exactly half-way" between the two, in which case a separate phoneme must be posited. But practical problems are not always
solved by such a formulation, for two observers may well
disagree as to whether *a* really sounds more like *b* or more
like *c*. (Hockett, for example, assigns the stop in *spill* to
/p/, in part because it is, he says, a fortis; but Twaddell
describes it as a lenis.)
5. But, attempting to be consistent, I would also employ
/p/, /t/, and /k/ in transcribing phonemically my own pronunciation of *disburse, misdemeanor,* and *disgust*.
6. It is sometimes possible, when working with recorded
material, to engage the needle in such a fashion that one of
these words is split right after the [s]. The word *boisterous*,
for example, can be so split on the record made by one of my
informants and the end of the word repeated at will. What results sounds like [driᵗs, driᵗs, driᵗs...]--the stop seems
voiced to my ears.

One further fact may be of interest to the reader. I have
carried out a little experiment with half a dozen children
who were old enough to pay attention but who had not yet
learned any spelling. I made it clear to them by examples
that when I said the first part of a word they were to finish it. Five of the six replied as follows:
Q. "When I talk this way *(whispering)*, I'm talking in a
whis--?"
A. " [bʌ] " or " [br̩]."
Q. "When you eat too much candy and your stomach is upset,
you have indiges--?"
A. " [dʒin]."
Q. "People call your mother 'Mrs.' They call your father
'Mis--'?"
A. " [dʌ] " or " [dr̩]."
Q. "Now look at what I'm doing to your wagon (*lifting it
up*). I'm lif--?"
A. " [diŋ]."
7. See Nathaniel M. Caffee, p. 128 in *Studies for William
A. Read*.
8. *Outline*, par. 499.
9. Several of my informants aspirate the initial voiceless
stops very heavily; see section 13.1.
10. Metropolitan speech does not differ in this respect
from those other types of American English with which I am
familiar and a similar statement, I feel, might be made
about them. Underlying the assertion that "voiced *t*" is distinct from /d/ in the tacit assumption that the intervocalic
consonant in *ladder* is a fully articulated voiced stop,
which is rarely the case. For an excellent study of usage in
another American dialect, see Victor A. Oswald, Jr., *American Speech*, XVIII (1943), 18-25.
11. In my own pronunciation and in that of some other New
Yorkers I believe that I not infrequently hear differences
in the length of the stressed vowels in pairs like *writer*
and *rider*, like those which occur in *write* and *ride;* in
pouter and *powder* I think I often make a similar length-
distinction. (I have not observed this difference in the
case of /i/, /e/, /æ/, /ɑ/, /ʌ/, and /u/: *bitter-bidder,
betting-bedding, latter-ladder, allotted-melodic, butting-
budding, putting-pudding.*) In so far as such differences
exist before identical consonants, a rigorous analysis would
presumably require the positing of two vowel phonemes in
each case of the sort. But the difference, if it is real, is
slight and one cannot be altogether sure that he is not im-
agining it. The subject is one that might profitably be in-
vestigated by instrumental methods.
12. Laterally and nasally ploded allophones of /t/ may
also occur before the nonsyllabic forms of /l/ and /n/ in
the emphatic articulation of words like *Scotland* and *witness*.
More commonly, however, the pressure behind the stop is weak

and, as the sides of the tongue or the velum drops down, no particular explosive effect is heard. In such sequences the stop sounds more like the unreleased variety heard in *that box*.

13. E. H. Babbitt in 1896 reported (*Dialect Notes*, I [1896], 464) that in uncultivated speech the voiceless stops were strongly aspirated, and added that "in the case of [t] the aspiration sometimes suggests an [s]."

14. In C. K. Thomas' "Jewish Dialect and New York Dialect" (*American Speech*, VII [1931-1932], 321-326), the question of a particular "substratum" language is left open, but it is nevertheless asserted that dentalized blade-articulation and the affrication of [t—] is Jewish dialect. His position is criticized by Robert Sonkin (*American Speech*, VIII, No. 1 [1933], 78-79).

15. By Dr. Max Weinreich of the Yiddish Scientific Institute.

16. The syllable-final [t] of Yiddish is often heavily exploded, frequently with an affricate release. This is another matter, however; see n. 19 below.

17. It is rather difficult to produce an alveolar tap with the blade of the tongue when the tip is pressed against the lower teeth. One sometimes hears, both in words like *city* and in those with orthographic *d* like *ladder*, a blade-articulated fricative, which might be described impressionistically as a distorted [ð]. I have observed this chiefly in the speech of Jewish students, which rather surprises me since I have not been able to learn of any similar articulation in Yiddish.

18. Babbitt (*Dialect Notes*, I [1896], 464) says that "a substitution of the glottal catch ... for [t] in words like *letter, butter* ... is common, though by no means regular, among the school-children." This is not true of contemporary pronunciation: the occurrence of the glottal stop in this position is very unusual.

19. But the regular affrication of the final stop seems to be a foreignism, and specifically a Yiddicism. As I have already indicated, this is the normal practice of Yiddish; and many persons who are bilingual in English and Yiddish or are the children of such bilingual speakers carry the practice over into English.

20. The contracted forms are pronounced in a number of ways by uncultivated speakers: for *didn't* I have heard ['didn̩(t), 'didən(t), 'ditn̩(t), 'di?n̩(t), din(t)] and, as a result of assimilation to a following velar stop, [diŋ], for example in *He didn't go yesterday*. In some cases, oral plosion is probably a foreignism. The nasal plosion of stops does not appear to occur in Italian, for example, and I have noticed that students who hear Italian at home often have particular difficulty with words like *didn't* and *wooden*. (Pronunciations like ['wudən], of course, are sometimes consciously employed by persons who have somehow or other acquired the notion that they are "more correct.")

21. *Action* and *lecture* may contain the same intervocalic sequences in less cultivated speech. See p. 43.
22. *Dialect Notes*, I (1896), 464.
23. But when the cluster /fθs/ in *fifths* is simplified, it is the /f/ which is lost more often than the /θ/.
24. Compare John Samuel Kenyon, *American Pronunciation*, sec. 185.
25. This is a not uncommon pattern in the speech of Columbia College freshmen who come from the city. In the 1890's Babbitt (*Dialect Notes*, I [1896], 464) reported that these uncultivated pronunciations did not occur at all in the speech of Columbia students, which is certainly not true today.
26. *Outline*, pars. 710-711.
27. *American Pronunciation*, sec. 189.
28. *Outline*, figs. 97, 98.
29. One rarely observes anything like the protrusion pictured in Jones' photograph, *Outline*, fig. 101. But exceptionally, when a syllable beginning with /ʃ/ is pronounced with emphatic stress or when a name like *Charlotte* or *Sheila* is spoken lento, as in reproach, the rounding and protrusion may be exaggerated.
30. Kenyon (*American Pronunciation*, sec. 195) says that in "ordinary speech" *miss you* is not /ˈmis juǔ/, but /ˈmiʃuǔ/, implying that the unassimilated pronunciations are not heard, or are very rarely heard, in natural speech. This seems to me a considerable exaggeration.
31. The Kenyon and Knott *Dictionary* gives only a British pronunciation for *Sydenham*. In New York City the name of the hospital in West Harlem is /ˈsaɪdn hæ̃m, – hɛ̃m/.
32. A complete spelling-pronunciation of this word, namely /ˈhoǔmədʒ/, is often used by students in reading.
33. I have departed from the usual practice here and classified /r/, /l/, /w/, and /j/ under one general rubric. All of them are voiced frictionless consonants in initial position, but in any initial cluster the first member of which is an aspirated stop, the phonemes are represented by voiceless fricatives. Such a classification seems to me neater than Kenyon's arrangement of /r/, /w/, and /j/ in one group, the glides, and of /l/ along with the nasals in another group, the sonorants.
34. Several of my informants, for example, #20 and #30, use phones of this sort.
35. *American Speech*, X (1947), 111.
36. One may occasionally hear pronunciations of *very* without the consonant from speakers whose articulation in general is extremely indistinct, but they are rare and untypical.
37. For these variations, see pp. 85, 63, 86. For the occurrence of the syllabic allophone of /r/, see below in this section.

38. Hans Kurath has stated that the best formulation of the usage of the "r-less" dialects is to set up a phoneme /r/ whose allophones include a [ə]-like vocalic glide and a "zero variant." (See *Studies for William A. Read*, p. 171.) According to this formulation, both [kɑ·r] and [kɑš] ([kɑ·]) are to be analyzed as containing /r/, and /r/ also appears, if I understand him correctly, in the "r-less" pronunciation of words like *stork* (and hence in *stalk* too, when this is homonymous). Leaving the question of phonetic similarity out of account, it may be noted that this conception requires that words like *fearing, sharing, barring,* and *pouring* be analyzed as containing an anomalous sequence /rr/, thus complicating the morphology." But even when a dialect may be described in such terms as these, it seems a rather confusing and cumbersome way of ordering the phonetic facts. Here, as in other cases where nothing is to be gained by innovating, I prefer to retain the older and more familiar formula.

39. See Jones, *Outline*, par. 757.

40. In my comments on the individual informants, I have noted the fact whenever I have observed them to pronounce /r/ in words of the group discussed here.

41. *Outline*, par. 760.

42. I can remember learning as a boy to avoid the pronunciation /ˈdrɔšrəŋ/ because of the criticism of my parents. But I cannot remember ever being criticized for pronouncing /r/ in words like *china*. No one ever seemed to notice it after an unstressed vowel.

43. Among my informants, #31 is the only one in whose speech this type of articulation occurs.

44. It is not the most common type on all levels and in all age-groups. Among Columbia College undergraduates, the most frequent pattern is the mixed one referred to in the next paragraph of the text.

45. Thomas (*American Speech*, XVII [1942], 154) says: "None of these intrusive [r]-colorings seem to depend on the presence of an initial vowel in the following word; they are quite as likely to occur before consonants or at the ends of phrases." This seems to me an overstatement.

46. The varying pronunciation of words like *cord* and *harm* might reasonably be expected to result in the occasional introduction by such speakers of /r/ into words such as *fraud* and *balm*. (See Robert J. Menner, *American Speech*, XII [1937], 167-178.) On my records the pronunciations [ˈθi·rtəz] *theater's* (Informant #14) and [kɑ·rb] *cob* (Informant #4) occur, but such hypercorrect forms are surprisingly rare.

47. *American Pronunciation*, sec. 311.

48. *Outline*, par. 833.

49. In the speech of those few persons who pronounce /j/ in words like *lunacy* and *absolute*, this type may also occur in the cluster /lj/.

50. In the speech of Informant #31, the word-final [l] is often very "clear."
51. See Jones, *Outline*, pars. 659, 662, and 274, n. 14.
52. For a similar pronunciation in Bermuda, see Harry Morgan Ayres, *American Speech*, VIII, (1933), 3-10.
53. Or a single phone, the voiceless labio-velar fricative.
54. Among my informants, #1, #8, and #34 are the only ones who regularly pronounce /hw/; several others do so occasionally. It may be that the /w/-pronunciations have become much more frequent in the past two generations. In 1896, F. H. Babbitt wrote (*Dialect Notes*, I, 464): "*wh* is not infrequently voiced, though the rule is for the voiceless sound, as in most parts of America." But even among very elderly New Yorkers, I have observed few who consistently pronounced /hw/.
55. *American Speech*, XVII (1942), 154.
56. Most of the texts written by the local teachers of elocution condemn this homonymy as an error, a fact which I find rather odd in view of the well-known predilection of these teachers for Southern British English.
57. For a similar observation, see William Cabell Greet, *American Speech*, VI (1930-1931), 403.
58. I am told that in some parts of the country this pronunciation may be heard in cultivated, but old-fashioned speech. In the city I have observed it only a few times, and always in the usage of persons of limited education.
59. On my records there are a few instances of /j/ being introduced into words like *afternoon*. Such hypercorrect pronunciations similarly indicate that the use of /j/ is often adopted and not part of the speaker's "natural" habits.
60. In less cultivated speech, the consonant is sometimes very much weakened in such words and the preceding vowel shows compensatory nasalization. For the parallel weakening or loss of /n/, see the next section.
61. But I have very rarely heard /n/ in place- and family-names like *Reading, Wheeling, Harding,* and *Pershing*.
62. A true palatal or alveolo-palatal nasal may be heard as an individual abnormality in unstressed final syllables (*reading, nothing,* and the like). The speakers who use it pronounce the normal velar after stressed vowels. Among my informants, #5 pronounces in this fashion.
63. The occurrence of /ŋ/ in such words is undoubtedly the result of assimilation and not of hypercorrect pronunciation. The frequently mentioned use of /ŋ/ in words like *kitchen* and *captain* by less cultivated speakers who are attempting to avoid /n/ in the participial forms I have never observed in New York City.

THE VOWELS AND DIPHTHONGS OF STRESSED SYLLABLES

1. There is nothing specifically metropolitan about this: as Jane Zimmerman has remarked (*Proceedings, Second Con-

gress, p. 299), it is rather generally true of American English that the front vowels, compared with those of Southern British, tend to be shifted somewhat toward the central position.

2. E. H. Babbitt, writing fifty years ago, described the vowel pronounced by many uncultivated speakers as "high-mixed or mid-mixed" and very close to the Eastern New England or Southern British vowel of *her, bird (Dialect Notes,* I [1896], 461). It is doubtful whether anyone would hear much resemblance between these vowels today. I might add that I have read and reread Babbitt's article with a good deal of bewilderment. Undoubtedly, very considerable changes can occur in a given dialect in the course of a half century, but some of the pronunciations which Babbitt speaks of as being very common in the 1890's I have not heard even in the speech of persons born before the Civil War. Certain of his statements were almost surely erroneous; see below, p. 142, n. 26, for an example.

3. When Thomas writes *(American Speech,* XVII [1942], 32): "The vowel [ɛ] is less often centralized than in upstate speech or the downstate speech of Babbitt's time," he and I are probably not speaking of the same thing. With one exception the words he cites are ones in which the vowel is followed by /r/. Now, the centralization and "*r-coloring*" of [e] in words like *very,* which is so frequent in many types of American English, is relatively rare in New York City. But the rather retracted placement of the vowel, before all consonants including /r/, is rather common.

4. The few examples of other vowels in these words reported by Thomas (*ibid.*) are, I imagine, chiefly from the other downstate counties. I have not heard the pronunciations mentioned from New Yorkers, with the exception of /eɪ̆/ in *eggs,* which I have once or twice noticed.

5. For this pronunciation in earlier English, see Otto Jespersen, *Grammar,* I, 3.114. It occurs several times on my records. I myself used to pronounce /ˈredəʃ/, as do the older members of my family.

6. Thomas's statement that the vowel is sometimes "relatively high and tense" (*American Speech,* XVII [1942], 32) results from a failure to make the proper phonemic analysis. These higher, tenser vowels occur, but they are not /æ/. (See the next paragraph.) A similar failure results in his recording of /e/ as frequent in words like *careless,* which is likely to suggest to those unfamiliar with metropolitan speech that many New Yorkers pronounce *careless* and *zealous* as rimes. The use of [e] in such words does occur in the speech of those whose first language is Yiddish: Yiddish-speakers often do not hear the length-distinctions of New York English (for example, the one is *pock-park, shop-sharp*) and so substitute [e] for /ɛə̆/. But the substitution is always a foreignism.

7. For the references, see p. 143, n. 39.
8. But *chocolate* is an exceptional word; see below and p. 84.
9. But see below and p. 84 for /oʊ̆/ in some of these words. And see p. 82 for the occasional riming of *sorry* and *starry*.
10. In these two words, /ɑ/ is rather common among New Yorkers of foreign parentage, in whose speech /ɑ/ often occurs also in certain other words, for example in *accompany, come, some*. In the pronunciation of those whose first language is not English [ɑ] is of course one of the regular substitutes for /ʌ/, however spelled.
11. But there are occasional "stylistic" distortions in uncultivated speech in which the quality may approach that of [ɑ], for example in *Shut up!, Cut it out!*
12. *American Speech*, XV (1940), 372-376.
13. When the vowel is noticeably longer and has a glide, so that *blood* and *blurred* are not identical, another phoneme must be posited. See p. 86.
14. For the common pronunciation of this word and *aren't* as disyllables, see p. 46.
15. As I have noted in section 13.1, several of my informants, for example #27 and #30, frequently pronounce these retracted variants.
16. New York students often question the transcriptions in the Kenyon and Knott *Dictionary*, where the equivalent of /i/ is usually employed in words of this type.
17. *American Pronunciation*, sec. 120, and "Guide," *Webster*, sec. 68.
18. See Jones, *Outline*, par. 437, n. 20, and *Dictionary*.
19. I have already dealt with this matter in *American Speech*, XV (1940), 372-376. Certain minor inaccuracies in that article are corrected in the following pages and above on p. 63.
20. A number of my informants have very mixed patterns in the pronunciation of these words. See my comments on their usage in sections 13.1 and 13.2.
21. Also to be included are *Berkeley, Berkshire, clerk, derby, Jervis*, the element *-worth* in names like *Leavenworth, Wadsworth, Wordsworth,* and lastly the word *hearth*, which a few of my older informants pronounced so as to rime with *birth*.
22. In the speech of a few uncultivated speakers, *enjoy* seems to be an exceptional word. I have occasionally heard diphthongs like [ɜɪ], [ʌɪ] pronounced in it when it was followed by an initial consonant, as in *Enjoy yourself*.
23. Several years ago Professor V. A. Oswald first called my attention to the usage of certain New Yorkers who occasionally pronounced words like *hurt* and *hate* alike. (For diaphones of /eɪ/ with a very retracted first element, see p. 65.) These persons do not ever regularly and consistently pronounce such words as homonyms, but the more advanced

varieties of the one diphthong and the more retracted varieties of the other may sometimes coincide. I was interested to note that in a story written in "New Yorkese," published in *The New Yorker,* John O'Hara represents the metropolitan diphthong, not by the usual *oi*-spelling, but by *ai* and *ey*. (See "The Heart of Lee W. Lee," *The New Yorker,* September 13, 1947, pp. 29-31.)

24. A woman from the Bronx whom I interviewed briefly furnishes an extreme example. In *birth,* she pronounced a diphthong close to my [ɔɪ̯] but with less rounding; in *words,* she pronounced one close to my [eɪ̯] but with a slightly more retracted first element.

25. It is actually more common than I indicated in my former article.

26. Babbitt *(Dialect Notes,* I [1896], 463), after remarking that the New York diphthong "is very close to the French sounds heard in *feuille,"* adds: "I used to get some New York boy to pronounce *fir* to illustrate the French sound in my classes." This statement is rather bewildering. For /ɜɪ̯/ *never* occurs in words like *fir,* even in the speech of those who were already adults when Babbitt wrote. (Nor is it pronounced in such words by Coastal Southern speakers who employ the diphthong in *worse* and *earn.*) It is possible that what Babbitt really did was to have the student pronounce *first* and then repeat, dropping the final consonants.

27. As I have indicated on p. 5, I have several times heard pronunciations like /ɜɪ̯l/ *oil* from elderly speakers of a cultivated sort, but their practice was quite unusual.

28. This statement may be illustrated by reference to the usage of Columbia College freshmen who come from the city. Of this group it may be said that the majority speak neither cultivated English nor the most extreme forms of uncultivated New Yorkese. In their speech such metropolitan characteristics as the blade-articulation and the affrication of alveolar stops, the use of a dental affricate or dental stop in place of the initial fricative [ð], and the strong retraction of the first element of the diphthong in *time* are rather common. But the occurrence of /ɜɪ̯/ in *join, oil, oyster* is much less frequent, although not unknown.

29. This explanation of the occasional occurrence of [r̩] and [r̩ɪ̯] in words spelled *oi* is essentially that advanced by Menner in *American Speech,* XII (1937), 167-173. In my earlier article I criticized this explanation on the grounds that "those speakers who use r-colored vowels in words like *coil* did so only in these words and not in words like *curl."* I have since realized that when I heard an /ɜɪ̯/-speaker occasionally pronounce [kr̩l] for *curl,* nothing registered because I am used to this pronunciation; but that when he pronounced *coil* in the same way, it struck my attention immediately.

30. For example, *goiter* was pronounced [ˈgʌidə] by Informant #30.

NOTES

31. I transcribe with [æŭ] a diphthong, fairly common in metropolitan speech, particularly among younger speakers on the less cultivated levels, whose first element coincides with the vowel in *hat*. It must be remembered that this vowel is a somewhat lower and more retracted one than that which appears in *hat* in many other types of English (see p. 59). This New York diphthong is, therefore, not phonetically identical with one occurring in many parts of the South that is usually transcribed in the same fashion.

32. *Dialect Notes*, I [1896], 462.
33. See Jones, *Outline*, pars. 430-433.
34. *Fellow* is a partial exception, as in other regional types of English, since even the cultivated may reduce the vowel in familiar pronunciation. The pronunciation /'θʌrə/ for *thorough*, common in Southern British, I have rarely heard. *Borough* is sometimes /'bʌrə/ in phrases like *Queensborough Bridge*.
35. *Dialect Notes*, I (1896), 462.
36. These transcriptions are taken from Jones' *Dictionary*. In this work [əː] is the mid-central vowel of *third* and the asterisk is employed to represent the word-final variety of /r/, which is omitted before a consonant or a pause.
37. In the pronunciation of place-names in *-shire*, /iə̆/ is rather regularly used, with a few exceptions. In *New Hampshire* and *Chesire*, /-ʃə(r/ is probably the commoner pronunciation and is certainly so in educated speech. The unstressed vowel may also be heard, although less frequently, in other names of two syllables. In longer names, where the final syllable tends to be pronounced with secondary stress, /-ʃə(r/ is rare: I have not often heard it, for example, in *Worcestershire sauce*.

Spelling-pronunciations with /-ˌʃaĭə(r/ may sometimes be used by the less educated. I have heard *Berkshire* pronounced /'bɜ̆ĭkˌʃaĭə(r/ a number of times by the train-announcers at the New York Central's Harlem Station.

38. Often /-'piĭn/ in uncultivated pronunciation. The loss of /ə/ between a high-stressed diphthong and /n/ may also be observed in a frequent uncultivated pronunciation of *ruin* as /ruŭn/, riming with *moon*, and of *giant* as /dʒaĭnt/, riming with *pint*.
39. *American Speech*, V (1929-1930), 396-400, IX (1934), 313-315, XV (1940), 255-258; *Le Maître Phonétique*, LXXIV (1941), 17-18.
40. /ʒ/ is not included because it does not occur under these conditions after low-front vowels.
41. This group includes /εə̆s/ in the sense of "buttocks," which is not distinguished in pronunciation or spelling from *ass*, the animal.
42. But /æ/ in *Anna;* see below.
43. In the usage of many less cultivated speakers, the vowel in this word is actually followed by /v/, the stop

being omitted. Note that the short form, *ad*, is a word in which /ɛə̆/ may occur.

44. In the speech of many, *grammar* and *Grandma* constitute a minimal contrasting pair.

45. The name of the actor *Cary Grant* furnishes a rather odd illustration of differences between various metropolitan dialects. I, like many educated speakers, pronounce it [ˈkɛ·riĭ græ·nt]. Many of my students reverse it, as it were, and pronounce [ˈkæ·riĭ grɛ·nt].

46. Informants #1, #31, and #32 may serve as examples. In their speech, with insignificant exceptions, [ɛə̆, ɛ·] occurs only in words like *care* and *various*.

47. A number of my informants pronounce in this fashion. See my comments in sections 13.1 and 13.2.

48. A not untypical illustration is furnished by a woman student at the University who, while reading "Dover Beach" before a class, pronounced the words *land, strand, sand* in such a fashion that no one of them rimed with either of the others. Variation like this is extremely common in the speech of a number of my informants.

49. *American Speech*, XVII (1942), 32.

50. See my comments on the usage of Informant #37.

51. Not, of course, in the small group of words represented by *clerk* and *Berkshire*.

52. But /æ/ is more common, I think.

53. In this word /æ/ is unusual in New York speech.

54. But in *Colorado* I pronounce a short vowel, namely /ɑ/, and I have noticed that some other New Yorkers make a similar distinction. A half-dozen of my older informants pronounced *Alabama* as /ˌælə'bɑə̆mə/.

55. Also occasionally pronounced with /æ/ and /ɛə̆/.

56. But /eĭ/ is more frequent. I have not heard /æ/ in New York City. The short vowel /ɑ/ may sometimes occur.

57. Pronunciations that would be considered hypercorrect in British English may occasionally be heard. Informant #31, for example, pronounced /ɑə̆/ once in *grand*. I have heard similar pronunciations of *fancy* and *circumstance*.

58. But Informant #27 pronounces /ɑə̆/ in *codfish* and *hod carrier*.

59. Babbitt (*Dialect Notes*, I [1896], 462) recorded this word and *harmony* as homonyms. Possibly he took as a feature of the New York dialects something that is actually a foreignism: speakers whose first language is Yiddish often make mistakes through a failure to hear the difference in length between /ɑ/ and /ɑə̆/.

60. To be sure, the occurrence of /ɑə̆/ is not as frequent in cultivated speech; there is in particular less tendency to pronounce it in the derivatives of more than one syllable.

61. Although not unknown: see my comments on the speech of Informants #4 and #31.

62. The diphthong, as it is pronounced by some uncultivated speakers, occasionally sounds to the observer as though it began at a point *considerably* above higher low-back. I have heard the word *law*, for example, spoken in such a fashion that it seemed almost to coincide with my own pronunciation of the word *lure*. This impression, however, may be due in part to the strong rounding with which the first element is often produced.

63. A certain degree of retraction may occasionally be observed in the speech of several of my cultivated informants.

64. In less cultivated speech, the not infrequent vocalization of [-l] results here in a diphthong that is leveled under /oŭ/. The pronunciation /'oŭˌweĭz/ is very common. A similar pronunciation may be heard for *almost*.

65. Occasionally pronounced with /ʌ/, although this pronunciation is not so common as it is in some other types of American English. For the final consonant in this word, see p. 40.

66. I have sometimes heard /æ/ in this word from elderly speakers. Informant #30 pronounced it as /'fɛəsət/.

67. Sometimes pronounced with /ɑ/; in *Lawrence*, /ɑ/ is very common. And in words like this, in which both /ɑ/ and /ɔə̆/ are widely used, compromise pronunciations with [ɒ] are especially frequent.

68. This word is rather unusual: it is often pronounced by less cultivated speakers with /ɑ/, riming with *cobbler*, and also occasionally with /ɑə̆/.

69. See Jespersen, *Grammar*, I, 13.355.

70. In my family *lawn mower* is /'loə̆nˌmoə̆(r/. I have not observed, however, whether this pronunciation is used by other speakers.

71. See Jones, *Outline*, pars. 460, 466.

72. Monosyllabic pronunciations of these words (/dʒuŭl, kruŭl/) are not confined to uncultivated speech.

73. Among my informants, /ɜə̆/ is regular in the speech of #1, appears very frequently in the speech of #31 and #32, and occurs sporadically in the pronunciation of a few others.

THE VOWELS OF WEAK SYLLABLES

1. See *Outline*, par. 257, n. 7, and par. 262; *Dictionary* under *become, chieftain, devil, horrible, hundred, jewel, report*, and *system*.

2. See, for example, Jespersen, *Grammar*, I, 9.111, 9.113, 9.12, 9.141, 9.142, 9.143, 9.52, 9.53, 9.553, 9.63.

3. See "Introduction," section 91, and the body of the dictionary under *be-, de-, e-, -ed, -es, -ess, -est, -et, -ity, pre-, re-, se-*.

4. The frequent occurrence of [ə] in these syllables was noted a half century ago in metropolitan usage by C. H. Grandgent (*Die Neueren Sprachen*, II [1895], 449) and by E. H.

Babbitt (*Dialect Notes*, I [1896], 461). In these articles Grandgent was referring to cultivated, Babbitt to uncultivated usage.

5. Babbitt, *ibid.*, after referring to the frequent occurrence of [ə], adds: "A noteworthy exception is -tion, which is often pronounced [ʃin]." Two paragraphs further on he notes: "In *can* the weak form is [kin], which is often kept even under accent." He does not mention any further examples.

6. Vowels also occur that lie outside the range approximately set by the retracted lower high-front, and the intermediate mid-central positions. For example, there is [e] in one pronunciation of words like *exchange, embrace, entirely*; [æ] in one pronunciation of *advisory*; a monophthongal [o] in one pronunciation of *window-sill*; [uŭ] in *tissue*, and in one pronunciation of *unite*. It is debatable, however, whether in these cases one may properly speak of the vowels as being completely unstressed.

7. Throughout this section, when words like *desert* are cited, it is their "*r*-less" pronunciation which is referred to.

8. When such syllables are distinguished, it is by the reintroduction of full-grade vowels, not by the use of [i] and [ə].

9. Here, as in some other cases, a distinction may often be present in lexical pronunciation that disappears in connected speech.

APPENDIX A: PRIMARY INFORMANTS

1. In this section and the next the exact order of listing is without significance, but in a general way I have put the more cultivated informants first.

2. As the biographical comments show, this informant is a New Yorker of the upper middle class, of the third college-educated generation in his family. There are certain features of his pronunciation, however, which I have rarely observed in the speech of others of comparable background. The rather heavy aspiration of the voiceless stops is one of these; the occasional appearance of pronunciations like [stæ̆z] *stairs* is another.

3. In New York speech this substitution is not a dialect-feature, as it appears to be in uncultivated London English, but an individual idiosyncrasy.

4. It is possible that such pronunciations, sometimes at least, are hypercorrect. I have pointed out on pp. 75 and 78 that many speakers consider pronunciations like [mɛ̆s] *mass* and [dʒɛ̆z] *jazz* ugly and uncultivated; such persons may as a result of this feeling sometimes substitute [æ̆] for [ɛ̆] in words like *stairs*.

5. I mean by this that she employs the [w]-like [r], often made with a marked protrusion of the lips, which occurs in all varieties of English as an individual abnormality. This

phone is to be distinguished from the New York dialect-[r] described on pp. 45-46.

6. A number of assimilations occur of a sort which rather puzzles me. They all involve the assimilation of a final voiceless consonant to an initial voiced one: examples are [laɪ̆g ðis] *like this,* [spoŭg 'nʌθiŋ] *spoke nothing,* [tug 'daris] *took Doris.* In the introductory section I have made my general attitude plain regarding the question of foreign influence on New York English. In this particular case, however, I must record the fact that I have observed this type of assimilation chiefly in the speech of Jews, and I understand that it is common in Yiddish.

7. The assimilation of [ð-] to [-ŋ] is never complete. The result is [n-].

APPENDIX B: SUPPLEMENTARY INFORMANTS

1. The biographical information inclosed within quotation marks is from Dr. Lowman's notes. Ages are given as of 1941.

2. Here I would like to record the odd fact that many cultivated New Yorkers who employ /ɜɪ̆/ believe that they pronounce these words as "everyone" does and hear the less cultivated varieties of the diphthong as [ɔɪ̆], just as a Middle Westerner might.

SELECTIVE BIBLIOGRAPHY

13.4. In this section I have listed only those books and articles to which reference has been made in the text.

Ayres, Harry Morgan. "Bermudian English," *American Speech*, VIII (1933), 3-10.
Babbitt, E. H. "The English of the Lower Classes in New York City and Vicinity," *Dialect Notes*, I (1896), 457-464.
Bloomfield, Leonard. Language. New York, Henry Holt & Company, 1933.
Caffee, Nathaniel M. "Some Notes on Consonant Pronunciation in the South," Studies for William A. Read, pp. 125-133. Baton Rouge, Louisiana State University Press, 1940.
Grandgent, C. H. "English in America," *Die Neueren Sprachen*, II (1895), 443-467.
Greet, William Cabell. "A Record from Lubec, Maine, and Remarks on the Coastal Type," *American Speech*, VI (1930-1931), 397-403.
"Guide to Pronunciation," Webster's New International Dictionary, 2d ed. Springfield, Mass., G. & C. Merriam Company, 1934.
Haugen, Einar, and W. F. Twaddell. "Facts and Phonemics," *Language*, XVIII (1942), 228-237.
Hockett, Charles F. "A System of Descriptive Phonology," *Language*, XVIII (1942), 3-21.
Hubbell, Allan F. "'Curl' and 'Coil' in New York City," *American Speech*, XV (1940), 372-376.
Jespersen, Otto. A Modern English Grammar. 3d ed. Part I. London, George Allen & Unwin, 1928.
Jones, Daniel. An English Pronouncing Dictionary. 4th ed. New York, E. P. Dutton & Company, 1937.
——— An Outline of English Phonetics. 6th ed. New York, E. P. Dutton & Company, 1940.
Kenyon, John Samuel. American Pronunciation. 8th ed. Ann Arbor, George Wahr, 1940.
——— and Thomas Albert Knott. A Pronouncing Dictionary of American English. Springfield, Mass. G. & C. Merriam Company, 1944.
Kurath, Hans. "*Mourning* and *Morning*," Studies for William A. Read, pp. 166-173. Baton Rouge, Louisiana State University Press, 1940.
——— Review of A Pronouncing Dictionary of American English, *Language*, XX (1944), 150-155.
Menner, Robert J. "Hypercorrect Forms in American English," *American Speech*, XII (1937), 167-178.

Oswald, Victor A., Jr. "'Voiced T'--a Misnomer," *American Speech*, XVIII (1943), 18-25.
Sonkin, Robert. "In Re 'Jewish Dialect and New York Dialect,'" *American Speech*, VIII, No. 1 (1933), 78-79.
Thomas, Charles Kenneth. An Introduction to the Phonetics of American English. New York, The Ronald Press Company, 1947.
——"Jewish Dialect and New York Dialect," *American Speech*, VII (1931-1932), 321-326.
——"The Place of New York City in American Linguistic Geography," *The Quarterly Journal of Speech*, XXXIII (1947), 314-320.
——"Pronunciation in Downstate New York," *American Speech*, XVII (1942), 30-41, 149-157.
—— "Pronunciation in Upstate New York," *American Speech*, X (1935), 107-112, 208-212, 292-297; XI (1936), 68-77, 142-144, 307-313; XII (1937), 122-127.
Trager, George L. "A Note on [æ] and [æ^{1}·] in American English," *Le Maître Phonétique*, LXXIV (April-June, 1941), 17-18.
——"One Phonemic Entity Becomes Two: the Case of 'Short A,'" *American Speech*, XV (1940), 255-258.
——"The Phoneme 'T'--a Study in Theory and Method," *American Speech*, XVII (1942), 144-148.
——"The Pronunciation of 'Short A' in American Standard English," *American Speech*, V (1929-1930), 396-400.
——"What Conditions Limit Variants of a Phoneme?" *American Speech*, IX (1934), 313-315.
—— and Bernard Bloch. "The Syllabic Phonemes of English," *Language*, XVII (1941), 223-246.
Zimmerman, Jane Dorsey. "Representative Radio Pronunciation in America," Proceedings of the Second International Congress of Phonetic Sciences, pp. 291-302. Cambridge, Eng., Cambridge University Press, 1936.

WORD INDEX

abandon, 2
abbot, 76
Aberdeen, 76
aborigine, 87
absolute, 138
absolutely, 54, 76
absorb, 2
absorbent, 83
academy, 76
accent, 59
accept, 80
accessory, 30, 89
acclaim, 50
accompany, 141
account, 29
acid, 76
acme, 87
action, 30, 43, 137
actual, 43
actuary, 59
acute, 72
ad, 144
Adam, 23
Addison, 76
adhesion, 40
adhesive, 40
adjective, 76
adopt, 27, 28, 37
advertise, 76
advertisement, 143
advisory, 146
affectation, 76
Africa, 76
after, 76
afternoon, 139
again, 59
against, 59
aggravate, 76
agony, 76
Alabama, 144
album, 89
ale, 75, 78
Algeria, 74
all, 51
allotted, 135

almond, 80
almost, 71, 83, 145
along, 84
always, 71, 82, 145
am, 76, 78
Amherst, 42
Amityville, 77
among, 89
ampere, 77
an, 76, 89, 90
ancestors, 89
anchored, 89
ancient, 56
and, 76
anger, 60
angry, 31
Ann, 76
Anna, 143
Annie, 76
annihilate, 42
annoy, 69
anxious, 89
anything, 56
aperture, 43
apostle, 84
apothecary, 84
apparatus, 60
apply, 50
appoint, 20
appointed, 88
appreciative, 66
apt, 22
arbitrarily, 59
aren't, 46, 141
argue, 80
arm, 49
armature, 46
arrange, 44
arrested, 88
Arthur, 36, 48
as, 41, 76, 89
Asia, 41
ask, 2, 16, 75, 76, 79, 80
asphalt, 76
ass, 144

assume, 72, 73
Astor, 76
at, 23, 36, 89
Athens, 76
athlete, 76
-ative, 66
Atlantic, 77
atom, 23
atomic, 81, 89
attain, 23, 26
attempt, 18
August, 83, 89
aunt, 80
austere, 74
Australian, 90
Austria, 83
author, 83
authority, 35, 82
auto, 83
avenue, 76
average, 89
awning, 84
azure, 60, 76

back, 59
bacon, 57
bad, 76
badge, 76
badges, 76
bag, 76
baggage, 78
Bali, 80
balm, 81, 138
band, 77
bandage, 77
banded, 87
bandied, 87
bandstand, 28
banner, 77
barb, 80
barbed, 61, 82
bared, 76
bargain, 81
barn, 2, 61
barracks, 89
barrage, 44
bat, 16
bath, 76
bathe, 38
bathed, 36
bathing, 38

baths, 35, 76
batter, 60, 76
battle, 24
be, 88
be-, 145
beard, 6, 18, 48, 49, 74
beautiful, 87
beauty, 53, 54, 73
because, 40, 83, 87
become, 145
bed, 59
bedding, 135
Beekman, 30
beer, 73
beg, 59
beige, 41
Belden, 28
believe, 87
bell, 50
Belmont, 61
belong, 84
Berkeley, 86, 141
Berkshire, 86, 141, 143, 144
berth, 68
Berwick, 51
best, 16
bestial, 43
bet, 59
betray, 87
betting, 135
bid, 6, 15
bidder, 36, 90, 135
big, 58
bigger, 31
bill, 58
Bill, 50
bind, 55
Bingham, 42
bird, 139
Birmingham, 42
birth, 36, 85, 86, 142
bitter, 36, 90, 135
blade, 38
blame, 50
blast, 22, 38
blithe, 35
Blodgett, 81
blood, 62, 141
blower, 85
bluer, 85
blur, 63

WORD INDEX

blurred, 63, 141
boarder, 83
boasting, 20
boat, 71
bob, 80
Bob, 80
bobbed, 61, 80, 82
Bobbie, 80
bobcat, 81
body, 81
boil, 3, 70
boisterous, 89, 134
bold, 50
Bollard, 81
bolted, 24
bomb, 81, 82
bombed, 81
bomber, 81
bombing, 82
bon-bon, 81
bond, 81
bondage, 81
bonfire, 81
boogie-woogie, 64
book, 85
Boone, 72
boot, 72, 73
booth, 34, 36
booths, 35
border, 83
born, 83
borough, 143
borrow, 82
bosh, 81
bosom, 64
boss, 84
Boston, 24, 27, 84
Boswell, 81
botch, 61
bother, 81
bottle, 14, 17, 27, 32
bought, 83
box, 61
boy, 68, 69, 70
boyish, 68, 69
boys, 69
brag, 76
bragging, 76
branch, 43, 77
bray, 22
breadth, 25, 28, 29

breath, 29
breathe, 38
breed, 38
brewer, 85
British, 24
Bronx, 84
broom, 64
brooms, 55
broth, 62, 84
brother, 38
budding, 27, 135
builds, 39
bulb, 50
bulge, 44
bullion, 50
Burnham, 42
burst, 68, 70
business, 40
but, 32
butcher, 43, 64
Butler, 36
butter, 28, 33, 136
butting, 135
button, 32, 36
buy, 22
by-and-by, 55

cab, 22, 77
cabbage, 23, 76
cabbages, 89
cabin, 55
cabin-boy, 22
caddy, 76
cage, 44
California, 83
calm, 80
came, 55
camel, 77
camera, 47
camouflage, 41
camp, 77
can, 58, 76, 146
Canada, 77
candy, 77
canoe, 29
cap, 59, 60, 77
captain, 139
captured, 89
car, 30, 46, 47, 71, 80, 138
carburetor, 53
card, 3, 61, 80

card-trick, 81
care, 75, 144
cared, 49
careless, 88, 140
cares, 48
Carolina, 46
carried, 87
carrier, 58, 87
carries, 87
carry, 46, 60, 78, 87
cars, 48
cart, 3, 7, 60, 80
Cary, 78, 144
cascade, 76
cash, 76
cashable, 76
cashier, 76
Cashman, 76
casserole, 40
castle, 76
casual, 76
catch, 59
Catherine, 76
Catholic, 36
cattle, 28
caught, 41, 83
caught you, 43
cauliflower, 83
celestial, 43
cemetery, 59
center, 24
cerebral, 65
chalk, 62
channel, 77
Chapman, 22
chariot, 87
Charlotte, 89, 137
Chatham, 42
Cheshire, 143
chew, 55
chewer, 85
chic, 65
Chicago, 80
chicken, 30
chieftain, 145
chin, 43
china, 47, 138
chip, 15
chipped, 24
chock, 62
chocolate, 62, 84, 141

chorus, 83, 84
Christian, 43
Circe, 87
circulate, 54
circumstance, 77, 144
city, 23, 24, 28, 58, 87
claim, 29
clam, 55
Clara, 47
clean, 55
clear, 10, 50, 74
clearer, 74
clearness, 75
clerk, 86, 141, 144
cliff, 33
cliffs, 33
climbed, 55
clique, 65
close, 40, 41
closet, 88
cloth, 84
cob, 138
cobbler, 81, 145
cod, 3, 61, 80
codfish, 80, 144
Coentes, 58
coffee, 62, 84
coffin, 84
cogwheel, 81
coil, 5, 67, 69, 70, 142
cold, 28
collar, 50, 51, 61, 71
college, 44, 89
collie, 81
Colorado, 144
column, 53
combatant, 60
come, 141
comfort, 55, 61
comfortable, 61
comical, 81
comma, 81
commandment, 77
communist, 53
compacts, 24
compare, 29
compass, 61, 81, 89
conclusion, 57
concourse, 56
conference, 56
confidence, 56

Congo, 84
congratulate, 43
Congreve, 56
Conn., 81
Connecticut, 12, 89
conquest, 56
conscious, 43, 56
constable, 61
Constable, 61
Constance, 81
continent, 81
convent, 59
conversation, 56
cookery, 29, 30
coop, 64
Cooper, 64
cooperative, 66
copper, 61
coral, 62, 82, 84
cord, 138
corner, 83
corrupts, 24
corsage, 41
cost, 20, 23, 84
costume, 84
cot, 7, 60
cotton, 24, 27
cough, 84
could, 90
couldn't, 28
counter, 24
coupon, 54
courage, 63
course, 2
court, 49, 67
courtesy, 23
crab, 22
creamed, 28
creative, 64, 72
creek, 65
crew, 29
Crimean, 74
crises, 87
cross, 84
cruel, 85, 145
cube, 29, 53, 73
cubic, 54
cuckoo, 64
cud, 17, 86
cultivate, 24
culture, 50

cumulative, 66
cup, 49
cupful, 22
curb, 68
curd, 17, 86
cured, 49, 85
cures, 48, 85
curing, 85
curiosity, 85
curious, 85
curl, 5, 67, 68, 69, 142
current, 63
custard, 48, 89
customary, 59
cut, 16, 62, 63, 71, 141

Dad, 76
Daddy, 76, 78
dagger, 77
Dahl, 80, 81
daily, 65, 75, 78
dairy, 75
Daly, 75
damage, 77, 89
damp, 2
dance, 2
dancing, 77
dandruff, 77
daren't, 46
data, 60
daub, 83
daunt, 83
dawning, 84
de-, 58, 145
deaf, 65
dear, 47
dearer, 6
decay, 27, 28
declare, 87
decorative, 66
deeply, 50
defend, 87
de Kalb, 22
delirious, 58, 74
demolish, 81
den, 15
dentist, 89
department, 31, 87
depth, 22, 34
derby, 86, 141
desert, 89

WORD INDEX

desolate, 40
desolation, 40
dessert, 28
destroy, 69
destroyer, 67, 68
devil, 145
devouring, 71
diarrhea, 74
dictionary, 46, 59
didn't, 28, 29, 136
dig, 31
dime, 27, 28, 37
ding-dong, 84
diphtheria, 34
diphthong, 34
dirigible, 12, 13, 58
disable, 40
disarm, 40
disaster, 40
disburse, 20, 134
discretion, 29
discussed, 20
disdain, 40
disgust, 20, 29, 40, 134
dish, 40
dishonest, 40
dishonor, 40
dismay, 40
disorder, 40
disown, 40
disperse, 20
dissolve, 81
distinguish, 31
district, 24
ditch, 43
divine, 87
do, 72
docile, 84
doctors, 39
dodge, 81
dodged, 81
Dodgers, 44, 81
dodging, 81
doer, 72, 85
doff, 84
dog, 6, 31, 62, 84
doggerel, 84
dogma, 31
doll, 61, 80, 81
dolly, 81
dolphin, 81

Dominic, 81
don, 81
Don, 81
Donald, 81
donkey, 63, 145
Donna, 26
doom, 72
door, 83
Dora, 47, 62, 84
drab, 76
drabness, 76
dragged, 30
draw, 45
drawing, 138
dreariest, 87
drill, 45
dry, 27
dubious, 53, 87
duchess, 89
due, 53
durable, 85
Durham, 63, 85
during, 63, 85
duty, 54, 72
dwarf, 52
dwindle, 52

e-, 145
eagle, 65
ear, 74
earl, 69
easily, 87, 89
eastern, 24
eccentric, 30
-ed, 145
edged, 44
educate, 44
effective, 87
efficient, 87
eggnog, 80
eggs, 59, 140
eighth, 25, 27, 35
either, 38
election, 87
elongate, 84
else, 38
embrace, 146
emperor, 46, 47
emphasis, 55
empire, 67
employer, 67, 69

WORD INDEX

employs, 69
empty, 55
endanger, 59
engagement, 57
engine, 58
engineer, 58
England, 31
English, 31
enjoy, 69, 141
enjoyable, 68
enjoyed, 68, 69
enlargers, 81
enrage, 55
enthusiasm, 53, 54, 72
entirely, 146
err, 59
erring, 59
-es, 145
-ess, 145
essential, 87
-est, 145
esthetic, 38
-et, 145
eternal, 87
ether, 36
European, 74, 143
evasive, 87
everything, 56
exaggerate, 76
except, 59, 89
excessive, 89
exchange, 146
exclusion, 40
exclusive, 40
exhale, 42
exhaust, 42
exhibit, 42, 59
exhort, 42
exophthalmic, 34
experience, 74
exploit, 69
explosive, 40
extinguisher, 31

fabric, 76
failure, 65, 75, 78
fair, 16, 75
fairer, 75
fairest, 46
fairly, 75
fairness, 75

fairs, 75
fairy, 75
faith, 27
false, 83
family, 77
fan, 76
fancy, 77, 144
fanning, 76, 77
Fanning, 77
far, 16, 18, 46, 79
fare, 75
Farley, 81
fashion, 76
fasten, 76
father, 81
fatter, 76
faucet, 60, 83, 144, 145
fear, 10, 16, 74, 75
feared, 75
fears, 75
feathers, 89
February, 53
feeble, 50
feel, 10, 74
feeling, 56
fellow, 71, 143
felt, 24
Ferguson, 68
ferry, 75
feud, 54
fewer, 85
field, 50
fierce, 74, 75
fifths, 137
fifty, 33
fight, 37
filch, 43
fill, 10, 15, 33, 51
filth, 51
finding, 28
fine, 16
finger, 31
fir, 142
firm, 68
first, 49, 65, 142
five, 34
flag, 79
flame, 33, 50
flare, 78
Florence, 82
flounder, 24

fluid, 55
fluidity, 72
fly, 9
fog, 80
foggy, 80
folded, 24
folly, 81
fond, 81
food, 16
foot, 63
for, 63, 83
forbade, 65
force, 83
Fordham, 42
forehead, 61
foreign, 61, 82
forest, 82
fork, 18
forty, 83
forward, 71
fossil, 84
Foster, 84
four, 83
fracture, 43
fractured, 89
Francis, 77, 89
frankfurter, 64
fraud, 82, 138
free, 33, 45
fricassee, 40
friend, 28
friendly, 56
fringe, 44
from, 45, 63
frost, 84
froth, 35, 84
fruition, 72
full, 63
Fulton, 24, 27
fundamental, 28
fur, 46, 68, 86
furniture, 46
furry, 63, 69, 86
furs, 48, 69
further, 38, 68

gadget, 76, 88
Galilean, 74
garage, 41, 44
garb, 7, 9, 80
garble, 81

gargles, 7, 60
garrulous, 53
Gary, 78
gasoline, 76
gasp, 76
gasping, 76
gather, 60, 76
gaunt, 83
gazed, 28
genius, 90
genre, 41
geography, 81
giant, 143
give, 15, 30, 34
glad, 78, 79
glare, 30
glass, 50
glimpse, 55
glittered, 48
glossy, 84
glue, 55
go, 71
goal, 72
gob, 7, 9, 80
gobble, 81
god, 9, 80
goddess, 82
goggles, 7, 60, 81
going, 56
goiter, 69, 142
golden, 28
gone, 84
gong, 84
Gordon, 83
gosh, 81
gospel, 84
got, 61
Goth, 84
Gotham, 84
Gothic, 84
gnaw, 85
graduate, 88
graft, 76
Graham, 42
grammar, 77, 144
grand, 144
grandma, 144
Grant, 144
grass, 76
grassy, 76
gravel, 76

WORD INDEX

greatest, 89
green, 30
Greenwich, 43, 51
groom, 64
grovel, 81
guard, 9, 80
gubernatorial 53, 54

habit, 76
had, 42, 76, 78
haggard, 76
hair, 10, 75
half, 33
ham, 76, 77, 78
hammer, 55, 77
hammock, 89
hams, 76
hanged, 56
hanger, 56
happen, 22
happily, 87
happiness, 87
hard, 49, 66, 79
Harding, 139
harm, 81, 82, 138
harmony, 144
harsh, 80, 81, 82
Harwich, 51
has, 39, 42, 76, 78
hat, 70, 77, 143
hatchet, 88
hate, 141
hath, 76
haunted, 83
have, 33, 34, 42, 76, 78
Haverhill, 42
hazard, 76
he, 42, 88
health, 51
healthy, 51
hear, 17, 46, 73
heard you, 44
hearing, 73, 74
hearth, 141
heathen, 55
hedgehog, 42
height, 35
heir, 43
he'll, 74
her, 42, 63, 140
herb, 43

here, 18, 42, 46, 73, 74
he's, 41
hid, 58
hidden, 28
hide, 37
high, 66
him, 42
his, 42
historical, 42
hit, 18, 58
hoarse, 3, 72, 83, 84
hod carrier, 81, 144
hog, 80
hoggish, 80
hog-tied, 82
hoisted, 88
hold, 15
holiday, 65
hollow, 81
homage, 43, 137
home, 42
home town, 55
hominy, 81, 144
homogenize, 81
honest, 43, 81
honor, 43
honorarium, 59
hoof, 64
hoop, 64, 72
hoptoad, 61
horizon, 42
horrible, 61, 82, 145
horrid, 82
horror, 46, 47
horse, 3, 83, 84
hospital, 32, 84
hostler, 43
hot, 70, 79
Hotchkiss, 61
hotel, 42
hotly, 61
hour, 43
house, 16, 70
household, 42
hovel, 81
hover, 81
how, 70, 71
Hoyt, 69
huge, 42, 53, 54
hugging, 31
humble, 43

humidor, 53
humor, 54
humorous, 42
hundred, 12, 27, 45, 145
hundredth, 35, 38
Huron, 53
hurricane, 89
hurry, 63, 86
hurrying, 87
hurt, 65, 141

I'd, 66
idea, 2, 47, 73
idiosyncrasy, 56
I'll, 66
illusory, 40
I'm, 66
imaginative, 66
imagine, 76, 89
in, 56, 89, 90
inclosure, 57
Indiana, 77
indigestion, 135
initiate, 65
initiative, 66
insurance, 85
insure, 40
irk, 68
is, 89
issue, 41
it, 24, 89
it's, 27
-ity, 145
I've, 66

January, 53
jar, 15
jazz, 76, 78, 146
jazzing, 76
Jersey, 68
Jervis, 86, 141
Jesus, 40
jewel, 85, 145
job, 44, 80, 82
jobber, 80
John, 81
Johnnie, 81, 82
join, 67, 69, 70, 142
joint, 3, 67
jollity, 81
Joseph, 40

josh, 81
joy, 67, 68
June, 55

Kahn, 81
keen, 15
keg, 59
Kerr, 86
khaki, 80
kiddie, 23
kill, 20
kind, 29, 30
kindly, 56
Kirsch, 43
kitchen, 139
kite, 66
kitten, 27, 32
kitty, 23
knife, 66
knock, 61
knowing, 89

ladder, 23, 76, 135, 136
lagging, 31
Laird, 75
land, 144
language, 31
lantern, 24, 32
lapse, 22
Larchmont, 61
large, 9, 61, 80, 81
lark, 80
lasso, 12, 72
lathe, 35
lather, 76
laths, 35
latter, 23, 135
laud, 84
laugh, 76
laughable, 76
laughter, 76
launch, 83
launder, 21
laundry, 83
Laura, 83
laurel, 83
lavatory, 83
lavender, 24
law, 3, 47, 48, 67, 82, 83, 138, 145
lawn mower, 145

WORD INDEX

Lawrence, 62, 145
lawyer, 67, 68
Lazerus, 76
learn, 5, 11, 69
leave, 34
leaving, 55
lecture, 30, 43, 137
leer, 74
leg, 30, 59
length, 56
lengthen, 56
Lenox, 12, 89
Leonard, 89
let, 23, 27
let's, 27, 32
letter, 33, 136
lewd, 54
liberty, 23
life, 50
lift, 15, 134
lifting, 134, 135
lifts, 24
light, 23
lilacs, 12, 61
linger, 10
lingerie, 65
literature, 43, 46
little, 28
live, 34
lived, 34
liver, 34
liverwurst, 12
lives, 34
load, 50
loafer, 47, 48
lobby, 81
lobster, 81
lodge, 9, 61, 62, 80, 81, 82
Loeser, 12, 41
loft, 62, 84
log, 6, 80
logging, 80
loin, 5, 11, 69
loiter, 69
loll, 81
lollipop, 81
London, 28
loneliness, 87
long, 84
look, 31
looses, 87

loot, 72
lord, 84
lore, 47, 138
loss, 84
lost, 84
loved, 28
lower, 85
loyal, 68, 69
luckily, 87
Lucy's, 87
lugubrious, 54
lunacy, 53, 138
lunatic, 54
lunge, 44
lure, 145
luxurious, 41
lyceum, 74

mad, 76
madder, 76
maddest, 76
Madeleine, 76
Madge, 76
madly, 76
magazine, 76
majestic, 44
make, 29
maker, 29, 30
mammoth, 89
man, 2, 76
manly, 76
manning, 77
Manning, 77
mannish, 76
Mansfield, 77
mansion, 77
manual, 77
manure, 72
march, 66
marshmallow, 59, 71
Mary, 75
mashed, 40
mass, 76, 78, 146
Massachusetts, 76
massage, 41, 44
masses, 76
massing, 76
mast, 76
match, 59, 60
math, 76
mathematics, 76

matinee, 24
Maurice, 83
McCloskey, 84
me, 64, 88
measure, 59
medal, 28
meddle, 24
Medea, 74
meet, 36
meet you, 43
melded, 24
melodic, 135
Melpomene, 87
melted, 24
mere, 74
merely, 6
merry, 75
message, 38
metal, 24, 28, 29, 32
method, 36, 37
mill, 16, 55
Milly, 6
mirror, 6, 58, 74
misdemeanor, 134
miserable, 42
misery, 42
miss, 38
mission, 40
miss you, 137
Mister, 135
misty, 23
mob, 22
modern, 28, 81
moire, 12, 65
molasses, 89
Molly, 61
monger, 12, 61
monophthong, 34
monotone, 81
month, 55
months, 34
moon, 72, 143
Moorish, 85
moral, 62, 82, 84
more, 83
Mormon, 83
morning, 83, 84
Morrill, 82
Morris, 82
Mosholu, 81
Moslem, 81

moss, 84
moth, 84
mother, 36, 38
moths, 35
motto, 61
mountain, 24, 32
mourning, 72, 83, 84
mouths, 35
much, 43
Muriel, 85
mush, 43
music, 89
mute, 53, 54, 73
myriad, 74
myrtle, 24
mysterious, 58, 74
mystery, 23
mythical, 34

nagger, 77
naphtha, 33
Nathan, 55
near, 73, 74
nearly, 73, 74
neglect, 87
Negro, 65
neologism, 64
nephew, 33
nest, 16
Nevada, 80
new, 16, 53, 54, 55, 72, 73, 86
New Hampshire, 143
newspaper, 39
nihilism, 42
ninety, 26
Noah, 85
noise, 16, 68, 69
nominative, 66
nonsense, 59
noon, 64, 72
Norma, 83
north, 83
northern, 38
Norwich, 43, 51
not, 32, 60
nothing, 36, 56
Nottingham, 42
nourish, 63
novel, 81
now, 71
now-a-days, 71

WORD INDEX

oaths, 35
object, 59
obscure, 53
obvious, 34
occur, 16, 86
occurred, 17, 86
occurrence, 63, 69
of, 34, 63
off, 84
offer, 84
office, 62, 84
officer, 62, 84
officers, 89
offices, 89
official, 33
often, 84
Ogden, 27, 28
oil, 14, 69, 142
olive, 61, 66, 81
Oliver, 81
Omaha, 80
omelet, 66
on, 55, 61, 81
once, 38
onion, 53
only, 56
open, 22, 55
ophthalmia, 34
ophthalmologist, 34
ophthalmology, 34
oracle, 84
oral, 62, 72, 83
orange, 62
orator, 62, 82, 84
orchestra, 47, 59, 83
ordered, 83
Oregon, 82
origin, 82
orphan, 83
Oshkosh, 81
ostrich, 43, 84
Oswald, 81
other, 28, 38
our, 71
ours, 71
out, 32
oven, 55
over, 88
overture, 43
Ovid, 81
oxen, 61

oyster, 142

package, 31
paddle, 28
pajamas, 80
pale, 75
pan, 6
pansy, 77
paramount, 61, 71
parent, 78
park, 140
particular, 53
passing, 78
passionate, 76
path, 36, 76
paths, 35, 60
Patricia, 21, 65
paunch, 83
paw, 20, 83
peace, 16
pedal, 24
pen, 6
pencil, 89
penniless, 87
penny, 26
Peoria, 64
percolate, 54
percolator, 54
perhaps, 21, 45
period, 58, 74
periodic, 87
Pershing, 139
Persia, 41, 68
persuasive, 40
pet, 65, 75
petal, 24
pew, 54, 72
photograph, 76
photographer, 81
photographic, 76
piano, 64, 71, 72
picture, 88
pier, 75
Pierce, 74
piercing, 73
pill, 20
pin, 6
pint, 143
pipe, 66
pit, 15, 16, 73. 87
pitiful, 87

164 WORD INDEX

plaid, 20
planner, 47
planted, 88
plasma, 76
plastic, 76
play, 50
pleasure, 41
pock, 140
pocketbook, 27
pod, 80
poise, 68, 69
pole, 50
policy, 81
pollen, 61
pomp, 81
pompadour, 81
poor, 16, 20, 46, 85
poorer, 85
poorly, 48, 85
population, 53
porch, 83
pork, 83
port, 48
poses, 87
posies, 87
possible, 2, 84
poster, 21
pot, 16, 66
pound, 20, 21
pouter, 135
powder, 135
power, 71
pre-, 58, 145
prefer, 87
prehistoric, 42
prepare, 87
prepared, 45
prescription, 45
pretend, 87
pretty, 26
prisoners, 89
probably, 23
procedure, 44
profit, 20, 84, 88
projectile, 89
prong, 84
prosecutor, 84
puberty, 54
pubic, 54
pudding, 135
pulpit, 63

pure, 20, 53, 72
purity, 85
purr, 63
purse, 68
push, 16
putting, 135

quarantine, 82
quarrel, 82
quarry, 82
quart, 83
queen, 29, 52
Queensborough, 143
question, 20, 41, 43
quick, 52

rabbit, 76
radiator, 60, 87
radio, 27, 60
radish, 12, 13, 59, 140
radium, 87
raffle, 76
raft, 33
rafter, 33
rafters, 76
rag, 76
ragged, 30, 76, 78
raise, 39
raised, 39
raises, 89
ram, 76
ramble, 77
ramming, 76
ransom, 78
rare, 46
rather, 80
ration, 60
rattle, 28
re-, 58, 145
reached, 43
reaction, 64
read, 28, 41
reading, 56, 89
Reading, 139
real, 74
reality, 64
really, 74
rear, 46
recognize, 31
recuperate, 54
red, 44, 49

WORD INDEX

reduce, 87
reed, 10
reel, 74
regime, 41
regret, 87
regular, 53
rehabilitate, 42
relation, 50
remunerative, 66
report, 87, 145
resign, 44
resource, 40
resourceful, 40
resume, 53, 54, 72
return, 14
revolver, 81
ribs, 22, 23
rid, 10
ride, 9, 15, 66, 135
rider, 135
rigging, 31
right, 23, 32
ring, 56
ripeness, 22
risk, 20, 38
risky, 29
riveter, 23
road, 16
robbed, 22
robber, 22
Robert, 81
rock, 60, 62
rod, 28
rode, 71
Rogers, 81
romp, 81
rompers, 81
roof, 64, 72
room, 64
root, 64
rosin, 81
Ross, 84
rotten, 61
rouge, 41
rouged, 41
rower, 85
royal, 68, 69
rub, 23
rubbing, 55
rude, 38
rugs, 30

ruin, 143
rule, 55, 73
runner, 55
running, 17, 134
runs, 39
rupture, 43

sack, 60
sad, 28, 76, 78
sadden, 76
saddle, 76
said, 27
sail, 65, 75, 78
sailor, 75, 78
salad, 27, 90
salt, 83
salve, 76
salves, 76
Sam, 76
same, 65
Sammy, 76
Samoa, 85
Sampson, 55
sand, 144
sandwich, 43, 56
sapphire, 76
Sarah, 45, 75, 78
sarsaparilla, 12, 13, 76
sat, 60
sauce, 83, 84
saunter, 83
sausage, 83
savage, 76
Savarin, 76
savior, 34
saw, 48
Sawyer, 67, 68
say, 65
scarce, 48
Schermerhorn, 12, 13, 58
school, 29
science, 67
scoff, 84
Scotland, 36, 135
scrawl, 29, 45
se-, 145
seal, 38
search, 43
seasonal, 89
seat, 64
secret, 23

secretariat, 59
security, 85
seduce, 87
see, 64
seed, 64
selective, 87
sell, 51
seminary, 46
sender, 24
series, 74
serious, 74
seriously, 74
serve, 68
seven, 55
seventy, 24, 55
shad, 76
Shah, 47, 80
shallow, 60
share, 46, 75
shared, 75, 76
sharp, 7, 48, 60, 80, 82, 140
she, 88
sheaths, 35
sheer, 73
Sheila, 137
she'll, 74
shine, 40
ship, 15
ships, 22
-shire, 143
shirt, 68
shoe, 72
shone, 84
shop, 7, 60, 82, 140
shopping, 21
shores, 48
short, 83
should, 90
shrill, 40, 45
shut, 141
shuttle, 24
sickness, 30
signature, 31
silly, 74, 87
Sinatra, 47
since, 55
sing, 16
singer, 10, 31, 134
singing, 31
single, 31
sings, 56

sinker, 10
sit, 25, 27
sixths, 34
skill, 20, 21, 90
slant, 77
sleep, 50
slight, 38
slipper, 21, 22
slipping, 55
slumber, 21
small, 83
smooth, 36, 38, 55
snail, 55
sneer, 74
soap, 15
soda, 16, 17, 71
sofa, 47, 48, 88
soft, 84
Sol, 81
solid, 81
Solomon, 81
solvent, 81
some, 141
Somerset, 59
something, 55, 56
sonata, 47
song, 84
soon, 64
soot, 64
sore, 48, 83
sorrow, 82
sorry, 6, 61, 82, 141
sort, 84
sought, 84
sound, 70
source, 84
southern, 38
sower, 85
spasm, 76
spear, 73
speared, 48
species, 87
spew, 21, 53
sphere, 20
spill, 20, 21, 90, 134
spin, 38
spinach, 43
spirit, 74
split, 21
spoon, 64
spring, 21, 45

WORD INDEX

spur, 63, 86
squash, 81
squirrel, 63
stab, 76
stabbing, 76
stabs, 76
stairs, 78, 146
stalk, 138
stampede, 77, 78
stand, 16, 75, 78, 79
standpoint, 55
Stanley, 56, 77
starry, 6, 46, 82, 141
state, 65
status, 60
steal, 74
steeper, 47
Stephen, 33
stern, 68, 85, 86
steward, 85
Stewart, 85
still, 20, 21, 23, 90
stir, 63, 68, 85, 86
stirred, 69, 86
stirrer, 63
stirring, 63, 69
stirrup, 63
stirs, 63, 86
stomach, 89
stood, 63
stop, 2, 22, 60, 61, 62
storage, 62
stork, 138
story, 72, 83
strand, 144
stratum, 60
street, 45
strength, 56
strengthen, 56
string, 23
strong, 84
stuck, 63
student, 53
stun, 62
subcommittee, 22
subgroup, 22
subject, 59
submarine, 23
sudden, 28, 38
suggestion, 41, 43
suit, 54

suitable, 53, 73
superintendent, 54, 73
sure, 85
sureness, 85
surer, 85
surf, 68
Susan, 54
swamp, 62, 81
swan, 81
sweet, 52
Sydenham, 42, 137
sympathetic, 34
synchronize, 56
syncopate, 56
Syria, 74
system, 89, 145

taffy, 76
take, 31
taken, 57
taking, 30
tall, 23
Talmadge, 89
tanks, 36
tardy, 60, 81
telegrapher, 23
telephone, 50, 51
tell, 15, 51
tell you, 50
temperature, 12, 46
tent, 55
terrific, 23
terror, 46
textbook, 24
than, 37
tank, 37
thanks, 36
that, 23, 24, 25, 27, 32, 37, 38
that's, 27, 32
the, 9, 27, 28, 37, 38, 88
theater, 65, 73
theater's, 138
Theodore, 74
there, 37
thereof, 33
these, 37
thin, 15
third, 2, 3, 9, 16, 48, 67, 68, 70, 143
thirty, 35
this, 9, 15, 27, 36, 38, 40, 41

thither, 35
thong, 84
thorough, 143
those, 37
thought, 34
thread, 36
three, 36, 45
three-bagger, 76, 77
thrifty, 45
thrill, 34
throng, 84
Thucydides, 87
thwart, 34, 52
ticket, 31
tide, 23
till, 20
time, 14, 23, 26, 28, 36, 142
-tion, 146
tissue, 41, 146
to, 23, 24
toboggan, 23, 81
today, 23
toddle, 81
toddy, 60, 81
together, 23
togs, 80
Tom, 81, 82
tomato, 80, 144
Tommie, 81
tomorrow, 23, 82
tongs, 84
tonic, 81, 89
tonight, 23, 32
tool, 72
torrid, 61, 88
tortoise-shell, 40
toss, 84
tougher, 33
tower, 71
toy, 68, 69
toys, 68
transfer, 77
tray, 45
tread, 36
treasure, 59
tree, 36, 53
triumph, 55
troths, 35
trough, 35
truer, 85
truths, 35

try, 23, 26
tube, 53, 54
Tuesday, 53, 73
tune, 72
turn, 2, 3, 9, 49, 67
turpentine, 68
tweed, 23
twenty, 26
twin, 51, 53

udder, 38
un-, 61
ungodly, 80
unit, 53
unsafe, 62
unsure, 62
until, 58
Upton, 24
urge, 68
used, 39
Utah, 47, 80
utter, 38

valid, 90
valley, 58, 87
valve, 50
vane, 15
vanilla, 12, 47, 59
variation, 78, 87
various, 78, 144
vary, 75, 78
vehement, 42
vehicle, 42
Vera, 58, 74
very, 10, 45, 46, 49, 75, 137, 140
veterinary, 46
view, 53, 54
viewer, 72
village, 34
virulent, 53
vision, 15, 41
visit, 39
vocabulary, 76
volume, 2

Wadsworth, 141
waffles, 62, 84
wage, 16
wagon, 76
wail, 52

Waldorf, 83
walketh, 88
wallet, 62, 88
walnut, 83
Walsh, 83
Walter, 83
Waltham, 42
waltz, 83
wan, 81
want, 26
war, 16, 46, 83, 84
warbler, 83, 145
ward, 83
warmth, 55
warrant, 82
Warren, 82
warrior, 84
was, 39, 63
wash, 51, 62, 81, 82
washcloth, 81, 82
Washington, 81
wasn't, 63, 81
wasp, 84
Wasserman, 84
watch, 61
water, 84
watering, 45
wax, 51
we, 88
wealth, 36
we'll, 74
weren't, 46, 63, 141
west, 15
western, 24
wet, 52
whale, 52
what, 27, 32, 63
wheel, 52
Wheeling, 139
when, 42, 52
whet, 52
which, 15
whiskers, 20
whisper, 20, 21, 46, 135
whispering, 21
white, 42, 66
whoopee, 64

whooping cough, 64
Wickersham, 42
width, 25, 28, 29
will, 50
William, 50
Willie, 58
will you, 50
win, 55
window, 71
window sill, 146
wisp, 20
with, 29, 34, 36, 38
witness, 135
wonderful, 28
won't, 71, 72
woo, 51
wooden, 28, 136
wool, 51
wooly, 58
Worcestershire, 143
word, 68
words, 142
Wordsworth, 141
worn, 83
worse, 142
-worth, 141
would, 90
would you, 44
wreaths, 35
write, 135
writer, 135
wrong, 84
wurst, 41, 64

year, 15, 73
yeast, 53, 139
yes, 53
yesterday, 65
yield, 53
younger, 31
you're, 85
youths, 35

zeal, 39
zealous, 140
zone, 15
zoo, 72

DATE DUE

DEC 17 '79			